Percy Monkman
An extraordinary Bradfordian

Martin Greenwood

PlashMill Press

Published in 2018 by

PlashMill Press

Friockheim, Scotland

First Edition

Copyright © 2018 Martin Greenwood

Typography and Cover Design Copyright © 2018 Rod Fleming

The authors hereby assert all Moral Rights regarding this book in accordance with the Copyright Designs and Patents Act of 1988.

All rights reserved.

No part of this publication may be reproduced, stored in a retrieval system or transmitted in any form or by any means without the prior permission in writing of the publisher, nor be otherwise circulated in any form of binding or cover other than that in which it is published and without a similar condition being imposed on the subsequent purchaser.

ISBN: 978-0-9572612-9-7

www.plashmillpress.com

ACKNOWLEDGEMENTS

To my brother, Adrian, for many years of patient family history research into both the Monkman and Greenwood families, which has provided robust evidence about Percy's family background.

To Percy's family members and friends who are still alive and have given their time to share memories of him, including Iris Galey, Michael de Greasley, Ashley Jackson, Avril and Richard Newton and David Waddington.

To my second cousin, Drew Monkman from Peterborough, Ontario for unearthing three valuable audio recordings by and about Percy.

To my grandfather, Percy, for living the life he did and having the foresight to retain so many documents about it to make this biography possible.

Finally, **to my wife, Jenny,** for her invaluable support from the original idea to completion of the book.

Unless otherwise stated, all illustrations belong to Martin Greenwood.

Portrait of Percy Monkman on front cover in early 1950s by WF Briggs, Chairman of Bradford Arts Club (1948 to 1962) and Percy's friend.

CREDITS

The following organisations have kindly granted permission for use of their material:

Bradford Local Studies Library for use at the start of the book of a map of Bradford and in Chapter 11 of an aerial photograph of the Toller Lane area of Bradford

The *Telegraph & Argus* for use of articles about Bradford (Chapter 1), about Percy (Chapters 3, 4, 6 and 10), one by him (Chapter 6) and photographs of him (Chapters 4 and 10)

Oberon Books Ltd for use in Chapter 2 of an extract from *The Christmas Truce* by Phil Porter (2014)

Bradford Museums & Galleries Collections for use in Chapter 4 of Percy's painting *City Rains (1958)*

The Royal Bank of Scotland Group plc for use in Chapter 4 of four paintings by Percy and in Chapter 5 of two cartoons by Percy published in *The Westminster* staff magazine

The **JB Priestley Estate** for use of a couple of letters from JBP to Percy in Chapter 6

Pen and Sword Ltd for use in Chapter 6 of extracts from *Ashley Jackson: An Artist's Life* by Chris Bond, 2010

The Dalesman for use of three articles by Percy in Chapter 6 and for a posthumous article about Percy in Chapter 9 by his friend Ken Feakes

The Times – News Syndication for use in Chapter 7 of two photographs of Percy at the scene of the 1985 Bradford City Fire Disaster, one published in *The Sunday Times*

Contents

PREFACE

PERCY'S BRADFORD WORLD

PROLOGUE

CHAPTER 1 BRADFORD AND THE MONKMAN FAMILY

Early Victorian Bradford	1
Breaking the mould	3
Mid to late Victorian Bradford	4
Born into a tough world	8
School and first jobs	10
Training for the bank	12
Edwardian Bradford	13
Impact of World War 1	15

CHAPTER 2 'HUMOROUS ENTERTAINER'

Joining the army	17
Pre-war experience of entertaining	19
Entertaining the troops (First World War)	21
The Disorderly Room	25
Getting married	27
Entertaining at home in the 1920s and 1930s	28
Entertaining the troops again (Second World War)	31
Entertaining at home post-war	34
Examples of Percy's humour	36

CHAPTER 3 VERSATILE ACTOR

The Bradford Civic Playhouse	39
When We Are Married (1938 and later)	41
Growing reputation of the Playhouse	44
Other productions at the Playhouse	45
Life at the Playhouse	50
Other theatre work	51
Star of screen: *The End*	53

CHAPTER 4 PASSIONATE WATERCOLOUR PAINTER

Philosophy of painting	57
Early experiences	59
Painting and working (1919 to 1952)	61
Painting in retirement (1953 to 1986)	62
The portfolio of paintings	63
Commissions	65
Passion for painting	69
Bradford Arts Club	71
Yorkshire Watercolour Society	72
Publicity and exhibitions	73
Sales and gifts	75
Examples of paintings	76

CHAPTER 5 ALSO, A TALENTED CARTOONIST

Sporting cartoons	87
Cartoons of actors	89
Other opportunities	92
Pair of banking cartoons	94

CHAPTER 6 LOYAL COLLECTOR OF LIFE-LONG FRIENDSHIPS

Patterns of friendship	97
JB Priestley (1894 to 1984)	98
Tommy Crosby – friend from the First World War	105
Yorkshire artists – Percy's contemporaries	106
Friends from Bradford Civic Concert Party	110
Friends from Bradford Arts Club in the 1950s and 1960s	111
The tragic story of Iris (1930 to current day), and her mother Trudi	112
Roger Suddards (1930 to 1995)	114
Bronwen Nixon and her tragic end (1919-1986)	116
Ashley Jackson (1940 to current day)	116
Other friends	118

CHAPTER 7 LONG-SUFFERING BRADFORD CITY FAN

Playing football	121
Bradford City's golden era	122
The inter-war years	123
The post-war years	123
The Bradford City fire disaster	124
Other sports	126

CHAPTER 8 COMMITTED FAMILY MAN

The Monkman family	127
Growing up	129
Non-conformist background	130
A largely healthy lifestyle	131
A supportive wife	132
Differences from his brothers	133
Some very sad episodes	135

CHAPTER 9 TEN PERSPECTIVES OF PERCY

Article in *Telegraph & Argus* by Robert Arnott (December 1932)	139
The branch manager at The Westminster Bank, Bradford (August 1952).	140
Speech by Ferdy Roberts, life-long friend and President of Bradford Arts Club at the 'Percyversary' (May 1974)	140
'This is your life' by friend Joan Crib recited at the 'Percyversary' (May 1974)	142
Extract from article in *Telegraph & Argus* by John Hewitt (July 1982)	143
Letter of condolence from Sam Carter, friend from entertainment years (May 1986)	144
Letter of condolence from Rev RH McMurray Adam, minister at Shipley United Reform Church (May 1986)	144
Article in *The Dalesman* by friend Ken Feakes (April 1992)	145
Memories of family life by daughter Dorothy Greenwood (sometime in the 1990s)	147
A graphologist (date unknown but no later than the 1940s	148

CHAPTER 10 ARTISTIC ACHIEVEMENTS

Volume of activity	149
Self-taught	149
Professional standards	150
Awards for painting	151
Two celebrations in one year	152
Showcase of Percy's talent	157

CHAPTER 11 PERCY'S LOST CITY?

    A close-knit community   160
    Major social changes   161
    Percy's perception of troubled times   161
    A different Bradford today   163
    No longer a Bradford family   165

CHAPTER 12 EXTRAORDINARY BRADFORDIAN

    A big step in the world   167
    Unexpected impact of First World War   168
    Entertaining the troops in two World Wars   169
    A job in banking, a life in the arts   169
    High artistic standards in each activity   170
    Contrast with his three brothers   170
    Unusual friendships   171
    Sense of humour   172
    A life no longer possible   172
    Living to a good old age   173

FURTHER INFORMATION   175

APPENDIX 1 TIMELINE OF PERCY'S LIFE   177

INDEX   183

PREFACE

A Bradford celebrity

Towards the end of my grandfather's life a journalist wrote that Percy Monkman must have been the best-known person in Bradford. Of course this is subjective and cannot be proven, but there is no doubt that for many reasons he was extremely well-known and was certainly a Bradford celebrity for some 60 years, after he returned from military service in the First World War.

Most people's legacies relate to their work or occupation. But my grandfather had the most unremarkable of professional jobs. Rising to chief cashier, he worked in the same Bradford bank from the age of 16 to when he retired at 60, indeed in the same physical building, with just four years away, from 1915 to 1919, with the army in Northern France. Hardly worthy of a paragraph, let alone a biography!

Yet all his spare time – evenings, weekends and holidays – was so crammed with tremendous energy and artistic creativity, that he was an inspiration to all who came across him. By temperament, he was a night owl rather than an early bird, and so this hectic social and creative life outside work suited him perfectly.

However, this story would not have been possible if my grandfather had not also been a hoarder and if his grandsons had not inherited the same trait. He seems to have kept every document he ever received, every press cutting, every programme he appeared in, notes of every talk he ever gave, and thousands of other items, from review sketches to joke books and jottings on backs of envelopes.

Packed into all sorts of folders and envelopes, this treasure trove has lain unopened in my attic since his death over 30 years ago. At last I have been able to analyse these documents and made many discoveries that have amazed me despite my prior knowledge of the key parts of his life.

This, then, is the story of that extraordinary life of rich achievement distilled from a remarkable base of evidence.

Living with Grandpa

Although this book is primarily about the development of my grandfather's public persona, he was also the most important male role model in my life as I was growing up. Even now, over 30 years after his death and into my own eighth decade, I still refer to him as Grandpa, as indeed did all his immediate family, including my wife, our children, my brother's wife and their children, and even his own daughter and wife. Outside the family he was always just Percy. For the purposes of this book I have changed the habit of a lifetime and also called him Percy. However here in this preface he remains Grandpa.

Our relationship was much closer than a conventional grandparent / grandchild. When I was six years old, my mother became a single parent in extremely upsetting circumstances after my father left us. My grandparents took in my mother, brother and myself at a difficult time in their own life. In effect, my brother and I became their second family. Although we saw our real father, a teacher, every half-term,

Percy Monkman

Grandpa took on much of the father's role for us in our childhood and until we became students.

We lived with our grandparents for five years until a small bequest from an aunt allowed our mother to buy a house nearby. Then for the next ten years we spent just about every Saturday and Sunday at their house, partly because they had a television which my mother could not afford and partly because it saved my mother from spending on food.

Our family holidays as children and teenagers were funded and organised by Grandpa and right until he died we almost always shared Christmas with him.

From his viewpoint he had bought a house for his retirement, having seen his three children become adults with two of them married and with their own young families. Then, without warning, he found himself having to help bring up a second generation of boys and support his devastated daughter both financially and emotionally. Although this had a major impact on the rest of our grandparents' lives, we never heard either of them complain about what had happened, or even blame or become bitter about our father. He just got on with things and did his best to adapt to the new situation and make it work. We gradually learnt that he often worried about the future, especially about our mother struggling to cope.

He retired very shortly after we arrived back in their house in 1952 and I knew him over his long retirement of 33 years. When he died in his 94th year, I was nearly forty. This final third of his life was dominated by his obsession with painting. Our memories of him reflected both this time of his life and the unusual house that he lived in during most of those years. Later we became aware of his earlier interests, but we had little direct experience of them, except for a few times when we saw him perform as an actor and entertainer.

What kind of person was he to live with?

Amongst the hundreds of paintings where we lived was just one portrait of Grandpa, in his fifties painted by his Arts Club friend Bill Briggs (cover of book). This captures him very well with his trademark pipe and bow-tie, the twinkle in his eyes and head slightly cocked to one side. He was a small-medium sized man, about 5' 8" and weighed about 11 stone. Lightly built, he developed a little tummy but he was never overweight.

Whatever he was doing, he usually dressed in a suit, sometimes with a waistcoat; if not, then always in a jacket and corduroys. The suit would be good quality wool or tweed, or as in the portrait a beige lightweight material for the summer. He didn't do casual and never tried to dress as a Bohemian artist (eg with a painter's smock). With thinning hair on top, he usually wore a hat outside the house, as did many men in those days.

The clothes were always browns, yellows and greens, never blues, blacks or greys. His shirts were usually checked, never white or pastel shades. His shoes were always brown, never black. He hardly ever looked smart. His clothes always looked rather crumpled and a little grubby. He used his pockets for carrying his pipe and tobacco which inevitably spilt out, and for a sketch-book with pencils and pieces of charcoal. He usually carried some mints or sweets, but stained by tobacco they had to be washed first!

He was generally the centre of attention in any group or setting. He was never short of a word or a story. Something had always just amused him, or he just met somebody interesting. He did not mind at all being teased by us when we were children. He did not take himself

An Extraordinary Bradfordian

seriously and so he never made you feel intimidated or apprehensive. He was always good at entertaining children, telling jokes, drawing funny things, pulling faces. In his late eighties I remember him getting down on the floor entertaining his great-grandchildren, who now as parents themselves remember him with much affection.

I cannot recall him ever getting really cross or angry. In fact, he rarely showed any emotion. Despite his general good humour and the easy familiarity that he created, he was not a 'touchy-feely' kind of person. He was not the sort of person to kiss or hug us or still less say that he loved us, but you knew that he did.

As my brother and I grew up, our memories of Grandpa were based around his time he lived at 2 Kirklands Villas, Baildon to which he moved from nearby Bradford in 1951 shortly before he retired and where he lived for some 25 years after we had left home. Like much about Grandpa, this was a highly unconventional house. It was the servants' quarters of a large Victorian mansion built by a wealthy mill-owner that was split into three separate properties after the Second World War.

The house had character, but it was essentially a two-up and two-down with conservatory and garage attached. Admittedly the rooms were all a very good size, but with just two bedrooms in particular it was very impractical for a family unit of five plus my Uncle Colin who at that time had not yet married; and for several months in that first year a friend recovering from a traumatic personal tragedy. The house had attracted him, because it had a large conservatory that, apart from a leaky roof, was ideal as an artist's studio. It had also a splendid passion flower that grew to such a size each year that it seemed to lift the roof off. This gave the conservatory a tropical 'feel' at least in the summer.

The house boasted an ancient, clunky and expensive underfloor central heating system. It had no garden of its own, but the lounge overlooked a beautifully manicured garden at the front of the house that was entirely out of bounds to us and belonged to the main property. The lounge and conservatory were crammed with paintings stacked against the walls in every conceivable space. At the back of the house outside our front door was a yard that was suitable for playing football and cricket, except that it was a shared space with the immediate neighbours in the adjacent second property, which cramped its potential as a play area.

The strongest interest that we shared as boys with Grandpa was sport, especially football, and of course he stimulated that interest. One Wednesday afternoon in November 1953 (why was I not at school?) he took me to my first Bradford City game at Valley Parade when I was seven. It was an FA Cup replay that we lost, but even so I was hooked. For years we went to almost every home game and sometimes to away games, although like everything else in his life going places depended on lifts. Fortunately, his brother Harry and nephew Tony, both City fans, were usually happy to oblige. We spent hours dissecting games and players, arguing about who was good or who was not. Grandpa's favourites were ball-players such as clever inside-forwards or tricky wingers, the ones who created the chances.

In the summer he also stimulated our interest in cricket, taking us to Yorkshire's Bradford ground at Park Avenue or occasionally Headingley across in Leeds. However he was never patient enough to watch a whole day and so he would take you just for an afternoon.

He would happily play games with us – football

or cricket in the yard, or, on holiday, on the beach. He was always willing to take you to putting greens or 'pitch and putt' courses, but, although he was not a regular golfer, it was very difficult to beat him. In the conservatory there was a dartboard. We played countless games of darts, but almost always he would win, even if you thought you had him beaten. In the lounge we invented with him a game using a whole stack of beer mats that he had collected. I cannot recall just how the game went, but it involved throwing beer mats from one end of the lounge to the other to land on top of each other.

Although he was proud of our doing well at what was considered the best school in the area, he took little interest in our education. As, leaving school at 13, he had himself received only a basic education, he found it difficult to share in our much more advanced schooling. He just assumed that we were doing our best. This lack of interest did not matter to us, probably because our real father, a Cambridge-educated teacher, filled that gap for us more than adequately when he came to see us each half-term.

In fact, Grandpa was not much interested in books, unless they were books on art or books by his old friend, JB Priestley. I cannot recall him reading a book. His views on politics and current issues were middle of the road. He did not have strong convictions or hold impassioned or dogmatic opinions. By inclination, he was liberal, moderate and tolerant. He did read papers regularly and was very interested in local news and personalities from the Bradford *Telegraph & Argus* and the *Yorkshire Post*.

He was always interested in entertainment and entertainers. He did have strong views about people who did or did not make him laugh. He often referred to famous music hall comedians from the 1920s and 1930s such as Jimmy James. He liked music hall routines such as the famous Wilson, Keppel and Betty sand-dancing. Although he did not like much of the American entertainment that flooded the TV in 1950s and 1960s, there were some exceptions. The Marx Brothers were a great favourite of his, as were Charlie Chaplin, Bob Hope and Jack Benny.

He was a great fan of Tony Hancock, but much to our horror he really rated Charlie Drake and Benny Hill. However to our great surprise he did not quite see the humour of the *Goon Show*, *That Was the Week That Was* or *Monty Python* ('too near the bone', I hear him say). Their humour was perhaps too intellectual and surreal for him.

Grandpa's most common topic of conversation was painting. A talented painter in her own right, our mother shared this interest with him and my brother and I listened to countless hours of discussion and argument about questions such as what made a good subject, what was the best light for painting, what his friends at the Arts Club were painting, what the latest Arts Club gossip was, what exhibitions were coming up, what the papers had said about the latest exhibitions, which paintings should he submit to the next ones, what paints and papers were best to use etc. Our mother was not obsessed about painting in the same way as her father, but she was inevitably drawn into these discussions.

Life revolved around what Grandpa wanted to do. Trips out inevitably meant painting trips in the Dales (or occasionally in the Brontë country) and you had to find your own entertainment around this assumption. On one afternoon I remember making money from tips opening gates for passing cars on a gated Dales road, while Grandpa painted in a field nearby. Holidays too were built around

An Extraordinary Bradfordian

their painting potential – always in the Dales or on the Yorkshire coast or in the Lake District. Three years in a row he took us all to Scarborough in the week of the Scarborough Cricket Festival. We watched the cricket and he (and my mother) painted. A win-win all round on those occasions, but sometimes it did not work out quite so neatly and we were left kicking our heels.

With hindsight this might sound very constraining for teenagers, but it was our life and we saw that without his support it could have been a much more frustrating one. Moreover, good things did come out of our experience. For example, I learnt to develop obsessions of my own. Holidays in the Lake District led to a lifelong interest in fell-walking. Every fell in the Lake District had to be climbed and then, whenever possible, every Munro in Scotland.

His life style and outgoing personality also led to a stream of visitors. Every weekend people would drop in to see him, usually without prior warning, often to have a look at his paintings, sometimes to buy them. He had a very wide range of friends and acquaintances to add to the large Monkman family who almost all lived round about. Moreover, many of his friends from the worlds of theatre and art were rather eccentric. Listening to them was often interesting and life was rarely dull when he was around.

He liked going into Bradford on the bus and this almost became part of his social life. He always had errands to run, painting materials to buy, pictures to have framed, people to see. In school holidays I remember often going in with him. He would be sure to bump in the street to half a dozen people he knew and you would have to stand by and listen before you could move on. I remember him introducing me in the centre of Bradford to Bradford-born Sir Alan Bullock, then a historian of great repute and Master of St Catherine's College Oxford, whose father, a Methodist minister, Grandpa knew. Bound for Oxford University myself, I was introduced by Grandpa much to my embarrassment and completely inaccurately as a protégé of Sir Alan's.

This was by no means the only time he embarrassed me. He used his contacts all the time to help promote his paintings – people who owned galleries or organised exhibitions or worked in newspapers and magazines. Sometimes he seemed quite pushy and was never shy of asking favours, but he would always do his best to return them.

The only time that I ever remember being cross with him was at the end of my first term at university when to my horror I returned home to see that I was front page news in the *Shipley Times and Express* with a particularly embarrassing photograph of me in an academic gown from my matriculation. He had phoned the local paper with what I thought was a non-story based on my hitchhiking around Europe that summer and had not bothered to check with me first! Now it seems a storm in a teacup, but then I was overcome with embarrassment. The truth is that he was proud of what I had done and saw an interesting story and an opportunity to mention his name with mine. Well used to promoting what he himself did, he never dreamt that I might object.

He had a tendency to exploit people's good nature and no more so when he needed a lift which was often. Not having a car was a major issue for him. There were so many places he wanted to go to – not just places to paint, but exhibitions to visit and people he wanted to drop in to see. Going on the bus might occasionally be the answer, getting a taxi might often to just too expensive, but most of the time he just needed a lift. He developed a network of people he could ask for one. I cannot remember asking him the obvious question why he didn't drive himself. I did find out that he had taken a few lessons after the Second World War (I have the receipts). It seems, however, that he decided to use the money to help his sons buy a car so that they could take him to places! Unfortunately that was not a sustainable solution as they had their own lives to lead.

At the time his life seemed to us to be that of a typical grandfather and, as our barely-remembered paternal grandfather died when I was four, I had no other comparison. However, looking back I now see that in reality it was anything but typical. He was quite unconventional and was an inspiration of how to live a healthy, generous and fulfilled life.

PERCY'S BRADFORD WORLD

Key
1: Percy's birthplace (1892)
2: Percy's school (1896 to 1906)
3: Percy's place of work (1908 to 1952, except 1915 to 1919)
4: Percy's home (1901 to 1952)
5: Bradford City AFC
6: Bradford Civic Playhouse
7: Bradford Arts Club

Source: Bradford Local Studies Library

PROLOGUE

When Private Percy Monkman saw the poster in early 1916, he immediately sensed an opportunity. After all, now 23 years old, he had for several years collected a large number of jokes and funny stories, and knew he knew how to make people laugh.

He had hesitated a long time before joining up and his initial experience of war had so far been underwhelming. Never having travelled before, down in Catford, south-east London, he was a long way from his Bradford home, and had been bored for weeks, waiting for things to happen. Now stationed in Doullens near the Somme, he had spent most of the time in removing dying and injured men on stretchers from the mud of the battle front.

Why not? What had he to lose? A concert party in a nearby village hall sounded just right. People needed entertaining in such dark days. He found the organiser, asked if there might be a role for him, was auditioned and invited to join. This moment was to open up a new life for him.

CHAPTER 1

BRADFORD AND THE MONKMAN FAMILY

Going back generations, Percy Monkman's family had experienced hard lives in searching for work around Yorkshire. Eventually they settled in Bradford, one of the fastest growing towns in mid-19th century England. The family's fortunes reflected the changing Bradford society. Born in 1892 into a humble working class home, Percy attended school until he was nearly 14. After a couple of office jobs, at 16 he passed a banking examination and started to work at Becketts Bank (later acquired by the Westminster Bank). When he reached his majority at 21, in 1913 Bradford was an exciting place to live, full of potential and opportunity. But a year later the country was at war. Everything was to change.

Early Victorian Bradford

Before we continue the story of how Percy escaped the mud of the Somme, we need to jump back a couple of generations to describe the poor and very ordinary Bradford family into which he was born and against which his achievements, and those of his brothers, should be measured. What kind of place was Bradford?

'A stinking hole' is how Friedrich Engels described Bradford. Joint author with Karl Marx of the *Communist Manifesto* (1848), Engels knew a thing or two about such things from his extensive research into the condition of the working-classes in Manchester.

This reputation was the price of rapid and unconstrained growth over nearly 50 years.

At the turn of the 19th century, Bradford was a small rural West Riding market town, based around the four townships of Bowling, Bradford, Horton and Manningham. The town supported wool spinning and cloth weaving in local cottages and farms. From 1810 to 1850 the population grew from 16,012 to 103,778. The market town was transformed into an international, industrial city, the eighth largest in the UK (though not officially called a city until 1897). The demand for labour was extraordinary.

The reason was the development of textile mills. The combination of soft water from the hills, coal and iron in local places such as Bowling and, of course, sheep on the moors and in the dales created the opportunity for the expansion of factories making all types of textile, particularly wool and worsted cloth. There had been a tradition of weaving going back to medieval times when Kirkstall Abbey, a few miles away on the River Aire near Leeds, developed the craft and acquired lands around Bradford.

In the first part of the 19th century Bradford emerged as the centre for factory spinning, which replaced hand spinning, and then it took over as the hub of worsted factory weaving. It became a boom town of the Industrial Revolution. Within this period the capacity of its factories expanded 27-fold. It was estimated that two-thirds of the country's wool production was processed in Bradford. By the end of the 1840s, Bradford had become the wool capital of the world and, for a short time, was considered to be the most prosperous place in England outside London.

Percy Monkman

In the 1851 Census 70% of the adults in Bradford had been born elsewhere, two thirds of them in other parts of Yorkshire. It is no surprise that in the 1850s Percy's paternal grandparents abandoned the East Riding countryside and by sometime in the 1860s were working and living in Bradford. The families of Percy's mother and those of his future in-laws also gravitated, from shorter distances, towards Bradford in search of jobs in one of the country's fastest growing areas.

The city grew without any planning. It became a sprawling habitation filling the sides of the surrounding hills. Lacking any local government, it could not afford the most essential public services. It developed into an environmental disaster, symbolised by the change in Bradford Beck running along the running from the valley bottom to the River Aire at Shipley, three miles away. Remembered by old men as a clear-running beck where they had once fished for trout, it became a foul stream of chemical effluent. Frequently obstructed with all sorts of refuse, it also flooded regularly. In the words of the Health of Towns commissioner, Bradford was in 1845 the 'dirtiest, worst regulated town in England'.

Overcrowding, lack of clean water, ineffective sewage management and increase in smoke pollution made Bradford an unhealthy environment. Disease was rife. There were, for example, periodic outbreaks of 'English cholera'[1], which would kill hundreds of people at a time, such as the one in 1849 that claimed 426 deaths.

The historian JB Morrell described Bradford in the 1830s and 1840s as *'a raw and rough place'*. Promiscuity and drunkenness were notorious. It had 40% more brothels than places of worship. Yet there was some pressure to change. There was, for example, a strong temperance movement; in 1837 the first permanent Temperance Hall in England was opened.

---

1 English cholera referred to a gastric ailment of uncertain cause, accompanied by diarrhoea.

An Extraordinary Bradfordian

Breaking the mould

The fortunes of the Monkman family were intertwined with the rise of Bradford.

Three of Percy's grandparents died before he was born. The fourth, Robert Monkman, his father's father, lived until Percy was 15. Robert came from Langton near Malton in the East Riding. The Monkman family's roots were in rural life, tied to working on the estate of the 'big house', in this case Langton Hall, whose owner, Colonel Norcliffe, also owned all the houses in the village and most of the land around. In the 1851 Census Robert was a 17-year-old page at another local 'big house' and, just one year later, married Harriet Cooper (1833 to 1868) from Wetwang, also in the East Riding.

Robert Monkman (1834 to 1908), the only grandparent that Percy knew

One of a family of six sons, Robert was the first to break with the past and seek a job in the town. In the first instance the young married couple moved to York, where he worked as an inn waiter. In the 1861 Census he was a gardener and Methodist preacher working in Low Ackworth, near Wakefield. By this time he had four children.

Around 1864 he moved to Bradford. In 1868 his young wife died on New Year's Eve at a Manningham address of 'English cholera', leaving Robert, at the age of 34, a widower now with eight children. The sixth child was Edwin, Percy's father.

Seven months later on 1 August 1869 Robert remarried, but his second wife Roseanne, who was 12 years younger, was not living with him, less than two years later, by the time of the 1871 Census when he was an insurance agent in Bradford. Ten years later she found herself in prison for larceny after a second offence, according to a record from the courts in Chester. In the meantime Robert became a dyer working in a mill and started to live with a Harriet Leaf, whom he later married bigamously, but not until he had had a further four children with her.

With 12 children, three wives, many different jobs and also, apparently according to stories in the family, a drink problem – yet remaining a lay preacher – he certainly lived a colourful life. Nevertheless, he showed the 'get-up-and-go' attitude that characterised the later Monkmans. Having survived to be five years old in 1839, Robert could have expected to live till he was 55. He died at 73 – a good old age for the time. Two generations later, Percy, too, was to break the mould in his very different way and also live well beyond his life expectancy.

Percy's daughter Dorothy recalled that her father hardly ever mentioned his grandfather. Yet Robert's last known address in Victor Street near Lister's Mill was very close to where Percy lived in his early years. If Percy was a little distant with his grandfather, then the likeliest explanation is that, as one of twelve children, Edwin might not have been close to *his* father.

In contrast, Percy's maternal grandparents lived more straightforward, though very humble lives. His maternal grandfather was Thomas Collins (1823 to 1863) from Elland in the West Riding. He married Rhoda Greenwood (1836 to 1876) from Heaton, where they both lived and died. Thomas was a stoneworker and Rhoda a factory weaver before marriage. Martha Ann, Percy's mother, was their only child.

So, both sets of grandparents had settled in Bradford after being born elsewhere in Yorkshire. Going back one generation further, all of Percy's great-grandparents were also Yorkshire-born, from the three ridings of Yorkshire, and most moved around in search of jobs. For over 100 years Percy's family on both sides had deep Yorkshire roots and strong connections with Bradford. It is no surprise that Percy himself never moved away and always strongly identified with both Bradford and Yorkshire.

Mid to late Victorian Bradford

The first public services

In the second half of the 19th century living conditions in Bradford very gradually got better since the horrors of the first half.

After a long public debate with petitions for and against, a municipal Corporation was formed in 1847 to run the city, composed largely of its major entrepreneurs. It slowly started to improve the running of the town. Its first act was to create a police force, maintaining public order being previously the role of the army. A few years later it introduced a fire service, replacing private insurance companies, and street lighting in the more well-off areas. In 1854 it brought in building regulations which improved the quality of new working class houses, although badly-built dwellings built before then remained for decades. Much later, in 1877, it began the work of extensive slum clearance.

In 1854 the Corporation also purchased the private water company set up in 1744 to supply piped water to the minority in Bradford who could pay. In the 1860s and early 1870s, not before time, it created a network of drains and sewers.

Sir Titus Salt

Alongside the public investment, some enlightened factory owners started to realise that it was in their interest to ensure that workers did not live in squalid conditions and an unhealthy environment.

The innovator who led the way was Sir Titus Salt. In 1833, age 30, he took over his father's business, created a new worsted material using alpaca wool, made a fortune and within 20 years had become the largest employer in Bradford. In 1848 he became its second mayor. At first he tried, unsuccessfully, to clean up the pollution, but then found another way. He used his fortune to buy a green field site, by the River Aire, three miles outside the city and, crucially, by the new railway line to Leeds, London and Scotland. Here, at what became known as Saltaire, he built a very large worsted factory and a model village, with houses for the workers, bathhouses, an institute, hospital, almshouses and churches. Although this did not solve the problems of the large numbers left in the city, it did demonstrate the need to improve living conditions for the workers. Today it is a World Heritage Site.

Salt was also the first Bradford employer to support a ten-hour working day for all his workers, when the usual working day was 12 hours or longer. The 1847 Factory Act made this a legal requirement and a succession of further Acts up to 1895 gradually improved working conditions in the mills. For example, the 1850 Factory Act brought in the Saturday afternoon closure of workplaces and the 1874 Factory Act reduced working hours by half an hour a day and permitted children up to 14 to work part-time only, to provide for their schooling.

Samuel Lister

Another Bradford industrialist who had an equally large impact was Samuel Lister, who invented a new way of spinning yarn and built Lister's Mill, which dominated the skyline and life of Manningham. Although a public benefactor, he was no enlightened employer like Titus Salt. His behaviour to his large workforce when he attempted to cut its wages by 25% led to a strike in 1891. In turn this led directly to the creation of the Independent Labour Party in 1893 at a famous inaugural meeting in Bradford attended, amongst others, by Keir Hardie and George Bernard Shaw. It became the modern Labour Party.

Child labour took some time to disappear. The law-enforced improvement in working conditions came a little too late to stop Percy's mother, Martha, from having to work as a seven-year-old in Lister's Mill.

On the other side of Percy's family, almost all of Robert Monkman's children are known from the Census in 1881 and 1891 to have worked in the mill, most likely Lister's Mill, where he also worked and near where he lived.

WE Forster and education

Another factory owner and philanthropist with strong Bradford connections was to have a big say in improving education, a service where provision had also been pitifully weak. Proper schooling was only available for those whose parents could pay. A southerner by birth, WE Forster moved north to build a factory in Bradford before becoming a local MP and then a Minister of Education. He introduced, after much debate, the 1870 Education Act which guaranteed education for all children in England and Wales from the age of five to thirteen, although attendance was not made compulsory until 1880. Again, this piece of legislation came a little too late for Percy's other parent, his father Edwin, to benefit from, which might have had an impact on Percy and his brothers. Edwin's own lack of a proper education may well have led him later to discourage his boys. What had been good enough for him was good enough for them.

(WE Forster also gave his name to Forster Square in the centre of Bradford, one of two rail termini and overlooked by the bank where Percy later worked all his working life. This view would also turn out to be the subject of one of his most popular paintings.)

Percy Monkman

Non-conformism

The rapid growth of Bradford brought with it some interesting trends in religious belief. The 1851 Census showed that 60% of those attending church on the day of the Census were nonconformists, three times as many as those who attended the established Church of England. This made Bradford the most intensely non-conformist town in England. The growth was centred on Baptists, Congregationalists and some Methodists. In the case of the first two groups, the growth came mainly from the arrival of immigrants, who brought with them their non-conformist identities; in the case of the third it came from conversion of the godless and Anglicans. Sunday schools were an important part of the chapels that sprang up; for many children they offered the only free education.

Percy's parents were both strong Congregationalists, especially his devout mother, Martha. His upbringing in such a household was to have a strong influence on his life.

Growth in leisure time

The gradual easing of working hours encouraged the concept of leisure time. This, in turn, encouraged the development of many different activities such as choral singing, allotments and sport. A rapid rise in the number of young adults encouraged participation in team sports in Bradford, starting with the formation of Bradford Cricket Club as far back as 1836 and continuing with clubs for football in 1863 and in 1871 for rugby union. Sport as a spectator activity naturally followed.

The opening of public parks offered recreational activities and encouraged new types of events such as galas and brass-band concerts as well as providing much needed fresh air in a polluted city. The first was Peel Park in 1853, funded by public subscription. Then in 1870 the Corporation purchased land in Manningham from Samuel Lister to create Lister Park. On its opening a year later, the *Bradford Observer* wrote: *No place in the kingdom has more need of open recreation grounds, in which the people recruit their wasted energies and breathe fresh oxygen unto their smoke-dried lungs after the day's work in the narrow streets and vitiated atmosphere of the town.*

Civic pride

During the second half of the 19th century Bradford gradually started to acquire the buildings that indicated growth in civic pride and growing interest in culture. St George's Hall was opened in 1853 as a venue for concerts and meetings with a capacity of 3,500. It is now the oldest such venue in the UK still in use. A correspondent from the *Illustrated London News* on a visit north that year suggested that the city had emerged out of the shadow of its neighbour: it was now *'Leeds near Bradford'*, he proclaimed. The influential German community played a major role in the funding of the new building. In this concert hall the Manchester-based Halle orchestra started in 1865 with annual seasons of subscription concerts.

In 1864 the city's first theatre, the Theatre Royal on Manningham Lane, was built with a capacity of 1,800, to meet the demand for live theatre. The city's first large hotel, the Victoria, was opened in 1864 near one of the two rail termini (now Bradford Interchange). In 1890 a second such hotel, the Midland, was opened near the other terminus (now Bradford Forster Square).

Alongside such cultural venues, new buildings appeared to meet the demands of the wool trade. The Wool Exchange, the first building built from local Bradford stone, was opened in 1867 with the foundation stone laid by Prime Minister, Lord Palmerston. It was seen as an important design commission in the style of Gothic Revival architecture, but attracted public criticism from John Ruskin, the leading English art critic of the day, when invited to come to Bradford to judge competitive designs. Today it is a small shopping centre, with Waterstones the main store. Less controversial but arguably more important for the Bradford skyline, which they still dominate, were the large export warehouses built between 1860 and 1874 in the area now known as Little Germany.

The biggest symbol of civic pride was the new Town Hall opened in 1873, to compare with similar buildings in Leeds, Manchester and nearby Halifax. This, too, was designed in the style of Gothic Revival with a distinctive bell/clock tower. In the 20th century it was renamed City Hall.

Between 1850 and 1875, more important than investments in buildings, was the emergence in the generation, also Percy's father's generation, of talented individuals who became national names in the arts. The two most famous were sons of German immigrants – the composer Frederick Delius (1862 to 1934) and the artist William Rothenstein (1872 to 1945). Both attended Bradford Grammar School. Up to this point any prominent Bradfordians had been factory owners.

Alongside all these improvements in the quality of life, the population continued to grow. By Percy's birth in 1892, the population had nearly doubled again from 1851 to around 200,000. Immigrants now came from further afield, a process that had started in the 1840s with the Irish and continued with Germans (many of them Jewish) and Italians in the 1850s and 1860s.

In 1897 Bradford was officially granted the status of a city.

Percy Monkman

Born into a tough world

Percy's parents

Born in Hemsworth, a coal-mining village south of Wakefield, his father Edwin (1864 to 1950) was described on Percy's birth certificate as a 'hawker'. He sold fruit and vegetables from a horse and cart before moving up in the world – and up the hill, half a mile or so further out of the city to Toller Lane, where Manningham joins with Girlington and Heaton. Here he bought a greengrocer's shop. By the time of the 1901 Census he had become a 'fruiterer and shopkeeper' and ten years later he was a 'fruit dealer'. By the 1921 Census he described himself as a 'fruiterer (Master)'.

In November 1890 he married Martha Ann Collins (1862 to 1944), a local millworker from Heaton. Martha's life centred around her family and the local chapel. No doubt influenced by stories of having an alcoholic father (who died when she was a baby) and later a drunken father-in-law, she was a strict teetotaller.

Both Percy's parents had a tough upbringing. His father was part of a big family, doubtless crammed into a small house and struggling to make ends meet. When he started to work, he got up early every weekday morning to go to the market to buy the vegetables that he sold to make his living. In contrast, Percy's mother was orphaned at 13, with no siblings, and was then raised by an aunt. As a little girl she was used to early waking from the age of 7, working as a part-timer at the nearby Lister's Mill in Manningham as well as attending elementary school. When she started at the mill, it was said that she was so small that she had to stand on a stool to reach the machinery!

Edwin and Martha married on 17 November 1890 at Heaton Baptist Chapel in Manningham. Within a year she miscarried twin sons.

Arrival of Percy

Never a morning person, Percy Monkman was often amused to sign himself off in later life as PM. He was, however, a morning baby, born at 10.30am on 11 August 1892 at 6 Bavaria Place, Manningham. Unusually for the time Martha was nearly 31 years old when Percy was born and was nearly 42 years old when the fifth and youngest son (Frank) was born.

Manningham was one of the four main townships that had formed what became Bradford. The address was far less imposing than it sounds, a side street of small terraced cottages of which only numbers 2 and 4 remain today, as shown in the photograph above. Many street names in Manningham and surrounding areas have a German origin, reflecting the influx of Germans (often Jews) in mid and late Victorian times to manage the woollen mills.

Percy's birthplace today

An Extraordinary Bradfordian

The birth was very much a family affair. Acting as the midwife was cousin Jinny, Percy's father's cousin, then in her early 20s. Midwifery was quite unregulated with no compulsory training until the 1902 Midwives Act. The practice was that mothers-to-be who were not from well-off homes and could not afford doctors would be helped in their confinements by a suitable female relative. With no sister, mother or mother-in-law, Martha chose her husband's cousin. Jinny was to help bring into the world all the five Monkman boys. It must have been unusual for the time that such a midwife was not a mother herself and also six years younger than the mother with her first baby. As Martha had had a miscarriage the year before, both mother and midwife might have had good reason to be very apprehensive about Percy's birth.

A year before his birth Jinny was recorded in the 1891 Census as a 'silk mill-hand'. This, then, might well have been not just her first experience of helping at a birth, but also the start of a new life for her. Many years later in the latest census available (1939) she described herself as a 'retired maternity nurse'. Percy's daughter was to remember that in later years Jinny also used to lay out bodies of those recently deceased – an unlikely combination of duties of life and death.

Jinny always lived in the Toller Lane area, remained unmarried and childless and died aged 92 in 1960. One of her earliest 'babies', if not her first, a 67-year-old Percy was to attend her funeral.

Percy and his mother circa 1893.

Apart from this photograph and the next one overleaf, we have little information about Percy's early years, except that he claimed, many years later, that his first stage appearance was made at Greenfield Chapel, Manningham, which his parents attended before they moved a mile or so up the road to Toller Lane. The occasion was a Jack and Jill duet with a girl, at the age of seven.

Percy Monkman

Percy, parents and two brothers (circa 1900)
Left to right: Percy (eight years old), Gordon (six years old) and Harry (four years old)

School and first jobs

Percy attended Drummond Road Board School in Manningham, built in 1887 as part of a second wave of school building in Bradford after WE Forster's Education Act of 1870. To this day it is still in use as a school. It is now known as IQRA Academy (Improvement Quality Respect Achievement), although the original name is firmly and proudly engraved into the building.

Stimulated no doubt by WE Forster's leadership, the new Bradford School Board created by the 1870 Education Act enjoyed a national reputation as a pioneer in education. Its Drummond Road school, still relatively new when Percy started there in the late 1890s, was considered to be a good school for its time. There is some sort of public record in the form of a log book for the 'infants' department' with an entry for each week.

An Extraordinary Bradfordian

Drummond Road Board School

The main concern was attendance, with problems reported regularly regarding sickness (measles, chicken pox and whooping cough) and occasionally bad weather. In addition the school was closed for special reasons. On 23 October 1899 the Barnum and Bailey show was in town. On 24 May 1900 it was Her Majesty Queen Victoria's 81st birthday and the laying of the foundation stone of the Cartwright Memorial Hall for a new art gallery in nearby Lister Park. (With nothing for the 80th or 82nd birthday, it must have been the combination of events that mattered)

The log book mentions visitors (eg School Board members, other headteachers) but has no references to parents or children. An HM Inspector arrives once a year and leaves a very bland comment. For example, on 30 June 1898 (when Percy was nearly six years old), he commented: *The infants continue to be well managed and the youngest are especially well dealt with'*. With its wealth of feedback, Ofsted only arrives 100 years later.

There is virtually nothing about the curriculum, except, curiously, a separate log book from the Housecraft Centre with detailed entries about cookery lessons, presumably for girls only.

Percy only ever talked about the art education that he received. His main memory, repeated many times in talks and interviews, was the *'pathetic'* teaching of art, which in no way helped him in developing his interest in later life. However, the school gave him the following positive reference, which gives no clue about this dissatisfaction.

Percy Monkman was a scholar in this school. He was a very observant, sharp, attentive boy. He has had some experience of office work. He is a very earnest lad and very anxious to do his best and get on.

According to his daughter Dorothy, Percy regretted that he was not allowed to go to a grammar school. Like many at the time, his father did not think education was very important.

An ornate school-leaving certificate from Drummond Road Board School

Not yet 14, Percy left school in 1906 and took a job for six months as an office boy for R Binns Stock and Share Broker in Swan Arcade, a famous old street in central Bradford where a little later JB Priestley also had a similar office job about which he wrote in some detail. A later reference stated that Percy *'satisfactorily filled the position, leaving on his own notice to fill a place thought to be of more advantage to him'*.

He then moved to Manningham Mills for six months, again as an office boy, this time

11

receiving a more specific reference, *'always being found to be attentive to his duties, punctual and honest'*.

Training for the bank

Like his grandfather Robert Monkman, Percy broke the mould of family tradition. In his case he sat and passed an entrance examination in order to work in a bank. For the first time a Monkman could imagine the concept of a career.

Becketts Bank (undated)

He joined Becketts Bank (Leeds) on his 17th birthday (11 August 1909). Founded in 1774, it was a mid-sized local bank with a headquarters in Leeds and, like many of the banks of its day, had grown as the sideline for a prosperous merchant. By the time it was bought out in 1921 it had 37 branches in Yorkshire and had the reputation of being *'one of the greatest English private banks'* according to the authority on banking history (WCE Hartley). In 1921 it merged with others to become the London County Westminster and Parrs Bank Ltd before its name was shortened in 1923 to the Westminster Bank. Eventually, after Percy's death and after another merger, it

An Extraordinary Bradfordian

became the National Westminster and then today's NatWest.

Percy had joined a bank with a strong reputation in Yorkshire and was to remain in that bank until retirement in August 1952.

In all his time at the bank Percy worked from the same office, at the bottom of Kirkgate in the centre of Bradford, with a view over Forster Square. The print at left, from around the turn of the century shows how imposing a building it was, facing the Midland Hotel (on the right hand side) built alongside the original Midland station (renamed in 1924 as the Forster Square station). Today the building lies empty with prominent To Let signs.

During the first year or two at the bank Percy completed courses with the Royal Society for the Encouragement of Arts, Manufactures and Commerce. In 1908 (aged 15) he had a Certificate in Book-keeping and a year later (aged 16) a certificate to show he had passed his Commercial Examinations – Elementary Stage for Shorthand.

Sometime in the early years at the bank Percy might well have taken Institute of Bankers examinations so that he could progress from an apprentice to a clerk (usually after two to three years), but we have no record of him doing this.

Edwardian Bradford

In 1913 Percy had his 21st birthday. What kind of place was Bradford at that time? What better way to describe life in Bradford when Percy came of age than to use the words of his boyhood friend?

JB Priestley, Bradford's most distinguished writer, in July 1968 described, in an article for the Bradford *Telegraph & Argus* centenary, what it was like to grow up in Edwardian Bradford. A contemporary of Percy, who lived very close by in the Toller Lane area in their formative teenage years, Priestley wrote this piece about Bradford in 1913:

If I raise that old 1910-1914 Bradford, I may be told that I am not really celebrating the place itself but the magic of long-lost youth. But I have long been in my guard against this, except, of course, when I have deliberately been using nostalgia. And if I had felt that Bradford was rather wonderful just because I was 17 or 18 then I ought to have felt that Leeds was rather wonderful too – and I never did. Leeds had the quantity, but Bradford had the quality.

Moreover, my life during these later teens had its drawbacks and limitations, I was working – and what would seem long hours now – as a junior clerk in a wool office and I did not want to be there.

Again I had very little money. Even when all allowance is made for the comparatively low cost of living then, I still had very little money and so could not buy half the things a teenager demands now.

The Bradford I knew so well satisfied me – no, delighted me – because it was comparatively small and compact and yet offered so much to a lively-minded youth. Let us first consider its size.

Percy Monkman

Except when the weather was very bad, you could walk everywhere, this saving your pennies and exercising your legs, but this did not count as walking-for-exercise, but simply as cheap and convenient transport.

As soon as you wanted some real walking, you turned your back on the city and made for the moors. And more than once on some particularly fine spring or autumn morning I would not walk towards Market Street, or the Swan Arcade office. but go in the opposite direction playing truant. It has always been a mystery to me why I was kept on in that office.

I can remember walking clean across Bradford and back, one Sunday evening, just to catch a glimpse of a girl at a Methodist Chapel service. That is how romantic we were – and how sensibly compact our town was!

Now consider what it had to offer us – three daily papers and a weekly, the Subscription Concerts on Fridays, the Bradford Permanent series on Saturday and superb choral singing almost any night; two theatres, two music halls, two or three professional concert parties and a surprising number of lively do's at various chapels; an Arts Club with its own premises; a Playgoers' Society giving public readings; one football club Bradford City that had won the cup not long before; several fine old pubs, from the George in Market Street to the Spotted House, easily reached from the military band concerts in Lister Park.

Bradford had some dismal regions which always bore names like Lilycroft and White Abbey, but in general it never seemed to me the ugly city that outsiders said it was..

When all the main buildings in the centre showed the same blackened stone and when on fine mornings a peculiar kind of smoky sunlight played with brightness and shadows from Town Hall to Forster Square, the effect could almost be enchanting. I may have preferred the moors but my eyes enjoyed a little feast going in and out of Swan Arcade.

Bradford was my metropolis. I felt it offered me everything I really wanted. And, although the 'Bradford millionaire' (See TS Eliot and others) came to be accepted elsewhere as a representative unpleasant type, bluntly aggressive and insensitive, I did not know any millionaires, but on the other hand I did know quite a lot of people who were lively, intelligent, responsive to the arts.

Indeed the Bradford of 1910-14 and then the early 20s did produce an unusual number of men and women who made names for themselves. However I must admit that the period just before the 1914-18 war was a good time for a youngster to be living in a place like Bradford. To begin with we did not realise how Europe might soak itself in blood, how our society might turn almost suicidal. The terrible casualty lists had not yet arrived..

Yes, as enthusiastic and hopeful youths, we were lucky in our teenage time. But I also think – and will never stop thinking – that those of us who lived in Bradford were lucky in our town too.

Note: Interestingly, Percy is referenced by JB Priestley in the *Telegraph & Argus* article containing this extract as possibly the only friend now alive (1968) who was qualified to compare pre-1914 Bradford with Bradford now. JB Priestley was himself not in that situation, as he never came back to live in Bradford after 1922, though a regular visitor over later years.

Furthermore, in the preface of a biography of Fred Jowett of Bradford, a leading left-

An Extraordinary Bradfordian

wing Labour politician and MP in the city, JB Priestley wrote in 1946:

The Bradford of those years was no ordinary city. In those pre-1914 days Bradford was considered the most progressive place in the United Kingdom. I am prepared to bet that Bradford produced more well-known people – musicians, scientists, writers, performers and the like than any place, anything like its size in the whole kingdom.

These descriptions of Bradford in 1913 that Percy would surely have related to show it to be a place of potential and encouragement with a culture that stimulated social and artistic activity. Percy's own story would eventually bear this out.

The city had come a long way from the dreadful state it experienced in the youth of his grandparents in the 1830s and 1840s.

Impact of World War 1

A year later Britain was at war. This was the start of four years of the most dreadful battles that the world had ever seen, with levels of casualties never before or after experienced. For men like Percy, 22 years old in 1914, full of optimism and enthusiasm, with his adult life stretching out in front of him and everything to live for, the First World War changed it all for ever. Young Bradford men were to suffer greatly. Thankfully in his case, Percy survived and things turned out remarkably well, setting him firmly down a new path for a life that he could never have anticipated before he joined the army.

Percy Monkman

CHAPTER 2

'HUMOROUS ENTERTAINER'

Unexpectedly, the First World War gave Percy an opportunity for a new life that he grasped firmly with both hands. He spent much of the war as a comedian in an entertainment troupe that ran concert party shows for soldiers just behind the front line. Back in civilian life he continued his entertainment career with great success throughout the interwar years. In the Second World War he was back at entertaining the troops, this time groups of returning servicemen across Yorkshire. His career in entertainment extended further until the end of the 1960s when he was nearly 80 years old.

Joining the army

Britain declared war on Germany in August 1914. Caught up in the enthusiastic surge of joining one of the new local 'Pals' battalions, Percy's two younger brothers both joined the 16th Battalion of West Yorkshire Regiment (together with the 14th Battalion, known as the Bradford Pals). Six weeks after the declaration of war on 21 September his brother Harry (just 18 years old) joined up with the Bradford Pals. One thousand young Bradford men joined within a week in September. Their names, including Harry's, were published in the *Telegraph & Argus.* His 20-year-old brother Gordon followed Harry ten weeks later, on 7 December (their remaining two youngest brothers were still at school).

However, Percy waited. He already had a good job and a promising future. He was optimistic. The war might be over soon. He would do his duty, but he just was not very keen on fighting. In the end, as the war continued and conscription became a likely reality, Percy decided to join the Royal Army Medical Corps (RAMC), where he became a stretcher-bearer ('paramedic' in today's parlance). The differences in timing and regiment are interesting. Why did Percy join the RAMC and do so a year later than his two brothers? In 1914 Percy had been established in the banking profession for five years and may have been reluctant to sacrifice that start in his career, whereas his two younger brothers had only just started working life – Gordon as a wool merchant's apprentice and Harry as a manufacturer's clerk.

Percy was known to have pacifist sympathies without ever seriously considering being a conscientious objector, but we have no record of why and how he started army life in a non-fighting arm, unlike with his two brothers. However, enlistment was voluntary until late in 1915, although talk of conscription was in the air and finally arrived on 27 January 1916 with the Military Service Act. Percy might have reasoned that, with the war lasting much longer than first thought, it was a choice of enlisting as a volunteer now in a non-military role or being conscripted later direct into the front line.

Three months before he joined up, Percy completed a course on First Aid to the Injured with St. John's Ambulance. This was not requested by the army. Maybe he thought that it would help with his application or maybe he just wanted to test the water. He never showed any interest in such work after the war.

Did this delay cause any tension and argument in the family, or indeed in the local community? It would be very interesting to hear the discussions about these points, but we have no record or real clues as to what people may have thought and said.

After all the delay, the start of his time in the army was nothing to write home about. In early 1916 he wrote a postcard from Catford in South-East London where he was first stationed: *'Well, there's scarcely anything at all to write about. We are just passing the time along here and things are moving pretty slowly. We are thinking we shall never get out of England before the end of the war'.*

But get out of England they did! When he arrived in France, the kind of scene that he experienced is captured by a photograph of an ambulance being pushed out of the mud with a cryptic comment by Percy scrawled at the bottom *'Not ours, but the mud is typical'.*

We have a good record of how, once in the RAMC and stationed in Doullens (in the Departement of the Somme) Percy had the break that helped him escape the mud and, more importantly, shape his life during and after the war. He left behind the notes of a talk he gave in 1950 about his First World War experiences.

Percy (sitting on extreme right) *in RAMC (Catford, early 1916)*

Ambulance stuck in the mud (1916)

An Extraordinary Bradfordian

Pre-war experience of entertaining

With hindsight, appearing with the concert party was a big break for Percy. How might he persuade those putting on this show that he was suitable for the job? Percy, in fact, had a real advantage. He had already built up a large collection of jokes and had some pre-war experience of performing to draw upon. Then, in the early days in Northern France, Percy arranged and played in many camp shows when he saw the poster.

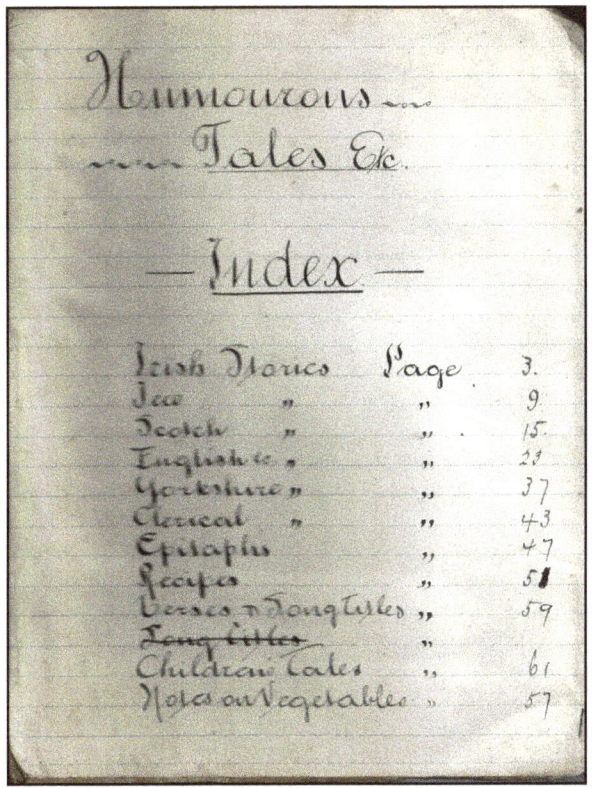

One of Percy's joke books

Percy's books of jokes bear testament to his great interest in comedy. The most significant contains hundreds of jokes (or 'gags' as he called them), some handwritten in pen or pencil, some typed and others copied from newspapers. The book is marked at the front with his initials PM in large letters. On the inside page is the statement: *The owner of this book is Percy Monkman, Comedian & Humorist, 106 Toller Lane, Bradford.* Underneath, it says *If this book is found, and if the finder would mind sending it back to this address, he would be suitably rewarded and his kindness much appreciated.* As for many comedians, his stock of humour was a major asset and losing it would be a nightmare.

The jokes themselves are classified by type of story – 'Irish, Jew, Scotch, English, Yorkshire, clerical, epitaphs etc, (in a somewhat non-politically correct way for today's tastes). The image gives the original handwritten list of contents.

We know for sure that as a 19 year old he appeared at the Girlington Congregational Cricket Club for 'A Grand Concert', being given third billing as a humorist. The programme shows that he sang *'Taking My Father's Tea'*, described as a humorous song, and that he appeared in a 'humorous sketch' entitled *'Mother-in-law'* in which he played the mother-in-law'.

This was followed by at least seven more appearances as a humorist in similar entertainments in the Girlington locality (ie within a mile or so of his home) before he joined up in October 1915. One of these was held at the Elite Picture House, Percy's local cinema. Here, he appeared as part of a troupe called 'The Uniques' and sang 'Sister Suzie's Sewing Shirts for Soldiers', a patriotic song much liked by soldiers. Interestingly, the programme carried an advertisement for 'E. Monkman – English & Foreign Fruiterer', who was, of course, his father, Edwin. Percy also appeared at an open air charity concert at the Royal Infirmary, Daisy Hill, which adjoins Girlington.

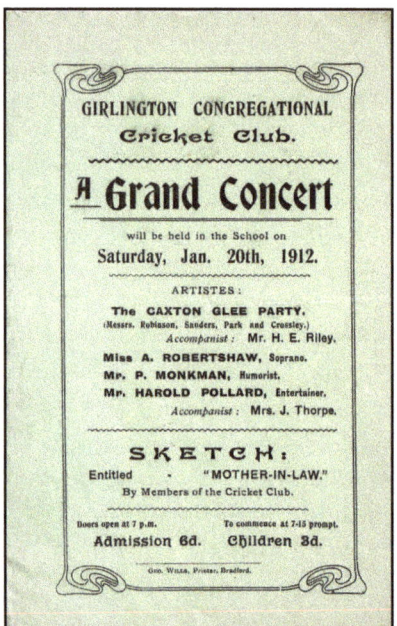 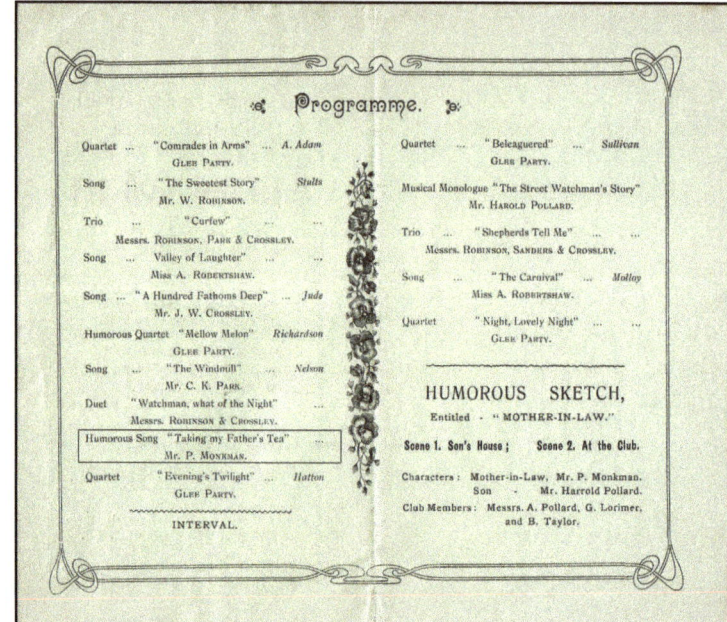

Percy's first concert (12 January 1912)

One photograph (right) remains from these early stage appearances. It was taken six weeks after Britain declared war on Germany and two days before brother Harry joined the Bradford Pals. The message 'Yours to a cinder!' indicates it was hard work.

Percy the young performer (September, 1914)

Entertaining the troops (First World War)

Entertaining troops behind the front line became an important issue because of the boredom that soldiers experienced before they became involved in military action.

A very effective dramatisation of how this might have happened takes place in Phil Porter's play *The Christmas Truce*, performed at the Royal Shakespeare Theatre at Stratford-upon-Avon in autumn 2014, to mark the centenary of the first months of the war. The main action starts when, out of boredom, one of the soldiers suggests an impromptu concert party:

Faulkner (Colonel):	How's morale?
Bruce (Private):	Rather low just now. Though perhaps I could do something about it.
Faulkner:	Go on.
Bruce:	Perhaps if I arranged a concert, Sir. Rope few chaps in. Sing a few songs, tell a few jokes.
Faulkner:	I'm not sure if anyone's in the mood for a party, are they?
Bruce:	But that's the idea, Sir. Take them out of it for an hour or two, give them something to smile about.
Faulkner:	No, I don't think so.
Bruce:	I promise you, Sir, it's what they need. Christmas is coming, they thought they'd be home by now. Trust me they'll be better soldiers for it.
Faulkner:	All right, you can have your party. Just don't expect me to get up on stage.
Bruce	Wouldn't dream of it, Sir.

Source: *The Christmas Truce* © Phil Porter, 2014

One can very easily imagine Percy being Bruce, especially with the confidence from his pre-war experiences of entertaining and his evident enthusiasm for it.

This early experience must surely have stood him in good stead for this audition. *'It was the very beginning of entertainments for the troops but it was so popular that in the end there were hundreds of concert parties. We started with cotton pierrot costumes and ended up with a show you could have put on in the West End'*, he was to say years later in an interview.

The players that he joined were all amateurs from a Liverpool regiment, the 13th Corps Headquarters. 'The Archies', as they were called, only had black pierrot costumes with red cloth buttons, a skull cap and white ruffle.

War throws people together. Becoming a member of a concert party entertaining soldiers night after night over two years will certainly have thrown together the group that called themselves the Archies – Percy and his new stage friends.

Percy Monkman

The Archies

The Archies (May 1918) Two rare pictures of the group.

(Left) Back row from left: WJ Mills, Alf Farling *('The deputy pianist. He is from the East Yorks and used to play at the Empire')* Jack Shotton *(our stage carpenter)*

Middle row from left: Charles Hopkinson, T Stilton Crosby

Front row from left: Percy, 'Rastus' the dog, JH Swift

(Below) Back row from left: Charles Hopkinson, Merlin Eaton *(tenor)*, Billie Mils, Ernie Becosez and Ray Ward *(baritone and manager)*

Sitting: Reg Graham

Front row: Tom S Crosby *(comedian)* and Percy

An Extraordinary Bradfordian

Here also are two images of Percy as a pierrot clown. At left is a photograph from 1916; at right, in a similar outfit, is a self-caricature, which may have been drawn some years later but has his initials PM, which he often used as a shorthand signature.

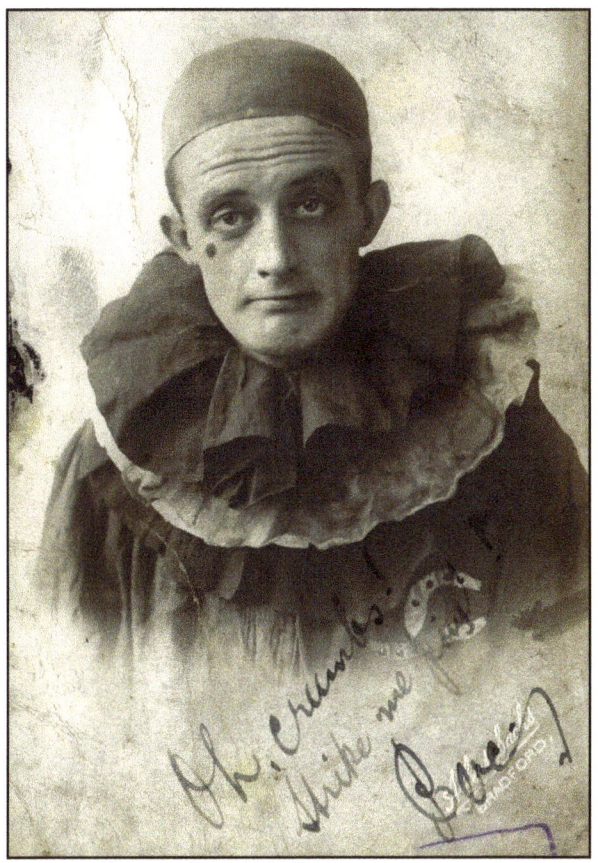

Percy as Pierrot clown (1916)

Percy as Pierrot clown – 'selfie' (undated)

Percy Monkman

An unpublished book by Howard N Cole (*Follies of the Forces*, written between 1936 and 1938) provides a credible history of such concert parties. Overall, there were 90 such groups in the Western Front. The book provides short notes about some of the groups, including The Archies: *'It was composed chiefly of gunners and was fortunate in including amongst them five ex-professionals'*. If this second point is true (at odds with Percy's point that they were all amateurs), then this would have helped to raise the standards of those who, like Percy, were amateurs.

According to the notes of his 1950 talk, Percy went on to say: *'The shows were a great success as there were no other kinds of entertainment for the forces and they were probably amongst the first concert parties in the British Army at that time (1916). The troops were getting bored and restless with no entertainment and so we were in great demand. New units in France were vetted and any professionals in their rank were drafted into the many concert parties. Standards rose rapidly and the Army realised that shows were a necessity for morale.*

Very soon we got a bigger wardrobe, portable lighting was acquired and eventually we had a full orchestra (all in evening dress) from London. No expense was spared – we even had a theatre built with tip-up chairs (from Paris). Heating was also installed by the Royal Engineers. The night before our first performance the theatre was burnt down. It was rebuilt in a fortnight by Chinese labour. By now our show was nearly fully professional. For me it was an invaluable apprenticeship in acting. A great experience working with professionals. We shared the theatre with other concert parties including Leslie Henson.[1]

We played sometimes under difficulties. Once on a moor under shellfire, we were dressed in white straw hats, life jackets and white trousers entertaining about 2,000 troops. Once we went to do a show in a village. We asked where the theatre was. It was in a barn packed to the roof with hay. We used the barn door for the stage, after all the contents were cleared.

Our show ran for two years, doing at least one show per day. Our last show cost over £2,000 to dress. Once we did a special revue for an RAF unit which was stationed near us. It was written very hurriedly. And at one point I gave a cue for one of our cast to enter, glanced in the wings and found the actor in question in the nude. I had to pad out till he was fit to enter!

In an unpublished and anonymous article about Percy, drafted towards the end of his life and otherwise generally accurate, the writer claims that *'At one such concert a General laughed so much at Percy's performance that he broke his chair. After the show he took Percy aside and said that he was wasted where he was, and would be transferred to the Entertainments Division'*. Did this refer to an informal concert party before he applied for and joined an entertainment troupe or afterwards? We will never know, but the story clearly refers to Percy being a great success.

---

1 *Leslie Henson (1891 to 1957) was an English comedian, actor, producer for films and theatre, and film director. He initially worked in silent films and Edwardian musical comedy and became a popular music hall comedian who enjoyed a long stage career. He was famous for his bulging eyes, malleable face and raspy voice and helped to form the Entertainments National Service Association (ENSA) during the Second World War*

(Source: Wikipedia).

The Disorderly Room

Percy's career as an entertainer embraced a variety of types of contribution – stand-up comedian, actor in comic sketch, comic writer and compere. He collected jokes and sketches from a variety of sources and it is often unclear when he is using his own material or material from others, including bought-in sketches.

In Percy's 1950 talk he picked out one sketch that was clearly very successful: *One of our most popular sketches (which a Liverpool friend and I wrote) was called 'The Disorderly Room' which I am told Leslie Henson used in London after the war.*

'The 'Liverpool friend' was Percy's wartime fellow-entertainer Tommy Crosby. The Disorderly Room is clearly one that Percy and Tommy wrote themselves. We also know that Percy used the sketch in peace-time entertainments, no doubt as a reminder of wartime humour.

A copy of the script exists, but at over 2,000 words long it cannot be easily reproduced here. Moreover, even the best of comic scripts (eg Tony Hancock, Monty Python) are a pale imitation of the performance.

The choice of material was sound. It was a satire of army life involving a pompous commanding officer, an earnest sergeant-major and an orderly clerk who had to do their bidding. It will have been popular with soldiers on the front line experiencing all sorts of horrors and deprivations.

We should also remind ourselves of the environment in which it was written. This was most probably one of the earliest, if not the first, comic sketch that Percy and Tommy had written either individually or in collaboration. The working conditions for script-writing must have been far from ideal – almost certainly, there would have been cramped and noisy conditions with little time to develop ideas and rehearse material and little help from anyone with greater experience in putting on comic sketches.

Sadly, there are no recordings of the actual performance, but the audience of servicemen will not have been the easiest of the audiences to make laugh. As it was performed so many times, we can assume that it was very funny to watch live; this is backed up by some contemporaneous reports.

For example a very interesting story emerges from Howard N Cole's book Follies of the Forces. It highlights Leslie Henson as the most famous and ambitious concert party leader of his day and his troupe called 'The Gaieties'. In 1918 he put on a performance in Lille, France, attended by Sir Winston Churchill. This was so successful that he was invited to put on a Royal Command performance for King George V and the Prince of Wales. This, too, was a great success. The book reports that the King was highly amused, especially by Eric Blore's Disorderly Room.

Percy recalled in his 1950 talk that had heard that Leslie Henson had used the sketch in London after the war. But here it was used before the end of the war in a Royal Command performance under somebody else's name!

Eric Blore was a comic actor who became a Hollywood star after the war but appeared during the war in concert parties. On the face of it, this is an example of straightforward theft of somebody else's material, which had already been used over 300 times by its originators. The sketch may possibly have been changed by Eric Blore, but the use of the same title suggests that it was still largely material belonging to Percy and Tommy.

In short, Percy's sketch highly amused the King and Prince of Wales, but he was not given the credit.

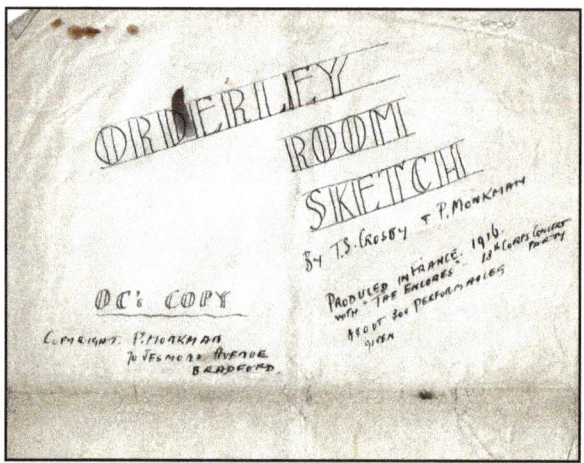

Original manuscript of The Disorderly Room (1916)

This cover of the original manuscript is marked as the intellectual property of TS Crosby and P Monkman. It shows that the original title was *The Orderly Room*. It also documents 'about 300 performances given', which would be over a two year period from perhaps mid-1916 to mid-1918 – a hectic and demanding schedule.

Finally, the manuscript states that it was performed 'with the Encores, 13th Corps concert party'. However the half-dozen or so photographs that remain indicate that the concert party Percy belonged to was called 'The Archies'. Howard N Cole's book refers also to The Archies as belonging to the 13thCorps, making no mention of 'The Encores' which only appears on this manuscript. A reference in one of Percy's talks later in life suggests that 'The Encores' was just an informal name being a weak pun of the sort that he made all his life: *'We were all on the staff of the 13th Corps – known as the 'Encorps'.*

The only existing journalist's account of a performance of *The Disorderly Room* comes from Robert Arnott with an article in the *Telegraph & Argus* (December 1932) after a post-war performance. *'The Disorderly Room' is everything that a military burlesque sketch ought to be. From start to finish it is always amusing and at times becomes riotously funny. Percy Monkman as the commanding officer is a scream and the other people who appeared with him last night seemed to play their parts as though the words had actually been written for them.'*

An Extraordinary Bradfordian

Getting married

Percy came back home on leave from time to time. Before the start of the war he had met Doris Northrop who lived nearby in Toller Lane. She was a secretary for a German Jew mill owner in the centre of Bradford. More than fifty years later Percy was to recall that first meeting on theirgolden wedding anniversary in a short speech to the family: *'Some 55 years ago on a chance visit to Toller Lane skating rink I first saw and was suitably attracted to a very smart girl – high-legged boots and a figure that attracted an artistic eye. That was Doris. The date was 1913.'*

On probably his last period of leave from the war they were married, five years later, on 13 September 1918 during a home visit weeks before the Armistice. A month before the wedding Percy had reached his 26th birthday. It was not just the war that influenced wedding dates. Most banks did not allow employees who earned below a certain amount to get married, as they believed that they would not be able to support a family. If employees wanted to marry before they were earning 'enough', they would have to apply to the bank's management for permission, and it was not always granted. As salary was very closely tied to banking experience, it is possible that Percy had only just started earning enough at age 26 to be allowed to be married.

Within five years of their wedding they had a young family of one girl and two boys.

Wedding Percy and Doris (13 September 1918)

Entertaining at home in the 1920s and 1930s

Back in Bradford with a new promotional letterhead

Percy was not demobilised immediately at the end of the war: he was kept back in Northern France for eight months after the Armistice. The RAMC completed a short form to confirm that he *'was retained in the Army by the Military Authorities and not demobilised until June 1919. This retention was due to no fault of his own, but to the exigencies of Military Service.*

Returning to Bradford, Percy immediately went back to his bank job, but also took steps to develop a career as an entertainer. He produced a personal letterhead and business card that built on his wartime experience. Promoting himself not as a Bradfordian, or even just a Yorkshireman, he indicated a level of ambition as a man of the north – *North of England concerts and late entertainer with the British Army in France.* There is no later record of him positioning himself like this as a Northerner. Perhaps he just came to realise that his selling point was more local.

He started to get bookings. The first recorded event was in December 1919, back at the Girlington Congregational Church where as a 19 year old he had made his first recorded stage appearance. He received two more bookings in early 1920 and nine bookings in the last quarter of 1922. It seemed to have taken a little time to get the momentum that he was to reach and sustain in the rest of the 1920s.

It is no surprise that some of Percy's correspondence in the early 1920s indicated attempts to find engagements and build contacts, eg letters to the BBC in Leeds and to the Windsor Hall, an entertainment venue in Bradford. He also received letters from others who were doing the same. For example, Harold Stead wrote to him in July 1921 with 'a vacancy for a good comedian in my party', (described as Halstead's Comedies, a Carnorous Carnival of Comedy). Nothing seems to have come from that opportunity.

Some fifty years later I asked Percy why he had not chosen entertainment as a professional occupation. I had seen him in action fronting a concert party and he seemed so confident, at ease and fitted for this role: surely he might have made it in radio and television. Indeed he had thought seriously about it, but Percy was cautious as well as adventurous. The steady job with the bank and the responsibilities of a young family (three children in four years) just seemed a safer option than stepping out into the unknown to face a precarious future, however much valuable experience as an entertainer he had acquired during the war.

During the 1920s and 1930s Percy participated in different capacities in 10 to 20 events each year, almost always in the winter months, for a wide range of organisations – church-based events (almost always non-conformist rather than the established church), political clubs (usually Conservative or Liberal), trade-based organisations, sometimes purely commercial ventures (eg interval entertainments at the cinema) and even a temperance union in the form of the Independent Order of Rechabites. The events were often described as smoking concerts (originally, musical men-only events to come for a smoke and chat about politics), ladies' evenings or bazaars (charity fundraising often linked with churches).

Generally speaking, the entertainments that Percy participated in did not enjoy wide press coverage, but occasional press comments about Percy are very positive. In 1924 the Huddersfield Examiner described him as *'a genuine humorist and distinctly clever'*.

There are hundreds of programmes, letters and other documents about this period of Percy's life with virtually no hint of any negative comment. Even where there is one, it is in the form of a back-handed compliment, as when a Bradford engineering company criticised one act by a Rex Hart in some Christmas entertainment organised by Percy in December 1921: *On the whole we were thoroughly satisfied with the entertainment, especially the conjuror and sketches. We think, however, that Mr Rex Hart's turn was not quite up to the standard of the others. We quite realise that we suggested that you should engage Mr Hart.* The company went on to invite Percy back for another three years.

One reason why Percy flourished as an entertainer in the inter-war years, when he was operating largely as an individual, was his flexibility and willingness to take on any assignment. In a letter dated 18 June 1935 a delighted Mrs Basil Hughes wrote to Percy after he stepped in to entertain at a nursing home:

I cannot thank you enough for your great good-heartedness in coming to my assistance so splendidly yesterday and at such short notice. Your entertainment was just perfect. The only fear I have is that today some of the patients may perhaps be suffering from broken ribs!

Diverse range of entertainments in 1920s and 1930s

Top row left to right: *Windhill Cricket Club, 6 October 1928, Wesleyan Reform Chapel, Denholme, 2 and 3 March 1929, Westgate Toller Lane United Methodist Church, 8 June 1929.*

Middle row: *Greengates Cinema, 9 January 1930, Bradford Musical Union, 5 April 1930, West Bowling Conservative Club, 27 February 1931, Independent Order of Rechabites, 4 February 1922.*

Bottom row: *Bank Officers Guild, 27 October 1922.*

Entertaining the troops again (Second World War)

The Second World War brought Percy back to entertaining the troops, but this time to returning troops and injured servicemen, rather than those serving on the front line, and the venues were scattered across Yorkshire, rather than barns in Northern France. Percy was ideally placed to lead on this in view of his experience in the First World War, then during the interwar years and, latterly, as an established member of the Civic Playhouse.

In the First World War the need for entertainment came out of the army itself, which provided the resources. In the Second World War the need was satisfied by a volunteer concert party under the auspices of the Bradford Civic Playhouse.

Percy as man with lute in the Bradford Civic Concert Party (July 1940)

Source: Bradford Civic Playhouse,1940

In November 1940 Percy became the Chairman of the newly-formed Bradford Voluntary Wartime Entertainers Association and organiser of what became known as the Bradford Civic Playhouse Concert Party, which had a pool of performers to draw upon when requests were made for entertainments. The types of organisation that called upon this concert partyincluded RAF Entertainments, the War Organisation of the British Red Cross and Order of St John of Jerusalem, the British Legion and the Veterans' Association. The venues ranged from RAF Dishforth, Harewood House (a large stately home converted into the Convalescent Hospital for Officers), to parks in Bradford (for open-air concerts as part of the council's Holidays at Home war-time initiative), cinemas andtheatres. Very soon they had an arrangement with Northern Command who helped organise and stage the events.

This quickly became a major undertaking for what was a voluntary effort. The Concert Party put on some 600 shows between 1940 and 1945. What mattered most, of course, was the quality of the entertainment. Percy received many positive reviews and comments. For example, the concert party on 15 May 1941 at Bradford's' Cartwright Hall in Lister Park mentioned above and was part of a civic reception, led to a couple of very warm letters.

Afterwards, the Lord Mayor of Bradford wrote to Percy: '*My most sincere thanks for their splendid concert. Their very talented work under difficult conditions was greatly admired by my guests.* This was supported by a separate letter from the event organiser who wrote: *Everyone said it was a most brilliant event and you kindly contributed to its signal success, also at very short notice. It does you great credit. There was a happy atmosphere and everyone enjoyed every minute of the whole evening. We are especially glad that your President and our own Guest of Honour, Mr JB Priestley, really enjoyed himself too ... again, thank you for your merry, witty, clever and delightful programme.*

Another heartfelt 'thank you' was received in 1942 from a Group Captain Commanding at

Percy Monkman

RAF Holme-on-Spalding Moor near York: *I am extremely grateful to you and your company for last Sunday's most excellent concert. When I tell you that yours was one of the most delightful concerts we have ever had on this station, I am not merely expressing a private opinion but that of all the personnel under my command, who were present.*

In his 1950 talk about his war experiences Percy said that *'We* (the concert party) *did 600/700 shows in evenings, all under the Northern Command . We often did four shows per week for troops and charities. Some of the venues were 30 to 50 miles away, and involved travelling in black-outs and many late nights. Through the war we had 38 performers in the party, although we never had more than nine in any one show.*

We once played in a concert at St Luke's Hospital in Bradford and had as guest artist Norman Evans (a variety and radio performer with a national reputation). One unforgettable show with Norah Blaney (famous music hall performer) was at Wakefield Gaol when one prison official's chair collapsed. Some of our outstanding venues were at the Leeds City of Varieties theatre, Selby Hippodrome, Ossett Town Hall and the Alhambra Theatre in Bradford. These were memorable occasions, never to be forgotten.

The impression is that Percy, the organiser and compere, participated in most if not all the shows in this period, even if the rest of the concert party chopped and changed. One cannot help thinking about Percy, time after time, arriving home after midnight and, not a natural early riser, having to get up early enough to get to the bank in central Bradford in time for a 9am start. This must have been a test of his resilience and his constitution.

Looking back over 50 years and more of entertainment, he must have thought this time, tiring though it may have been, as the most rewarding and successful of all the periods of his life. He was at the peak of his career as both organiser / producer and 'top of the bill' act, perhaps best captured by his promotional tag line: 'Yorkshire's King of Mirth'.

Yorkshire's King of Mirth (29 March 1942)

An Extraordinary Bradfordian

At the end of the war the Civic Concert Party as a whole received an official 'thank-you' from the Commanding Officer of Northern Command for its contribution to troops' welfare and morale, also naming Percy as its leader.

HEADQUARTERS,
NORTHERN COMMAND,
September, 1945.

THE termination of hostilities is a suitable opportunity for me to express, on behalf of all ranks of the Army and ATS under my Command, who have enjoyed the entertainment afforded by

Bradford Civic Concert Party.
(Leader: Mr. P. Monkman.)

my grateful thanks for their assistance during the last six years.

Long hours have frequently been entailed and entertainment has often been given under circumstances of difficulty and discomfort for the artistes, cinema operators and voluntary drivers concerned. There is no doubt, however, that the entertainment provided has been thoroughly appreciated, and without this voluntary help the entertainment which could have been given would sometimes have been on a very meagre scale.

Owing to the transfer of many ENSA and other professional parties to the Far East, Voluntary Entertainment for troops in England is still required, and it is my hope, therefore, that you will continue your assistance, which makes no small contribution to the welfare and morale of the troops.

Lieutenant-General,
General Officer Commanding-in-Chief,
NORTHERN COMMAND.

'Thank you' from Northern Command (September 1945)

Entertaining at home post-war

The pace of entertaining slackened after the hectic schedules of the Second World War. Inthe post-war years Percy appeared in a handful of events each year, usually with friends from the Civic Concert Party. The range of organisations was even more diverse than in the past, and included the NUT Bradford Branch, the Jowett Cars Horticultural Society, the Publicity Club of Leeds, the National Federation of Master Printers of England & Wales and the Perseverance Masonic Lodge (his first-ever appearance at a freemasons' event). In 1951 he also had the unusual experience of appearing with Harry Corbett and Sooty at an All-Star Charity Concert for West Riding Constabulary.

During the 1950s and early 1960s the old Civic Concert Party reappeared around New Year playing to packed houses for between four and six Old Time Music Hall shows at the Civic Playhouse, produced in the later years by Percy's friend Roger Suddards. The programmes typically had over 20 items, many of which had become strong favorites. One turn in which Percy appeared regularly was The Singing Waiters (photo below).

Percy as one of the four singing waiters (January 1958)

An Extraordinary Bradfordian

The splendid 'tongue-in-cheek' programme notes for the 1962 production, written by Roger, capture the spirit of the occasion:

This year's show has many of the Civic favorites – there is your own , your very own Rita Scully, Geoffrey Bryson in person, Harry and Joan Tout, Percy Monkman and Ted Nathanson. Harry and Joan, Percy and Rita with Audrey Woodrow and often others spend agood deal of their time doing Music Halls around and about in the city over the years – very often in remote and inaccessible places – for one good cause or another. Edwin Smith and Olive Kitchen are to be with us once more- their rendering of Excelsior is not just a rendering; it's a custom. Which is, of course, Music Hall. This was and still is the point of Music Hall – it is a familiar and, we hope, a happy patter.

This year we have a splendid melodrama – a surprise item, no, no waterfalls, which we think is tremendously funny. If the packet arrives in time, we shall also bring, at vast expense to the Management, a magician from China.

I suppose that the thing we enjoy about Music Hall most is your enjoyment. It's a bit depressing when the audience is quiet and gloomy, and wonderfully exciting when the audience joins in, hisses the villain and cheers the hero. For you are as much part of the show as we are.

We spurn the 'Victorian' Music Hall seen elsewhere, which is just a 20th century variety show dressed up in feather boas. Why put on wing-collars and grow side-whiskers to crack jokes about television? (A dig at the popular 1950s TV show Old Time Music Hall from the City Varieties at Leeds led by Leonard Sachs.)

Reading these warm words, Percy ('Direct from the Empire, Pudsey'!) must have been proud of his leading role in creating such a Concert Party and tradition of entertainment going back to before the Second World War. Moreover, the show was a sell-out, with queues for returns forming each evening.

The final event that Percy contributed to was on Friday 4 July and Saturday 5 July 1969, another Old Time Music Hall devised and produced by Roger Suddards. The programme featured many of Percy's friends from the Civic Concert Party days going back nearly 30 years earlier to the start of the Second World War: Mr Walter Williams who was the chairman, 'wonder boy' Geoffrey Bryson, Miss Rita Scully, *'our very own Madame'* Joan Tout, Mr Harry Tout, Edwin Smith and Olive Kitchen (*'two real aspidistras'*) and *'our spritely Mr Percy Monkman'*. Just short of his 77th birthday, Percy continued to attract press comment from the *Telegraph & Argus* when the show was reviewed: *'One of its stars was undoubtedly Shipley artist Percy Monkman, whose range of Yorkshire stories was almost inexhaustible.'*

Percy Monkman

Examples of Percy's humour

Percy kept numerous books of jokes and stories in 'gag' books. We have reproduced below a selection.

One-liners

Q: If you caught a man in bed with your wife, what would you do?
A: I'd kill his dog or break his white stick.

Golfer in bunker; missed 8 times

Two ants in bunker: let's get over the ball before this chap kills us

Limericks

Said the Duchess of Alba to Goya
Please remember I am your employer
So he painted her twice
Once dressed to look nice
And once in the nude to annoy her

A flea met a fly in a flue
Said the flea 'Let us fly'.
Said the fly 'Let us flee'.
So they flew through a flaw in the flue.

Bank manager's private cash account

Advert for typist	5s-0d
Typist's salary	£3-10s-0d
Taking wife to cinema	3s-0d
Sweets for wife	9d
Flowers for typist	10s-0d
Chocolates for typist	7s-6d
Typist's salary	£10-10s-0d
Taking wife to cinema	3s-0d
Sweets for wife	10d
Flowers for typist	12s-6d
Theatre with typist	£1-10s-0d
Taking wife to cinema	3s-0d
Sweets for wife	10.5d
Weekend with typist	£8-0s-0d
Taking wife to cinema	3s-0d
Sweets for wife	9d
Chocolates for typist	12s-6d
Flowers for typist	15s-0d
Doctor's fee for typist	£200-0s-0d
Mink coat for wife	£500-0s-0d
Advert for male typist	7s-6d

An Extraordinary Bradfordian

'Patter' (a fragment)

We have some goings on in our family. There's 37 of us you know; and the worst of it is we've only got three rooms – kitchen, back-yard and garden. And we've only got one chair in our house. We have to take it in turns to sit down. It's my turn three weeks next Friday.

My father's got a right job you know. He's a draughtsman down at Town Hall. Opening windows, you know.

He used to have a job before that, though, digging holes for telephone posts. And one day he'd been digging holes and he'd got the dirt out and placed it on one side of the hole when the boss came and said: 'Well, John, do you think you'll be able to get all that muck back in the hole'. My father looked at the hole a bit and then said: 'No, I think I'd better dig it another foot deeper'.

Old Time Music Hall – Chairman's remarks

Good evening, ladies and gentlemen. Welcome! Rest assured I've no intention of vociferating in verbal verbosity, vindicating or vilifying the virtuosities or vicissitudes of fellow vaudevillians, however vunderful they vill be. I'm just the Chairman and nobbut a Yorkshire lad.

And now the Bradford Playhouse Old Time Music Hall! If you think my jokes are old, they're meant to be. This is Old Time Music Hall. It's surprising how many of them turn up on television these days. If you've heard one of mine on TV, you'll know now where they got them from.

Percy Monkman

CHAPTER 3

VERSATILE ACTOR

In 1935 Percy joined the Bradford Civic Playhouse and became a fixture in the cast for over 20 years. He played in many diverse productions (27 in total), but the highlight was JB Priestley's *When We Are Married,* first played in 1938 and performed 66 times with five revivals (the last in 1958). He also occasionally appeared in other Bradford theatres. His final acting performance came, unusually, in the form of a cine film that won national recognition.

The Bradford Civic Playhouse

Bradford has a Civic Theatre, of which I happen to be President ... Even now, many people do not realise that there is a chain of such theatres, small intelligent repertory theatres organised on various lines, stretching across the country. Most of them have to struggle along ... this dramatic movement ... is of immense social importance – To begin with, it is a genuine popular movement, not something fostered by a few rich cranks. The people who work for these theatres are not by any means people who want to kill time. They are generally hardworking men and women ... whose evenings are precious to them ... and they are tremendously enthusiastic, even if at times they are also like all theatrical folk everywhere – given to quarrelling and displays of temperament ...These theatres are very small and have to fight for their very existence, but ... I see them as little camp-fires twinkling in a great darkness. Readers ... may possibly not care twopence if every playhouse in the country should close tomorrow. The point is that in communities that have suffered the most from industrial depression, among younger people who frequently cannot see what is to become of their jobs and their lives, these theatres have opened little windows into a world of ideas, colour, fine movement, exquisite drama, have kept going a stir of thought and imagination for actors, helpers, audiences, have acted as outposts for the army of the citizens of tomorrow, demanding to live.
Source: JB Priestley, *English Journey*, 1934

Very soon after Percy joined the Civic Playhouse in 1935, disaster struck in the form of a fire that completed gutted the hall, destroying all records and possessions. Having operated successfully for six years after it had broken away from its parent theatre in Leeds, the Playhouse was now homeless for two years. Its viability was in jeopardy before it started to re-establish the reputation covered in JB Priestley's description at left.

Fundraising became the top priority. There were many varied attempts. One of the most adventurous was a travelling theatre, when plays were performed on a borrowed lorry in public parks, school playgrounds, village greens, inn-yards and even a cattle market. Then, quite out of the blue, along came a patron who gifted the money and agreed to guarantee any mortgages. A new 299-seater theatre was opened in January 1937, equipped for both films and plays, in Chapel Street in the area of the city centre called Little Germany.

At the start of the Second World War, the theatre faced a second crisis with membership dropping steeply as a result of petrol rationing and the blackout: many members lived outside Bradford. Actors were also depleted by call-ups to military service. Despite forecast losses, performances were successful and the theatre stayed open for the duration of the war.

Percy Monkman

From 1935 to 1958 Percy was involved in 20 productions. Three returned for extra weeks and one (*When We Are Married*) was revived on five separate occasions over 20 years. Appendix 1 provides the full list.

Percy (right) as Herbert Soppitt in When We Are Married (October 1952)
Source: Bradford Civic Playhouse

An Extraordinary Bradfordian

When We Are Married (1938 and later)

The production of a new JB Priestley play was a landmark event in the story of the Civic Playhouse. To help keep costs down, the author (also the theatre's president) waived royalty fees for an amateur production of the play (which was also being performed for the first time by a professional theatre in London). Both productions started on the same day (14 November 1938).

All the local press reviews came to the same conclusion: the play was a resounding success.

The *Telegraph & Argus* review sets the standard:

The Yorkshire premiere and world amateur premiere of Mr JB Priestley's play **When We Are Married** *had a hearty send-off last night at Bradford Civic Playhouse where every one of 15 players is admirably cast.*

It is a rollicking, unpretentious comedy about three Cleckleywyke couples who, about to celebrate their silver wedding anniversaries, were suddenly told that they weren't married. What with the husbands being leading lights in the township and at the Lane End Chapel, the fat was properly in the fire.

The Civic production of this classic-to-be is an admirable example of teamwork in which each part dovetails into the next with a finish that never fails to please. There is no forcing of character or dialogue, and while each player gives a distinctive performance that lingers on the memory, the final picture we take away is of the comedy as a whole, done with polish and relish, and rare Yorkshire wit.

Bessie Pratt, Mary Whitehouse, Philip Robinson, Arthur Tetley, Jane Smith, Percy Monkman, Muriel Webster, Roni Vine, Walter Williams and Nora Fox have the largest chunks of this Yorkshire pudding; and Cleckleywyke will praise them all for their splendid work.

Source: *The Telegraph & Argus*, 1938

The *Yorkshire Post* published a notice in similar vein:

Mr JB Priestley has paid another compliment to the Bradford Civic Playhouse, of which he is president, in permitting the first presentation there outside London of his latest play **When We Are Married.**

The courtesy is returned in the most graceful way by a production which is almost faultless. Here is a play which needs a thorough familiarity with the West Riding character on the part of its actors, and, one may add, an equal understanding on the other side of the footlights be properly appreciated. In the Civic production these needs are fully met.

Three Yorkshire couples are celebrating the silver anniversary of their joint wedding day when they are told that the marriages were invalid and their reactions to the situation are the essence of the plot.

The action takes place 30 years ago, but it might just as well have been contemporary, except for the excuse that this period gives for a complete authentic set, complete with antimacassars, what-nots cluttered with ornaments, venetian blinds and the kind of pictures that used to make very good almanacs.

The couples have names we might expect – Albert and Annie Parker, Herbert and Clara Soppit, and Joseph and Maria Hellawell.

One of the men is noted for stinginess, another because he is hen-pecked and their wives are just as typical. Arthur W Tetley, Jane Smith,

Percy Monkman

Percy Monkman, Muriel Webster, Walter Williams and Roni Vine give them perfect verisimilitude.

The constant chuckles, rising intermittently to uproar, and guffaws of last night's audience were even more eloquent than the applause. Both Mr Priestley and the Playhouse have hit their mark this time.

Source: Yorkshire Post, 1938

It was a sellout every night of its two-week run and a third week was added immediately. It was revived two years later for two weeks (1940) and again for two more weeks two years on (1942). In 1944 it was revived for an outdoor production over eight nights in August across five of Bradford's most popular parks.

After the end of the war the revivals continued. Another two weeks' run was performed in 1952 and, finally, there was a fifth revival for one week in 1958, 20 years after the first production. In all there were 66 performances. Only three members of the original cast from 1938 played in the final revival of 1958. One was Percy.

Over the years the press reviews stressed the consistently high performances of all the cast and hardly ever singled out any actor, such was the teamwork of the production. In view of Percy's ever-present record, it was appropriate, perhaps, that on this final revival the *Telegraph & Argus* reviewer did pick him out for a special mention: *'Another splendidly played scene was between Percy Monkman and Mary Schofield who, as the Soppitts, never for a moment missed the true key of the characters of hen-pecked husband and domineering wife.'*

In celebration of its 40th anniversary in 1969 the Playhouse returned with a completely new production of the Priestley classic. On this occasion, the 77 year old Percy was in the audience, seated in the stalls. Unfortunately, we have no record of how he felt as he watched the play that had been such an important part of his life on stage over 20 years.

Overall, there is little doubt that *When We Are Married* was the most successful production at the Civic Playhouse in Percy's life, both commercially in its contribution to the theatre's finances during difficult times, and professionally in the reputation of it being one of the best amateur theatres in the country.

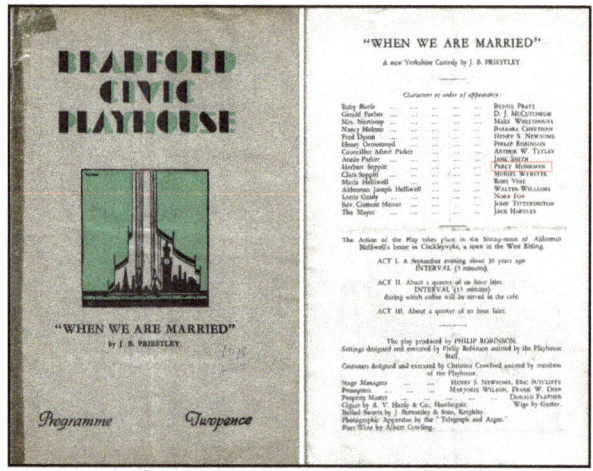

Programme for When We Are Married (1938)

It was certainly the highlight of Percy's acting career.

Percy is quoted in *The Rebel Tyke: Bradford and JB Priestley* by Peter Holdsworth, the *Telegraph & Argus* drama critic as saying that *'The Playhouse owed a great debt to* **When We Are Married.** *It saved the theatre financially because you could guarantee a packed house every time – at every performance'.*

Similar to *The Disorderly Room* comic sketch from the First World War (see Chapter 2), the stage performance that best defines Percy's acting talent lacks any recording from which we can directly assess his contribution. There is, of course, the script by JB Priestley that is generally judged to be one of his best plays.

An Extraordinary Bradfordian

Percy's performance indicates greater depth to his acting ability than one might see from a more typical production in which he appeared. Generally, he played the most significant comic part, which often led him to being singled out in press reviews, because he played these well and the audience laughed.

The hen-pecked husband that Percy plays in *When We Are Married* is by no means the most significant comic part. Judging by the press comments, he played this role in an understated way compared with the play's other two noisier and brasher husbands. He is a simple 'mister'; they are an alderman and a councillor. Percy always appreciated humour that was not overplayed. For example, Jack Benny, the American TV comedian appealed to him, because he was not a wisecracking comic, but relied on being a master of timing and extracting maximum humour from relatively few jokes.

One common theme of the press comments across the original production and its five revivals is the teamwork of the production. On several occasions reviewers say how difficult it was to pick out any single actor. Percy himself said later that he had never experienced such a complete performance with such a well-balanced cast, each so right for the part.

On one special occasion in 1942 the Playhouse took the production lock, stock and barrel to an audience of servicemen at RAF Linton-on-Ouse Aerodrome. In the audience was Sir William Rothenstein, Bradford-born artist (and also President of Bradford Arts Club from 1933 to 1934), who was the official war artist for the RAF; he recounted the occasion in his 1942 war book *Men of the RAF*, jointly authored with Lord David Cecil.

Setting off to RAF Linton-on-Ouse (1942)

Here we see the cast ready to get on the bus from Bradford. Percy is third on the right, with pipe, hat and bag in hand.

Sir William comments about the production: 'The play could not have been more genially, more amusingly interpreted. *Each of the players seemed by nature the character he was acting for was the play not about Bradford and Bradford folk?* (Percy often referred to his role as the hen-pecked husband Herbert Soppitt as being completely out of character.) *and the familiar Bradford speech was pleasant to my ears. I sent a note round to express my good fortune in being present and was invited to join the company after the play to enjoy sandwiches and coffee. It was a happy chance that I should then meet my fellow townsmen, and the ladies of the company.*'

So, Sir William was introduced to the cast after the performance.

Percy Monkman

Growing reputation of the Playhouse

On the eve of its 40th anniversary festival, the *Telegraph & Argus* drama critic, Peter Holdsworth, played tribute to the contribution to stage and screen by directors and actors who learnt their trade at the Playhouse. He wrote:

Among organisations which have benefited in recent times are the National Theatre (through Billie Whitelaw, Edward Petheridge, Robert Stephens and Judy Wilson), London's Royal Court Theatre (through its director William Gaskill), Birmingham Repertory Theatre (through its director Peter Dews who is the Playhouse President), the cinema (through Tony Richardson and James Hill) and television (through Bernard Hepton and David Giles).

During the 1940s and 1950s Percy rubbed shoulders with these up-and-coming stars, who helped set and maintain high standards of production that earned the Civic Playhouse a reputation that stretched well beyond Bradford.

A major influence on this growing reputation was Miss Esme Church (1893 to1972), a British actress and theatre director. In a long career she acted with the Old Vic Company, the Royal Shakespeare Company and on Broadway. She directed plays for the Old Vic, became head of the Old Vic Theatre School and then director of the Bradford Civic Playhouse, with its associated Northern School of Drama. Between 1943 to 1948 she produced seven plays in which Percy performed.

Already with a national reputation, in 1944 Esme took the position of artistic director at the Bradford Civic Playhouse, a career development which initially caused puzzlement, but the move gave her the opportunity to found her own school, the Northern School of Drama, at 26 Chapel Street, using the theatre facilities. The school's reputation grew rapidly and many notable actors trained there, including:

- Tony Richardson (1928 to 1991), an English theatre and film director and producer whose career spanned five decades. In 1964 he won the Academy Award for Best Director for the film *Tom Jones*. Born in Shipley, just outside Bradford, he attended Wadham College, Oxford, where he had the unprecedented distinction of being the President of both the Oxford University Dramatic Society and the Experimental Theatre Club (the ETC). He directed many famous productions (eg John Osborne's plays *Look Back in Anger* and *The Entertainer* at the Royal Court Theatre) and in the same period he directed Shakespeare in Stratford-upon-Avon.

- David Giles (1926 to 2010), too, born in Shipley, Yorkshire and educated at the local grammar school. He joined the Bradford Civic Playhouse, took part in the York mystery plays and after a course at RADA became a full-time man of the theatre.

- Bernard Hepton (1925 to current), British actor and director of stage, film and television. Born in Bradford, he trained at Bradford Civic Theatre school under Esme Church. He has extensive stage experience as an actor. He also played many famous parts on television (eg Caiaphas in the 1969 Dennis Potter play *Son of Man* and Toby Esterhase in the BBC adaptations of *Tinker, Tailor, Soldier, Spy* and *Smiley's People*)

- Sir Robert Stephens (1931 to 1995), a

leading English actor in the early years of Britain's Royal National Theatre. He was one of the most respected actors of his generation and was at one time regarded as the natural successor to Laurence Olivier. Aged 18 he won a scholarship to Esme Church's Bradford-based Theatre School.

The reputation of the Playhouse was enhanced not just by the talent of the actors but by the wide range of plays that were performed. Its programme was certainly not restricted to safe choices of popular middlebrow period comedies. In between the revivals of *When We Are Married*, for over 20 years Percy played in many different roles, usually comic, in many British and European plays, both classic and modern.

Other productions at the Playhouse

The first play that Percy appeared in was a 1935 production of a little-known Irish drama by Denis Johnston called *Moon in the Yellow River*. A couple of reviews singled out Percy's performance as a Captain Potts. The first commented: *Humour was a quality for which one was grateful when it came and it was admirably supplied by John Anderson and Percy Monkman.* The second commented: *John Anderson and Percy Monkman were very funny in their rural simplicity.*

The next production that Percy played in, in 1938, was the Russian classic, *The Inspector General* by Nikolai Gogol. Playing a Medical Officer of Health, Percy again earned an honourable mention with *The first act cameo of Percy Monkman, whose silence was more eloquent than much that was said was among the brighter impressions retained* (*Yorkshire Post*).

After the hit production of *When We Are Married*, the next really successful production was a little-known Soviet play in 1941 by Alexander Afinogenev called *Distant Point* in which Percy played the local stationmaster. The production was highly praised, with the *Yorkshire Post* saying: *Not for many months has a Bradford Civic Playhouse given such an enthusiastic reception to a play as to **Distant Point** last night. The acting was of extraordinary high order; the story simple but gripping.* No special mention was made of Percy this time, except to say that he was 'admirably cast,' as were many others (*Yorkshire Observer*).

Another landmark production starring Percy was the Restoration comedy, *The Beaux' Stratagem* by George Farquhar, performed in 1943 under the direction of Esme Church, the London director, the first time she had produced a play in Bradford. It was a 'racy production' and one in which Percy's performance was again singled out: The *Telegraph & Argus* commented that 'Percy Monkman kept the party going by his clever performance as the squire's amusing servant and won scores of laughs in this part, which fitted him like a glove. Another paper said that 'Percy Monkman makes of Scrub, Squire Sullen's factotum, a droll and cunning clown in the great English tradition', while a third wrote: 'But a good deal of the success of the play was due to Percy Monkman, whose untiring and amusing efforts as the squire's quaint factotum got most of the laughs.'

Percy's next two plays in 1944 make quite a contrast. The first was *The Corn is Green* by Emlyn Williams, in which Percy plays Mr John Goronwy Jones. This was a modern Welsh drama of its day about the difficulty of being a teacher in a Welsh mining village of the 1930s. Capturing Welsh intonations and diction was a challenge for the West Riding cast, but their efforts were praised for the 'perfect rendering of the Welsh dialogue' Again Percy

Percy (left) as Mr John Goronwy Jones in The Corn is Green (October 1943). Source: Bradford Civic Playhouse, 1943.

had an honourable mention in the press reviews: *'Among others who make excellent contributions are Percy Monkman (as Mr Jones with a preoccupation for saving souls)'.*

Percy then went into new territory again, as Engstrand in Ibsen's *The Ghosts*. This is not a major part, but it is certainly a far cry from the Percy's usual comic roles. One reviewer found that *'Percy Monkman portrays the hypocritical Engstrand with success'*.

As the Second World War came to an end Percy ventured once more in a different direction, playing famous comic roles from Shakespeare. In 1945 he played Verges, a 'headborough' (a parish officer), alongside Dogberry (a constable). The *Yorkshire Post* described it *'a polished performance, reaching a standard, the equal of which is rarely attained on the amateur stage and seldom surpassed even in the professional theatre'*, commenting also that *'the comic relief afforded by Dogberry and Verges is safe in the experienced hands of Newton Wood and Percy Monkman'*.

Percy as Verges in Much Ado about Nothing (May 1945). Source: Bradford Civic Playhouse, 1945

An Extraordinary Bradfordian

Percy as Trinculo in The Tempest (May 1946). Source: Bradford Civic Playhouse, 1946

A year later Percy played Trinculo I in *'The Tempest'*. Again the whole production was highly praised, with Percy attracting plaudits for his comic acting. One report praised him as follows: *'For the clowning scenes that are as sure of success today as they were at the Globe, a special word of praise is due to Percy Monkman and Leslie Griffiths, brilliant in drunken revels with Caliban'* (Telegraph & Argus). Another review said: *'But perhaps the laurels go to that violently-contrasting group, Caliban, Trinculo (Percy Monkman) and Ariel. The comedy scenes between the ignoble drunkards and the evil yet poetically tragic Caliban were outstanding'* (Yorkshire Post).

After these excursions into Shakespeare, Percy continued after the war to take on a variety of roles that led the local press to sing his praises.

In 1948 he appeared in James Bridie's *It Depends What You Mean* and a reviewer wrote *'There are several exquisite cameos – Percy Monkman as the old family doctor, for example'*. This was followed very quickly by *Quay South* written by Howard Clewes and directed by Esme Church. Unusually, this had a mixed review, but Percy was picked out for an *'excellent comedy character as the pathetic traveller in fancy goods'*.

Percy as Alexander Perry in Quay South (May 1948). Source: Bradford Civic Playhouse, 1948

Percy as the chaplain in The Lady's Not For Burning (September 1950).

Source: Bradford Civic Playhouse, 1950

He then appeared in *The Lady's Not for Burning, a* romantic comedy by Christopher Fry set in the Middle Ages. This drew the reviewer's comment *'Percy Monkman as the chaplain (*and two others*) all gave expositions of restrained character studies, the subtleties of which always evoked appreciative chuckles'* (Yorkshire Observer).

Three years later he played the part of a local fire brigade chief in John Whiting's *Penny for a Song,* an eccentric English comedy. One reviewer commented that *'A fine character study is given by Percy Monkman'* and another that *'Percy Monkman is convincing as the fire brigade chief whose main ambition in life is to quell fires'* (Yorkshire Evening Post).

(Right) Percy as Lamprett Bellboys in Penny for a Song (September 1953).

Source: Bradford Civic Playhouse, 1953

An Extraordinary Bradfordian

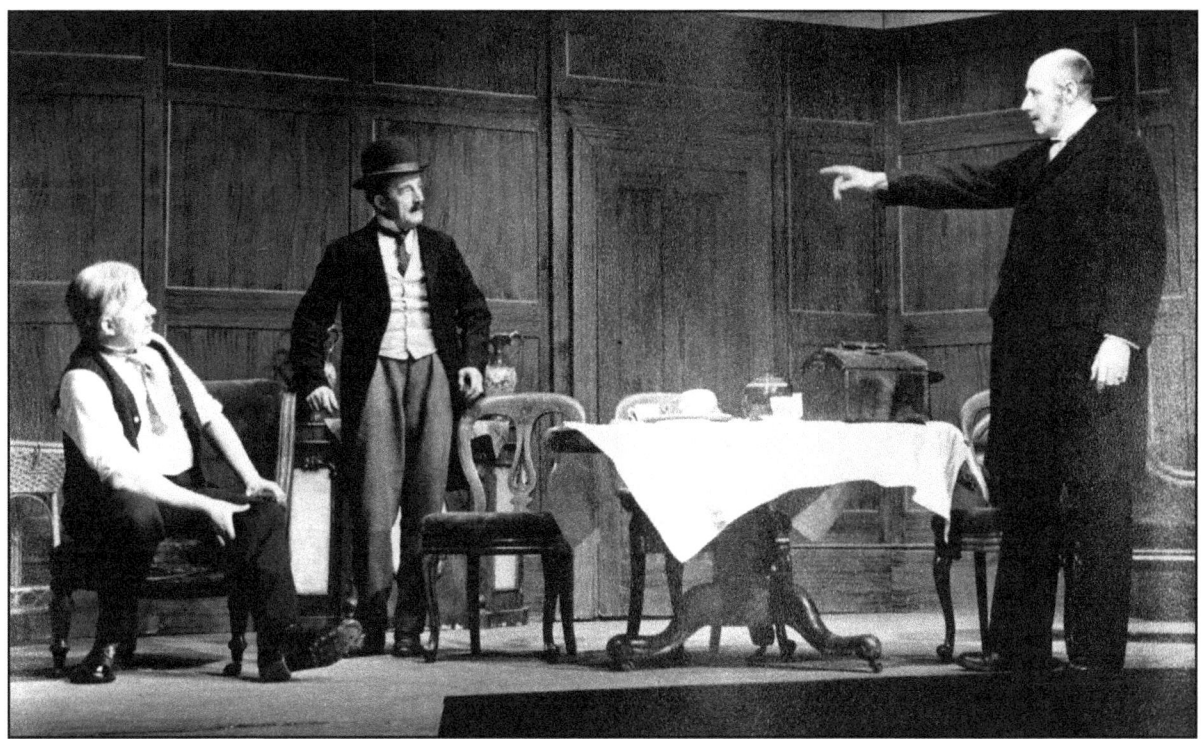

Percy as Jim Heeler in Hobson's Choice (October 1956).
Source: Bradford Civic Playhouse, 1956

Before the performance of *Hobson's Choice* in 1956, Percy had, unusually, one year when he did not appear in any production. The Civic's theatre programme, a spartan affair which communicated little except the cast list and next month's schedule, on this occasion commented that Percy had not played as regularly of late and it was good to welcome him back. The production was again reviewed in glowing terms – *'delightfully presented'* according to the *Yorkshire Observer* whose reviewer picked out Percy's performance as one of the highlights. *'Mention must be made of Percy Monkman excellent as one of Hobson's companions at the Moonrakers.'* Apart from one more revival of *When We Are Married*, this was the last time Percy appeared on stage at the Civic Playhouse.

Percy Monkman

Life at the Playhouse

For over 20 years the Bradford Civic Playhouse was a second home for Percy (or maybe third home, given his involvement with the Bradford Arts Club). Not only did he appear in a production on average at least once a year, but he had other commitments arising from his involvement.

On joining the Playhouse, Percy was soon noticed for his skills as an artist and he became involved in stage set design. He recalled being contacted by Philip Robinson, the director in the early years, with an urgent request. Philip had found out that Percy could paint. Percy continues with the story:

He (Philip) rang me up one Monday teatime 'Could I do a painting for a play they were doing?' Yes, I said, when do you want it? Tonight! It had to be a mountain scene typical of Norway so I found posters and cards from which to copy. I went down to the theatre for 6 o'clock and there was a canvas and paints ready to use. I painted the mountain scene in poster paint (which I wasn't used to). I got it finished by 7.30 when the curtain went up. We then dried it out over a radiator for Act 2 when it went on the set. Philip and I then also did 12 Old Master paintings, six apiece, and for another week 12 French impressionist paintings!

The years of the Second World War were particularly hectic times, because Percy made a new commitment. At the start of the war, a concert party was soon formed in which Percy took a leading role. This took shows to troops, hospitals and workers in Northern Command, across the whole of Yorkshire. Some of the members, like his good friend Harry Tout, were regular actors in the programme of plays, while others became involved just to support the concert party.

Percy was co-opted on to the Playhouse's general management committee and attended almost all meetings (every six to eight weeks), acting as the main link between the Playhouse and the concert party. This became a major activity during the war. Percy estimated that over 600 shows were given between 1940 and 1945. For example, in 1941, he reported about the new concert party's activities to the management committee:

The Concert Party maintained its activities during 1941, notwithstanding many difficulties, principally the call of members to the Forces and the occasional use of members for plays at 'Headquarters'. Although there was a period of almost three months, during which members were engaged in Civic plays, (and in this period no full concerts were given by the party), nevertheless 53 performances were given during the year, mostly to the services.

It may be stated with sufficient evidence to justify the assertion that the high standard that a Civic show expects has been maintained.

Approximately 1,000 miles were covered to give these concerts. Interesting shows were two well-known aerodromes, two visits to Harewood House and what was probably the first concert party show ever given at the Cartwright Hall, (when our president JB Priestley was the principal guest) and, to commence the year, 10 performances at the Civic Theatre.

A recent criticism from two sources of undoubted authority volunteered the opinion that our party and the Leeds Sylvans were the best amateur parties in the Northern Command. The members of the party never fail to utilize any opportunity of making Civic propaganda; and these opportunities occur frequently.'

An Extraordinary Bradfordian

For a voluntary group, this scale of activity is impressive. For nine months in 1941 it performed 63 shows, an average of seven every month. For Percy, as leader, this must have been demanding. Juggling dates, performers and programmes and communicating with event organisers are likely to have taken at least one to two evenings every week, ignoring the time spent on performance days.

This, then, was Percy's activity as an entertainer in 1941. The pattern was, in fact, repeated for the whole of the war.

Some years after the war the concert party returned as a regular feature around the New Year period, putting on some four to six evenings of Old Time Music Hall entertainment, between 1951 and 1962 (although the shows did not appear every single year).

Finally, Percy was responsible for an innovation that lasted many years. He instigated regular exhibitions of paintings by members of the Bradford Arts Club in the Playhouse bar and café areas, from which he also benefitted through sales of his paintings.

Other theatre work

Stage appearances were not totally restricted to the Civic Playhouse. As he gradually reduced his commitment to the Playhouse, Percy could be seen in other theatres with some ad hoc involvements.

For one week in 1947 he appeared for the Bradford Players at the much larger Alhambra Theatre (Bradford's main commercial theatre which showed touring companies). This is one of the oldest amateur operatic and dramatic societies in West Yorkshire: it still performs the annual pantomime at the Alhambra. The play was *Wild Violets*, a musical by and about youth. This was the first production at the Alhambra after being closed during the Second World War (unlike the Civic Playhouse). Percy was brought in with one or two others to give the largely youthful cast some experience.

Five years later, in 1952, Percy had, for him, an unusual involvement on the stage. For the first and only time he became a producer on behalf of the Bradford Diocesan Adult Religious Education Committee. The play itself was also unusual for Percy. *Count it all Joy* was a religious play commemorating the life of St. Cecilia, a Roman noblewoman in the third century AD who converted to Christianity. The *Telegraph & Argus* commented that *'Percy Monkman's production is effective and good use is made of both unusual lighting and the striking effect of recorded voices'*.

Finally, soon after his retirement move to Baildon in 1952, he appeared two years running for the local amateur dramatic group, the Baildon Players. That year he played a taxi-driver and *'gave a very entertaining little character sketch'* in *Treasure Hunt,* a whimsical Irish comedy, according to the *Telegraph & Argus*. A year later he played a much more substantial part in *The Happiest Days of Your Life*. This was notable for two reasons. First, he played a headmaster, a leading role when generally he had preferred supporting roles at the Civic Playhouse. Second, it was the only time that his grandsons saw him on the stage in a play.

The *Shipley Times & Express* reported that Percy *'too gave a great performance. His quiet unassuming manner intimidated by events but occasionally mixed with a sudden flash of fire usually directed on the wrong person, was a direct contrast to Mrs Dibb's* (headmistress of neighbouring school) *loud imperative commands. Percy Monkman, another player of great experience, gave an admirable performance as the dapper little headmaster *who allowed himself to be thoroughly henpecked by the girls' school headmistress, and in times of stress, to be ordered about by his own assistant.'*

Percy did not appear again for his local amateur dramatic group, which would have been a much less experienced group than the one to which he had become accustomed to at the Civic Playhouse. This might have helped to make his performance stand out.

An Extraordinary Bradfordian

Star of screen: *The End*

One of Percy's final acting assignments was the making of a film that won a national award as one of the Ten Best Cine-Films of 1960. This was the only time in his life when acting extended to film-making and it turned out to be highly successful. At a time when amateur cine-film-making was becoming very popular, this film satirises the process of making a film, by breaking every convention of good practice. There is just one actor (Percy) and he struggles to make an impact. The style is a Jacques Tati-like mime sequence with commentary added. The effect is one of humour at every twist and turn of the camera that gradually builds up to a climax.

Here is an article by the director of the film that explains in detail how it works. Bear in mind that it is written for the relatively technical readership of the weekly magazine *Amateur Cine World*.

Two years in the making, one day in the filming – that's the story of *The End*, one of the Ten Best Cine Films of 1960

*Like a Hollywood producer I can claim that **The End** was two years in the making. Of course, actual filming took only one day, the other 729 days representing the time it took the original idea to germinate and to be translated into a coherent movie.*

The germ of the idea was a camera specification sheet. I looked through all the features – backwind, built-in filters, variable speeds, parallax correction etc. What kind of film would result if the cameraman misused all these requirements? And what kind of excuses would he offer when his masterpiece was screened?

*I started by listing as many camera gadgets I could think of, together with the effects of misusing them. To this was added a series of sub-titles. From these still more ideas emerged, such as showing the cameraman's tripod **in** the picture and the results of a disastrous attempt at home processing. The latter idea came quite easily as I had just tried to reduce some unexposed film after it had been projected several times (I still don't know how all that oil got into the projector gate!)*

But here I had to stop. The shots I had listed looked fine individually, but there was no link to hold them together.

A year later I found the missing link. I had just been watching a holiday film in which all the shots of the actors (there were only two) were lost through underexposure. So why not make a film in which the actors' face is never clearly seen until it finally appears through the lab punch marks at the end of 'unedited' film. From this I completely rewrote the script, 'using the chap next door' as the central character. He would suffer all the indignities imposed by a merciless cameraman with increasingly painful results.

*The story was to open with a shot of the actor's legs: – Ah! That's him, **my actor!** The next's a better one of him!'. The commentator now rambles on about his camera, while the actor taps his foot impatiently and finally walks away. 'Oh! And I've got a backwind' says the cameraman, and the poor actor has to come back in reverse motion to his original position. We let him walk this in reverse rather than actually use reverse motion, to save having to make a cut in the middle of the shot.*

A big out-of-focus close-up of the actor's face follows, taken from three feet with the lens focused at one foot, accompanied by the comment 'Of course, 8mm is all right for beginners but for crisp sharp pictures give me 16mm every time!'

Next comes a three-stops, underexposed shot of the actor peering at the camera from the darkness, followed by a similarly overexposed shot. 'The sun must have come out!' says the commentator in surprise.

Getting tired of all this, the actor now tries to get into the centre of the picture, but – Oh! dear! some parallax trouble? Only his left hand side is seen right at the edge of the frame, and moving in doesn't help: the cameraman pans with him, keeping him at the edge all the time and mutters, 'He always stands in the wrong place!'

The actor gives up in despair and leans against a tripod, for which the cameraman seems to have no use – though he says 'I always take one with me wherever I go?'.

There is no rest for the actor. He is now driven from the picture by edge fogging which closes in on him like a fire, from both sides. The actor retreats at 64 f.p.s. but 'variable speeds are agreat help' says the cameraman and he is suddenly whisked away at 8 f.p.s.

We had to compensate for exposure when we filmed this, which meant stopping our actor in mid-shot, closing down three stops, changing the speed and then carrying on. We cut out the flash frames, and the cut then can hardly be detected.

A shot taken through a glass sheet smeared with Vaseline ('A haze filter is always useful.') is the prelude to worse happenings during which the actor is knocked down by a bad splice. In the final shot, which is supposed to be home-processed, the actor is deluged in a storm of spots and scratches.

I passed this script on to Eric Pollard, our producer at Wharfedale Films, for his comments. He made two important suggestions which I incorporated in the shooting script. One was that the films should start with The End title, as if it were being shown in reverse, and that when the end finally came the film should just die away. His second suggestion was that we replace the sub-titles with commentary, since they would slow down the action too much.

This meant background music and what could be more appropriate than The Blue Danube – that ever popular last resort for when you can't think of anything better?

Eric also criticised some of the commentary which set out to be deliberately funny. He felt that it should be done in a serious vein with the humour springing from the contrast between the absurdity of the visuals and the naivety of the commentator. We made the necessary alterations in the shooting script, from which we never departed during filming.

Once the script was finished we had only three weeks in which to do the actual production if we were going to make the Ten Best deadline. A local actor, Percy Monkman, agreed to star in the production and we arranged the shooting session for 4 December (in Bradford's Lister Park, doubtless never before used for such a venture). We had only that day for shooting, since after editing the film would have to be sent away for 'striping' and the commentary added

Of course the rains came. But struggling grimly forward, we managed to find a sheltered spot in the park and despite frequent stoppages caused by showers, all but two shots were in the can by 3.30pm. But by that time we were already shooting at full aperture and as darkness fell it looked as if we were beaten.

As despair settled on our little group we

suddenly realised that there was no reason why the remaining shots could not be taken indoors. Eric Pollard hastily organised a set of lights and shooting was completed at the local art club. (Note: this almost certainly would be Percy's suggestion to use the Bradford Arts Club, just five minutes' walk from Lister Park.)

Howard Wyborn

Source: *Amateur Cine Film* (23 November 1961)

Note: The film can be seen at http://www.eafa.org.uk/catalogue/3989 (the only known live recording of Percy performing).

Percy Monkman

CHAPTER 4
PASSIONATE WATERCOLOUR PAINTER

When asked for three words to describe his passion for watercolour painting, Percy replied 'fanatic, dedicated and impulsive'. He started in his teens, drawing ministers at chapel, and continued almost to the end of his days, taking advantage of every opportunity to paint. Retirement in 1952 gave him many more hours in the day to devote to painting, just when his commitment to entertaining and acting started to tail off. Largely self-taught, he believed strongly in being part of a community of like-minded painters so that he could learn from them. The Bradford Arts Club gave him this network for all his adult life. Exhibitions and sales also spurred him on to improve the quality of his output.

Philosophy of painting

When he set off with a bag full of pencils, ink, chalk, pastels, water colour and paper, to mooch about and have some fun, he was already on his way towards lighting up the existence of somebody he never knew. He had to feel happy and excited about what he saw and then get the thing down as quickly as possible and what he saw and enjoyed he recorded with speed and precision.

Catching a moment and holding it forever – every sincere artist tries to do just that.

Source: JB Priestley essay on Sir CJ Holmes (1868 to 1936), renowned art historian

As so often, Percy looked to JB Priestley to find the words for capturing his thoughts. He frequently referred in his many talks on painting to this definition offered by his friend.

During his retirement Percy was invited, on numerous occasions to talk about painting. He had about half a dozen standard talks with titles such as *It's a Funny Thing, Painting*, or *Adventures with a Paint Box* or *My Hobby is Painting*. He gave around 130 talks from the mid-1950s to the late 1970s. Audiences ranged from arts clubs to rotary clubs, townswomen's guilds and various church-related organ-isations. Whatever the title, the formula was a mixture of insights into the importance of painting, laced with many humorous stories of things that happened to him.

One story that he often repeated concerned an unexpected question from an unlikely source.

Early this year I was out on a painting exhibition with a friend in the Brontë country. When I had almost finished my painting, a small boy with an enquiring turn of mind said to me quite simply 'What are you doing it for?'. This was a question that I had never confronted before.

If I endeavour to answer that question, I can probably give you the clue to the prosperous times most of our art societies are experiencing at the current time. Firstly, I say that it is an enjoyable hobby because it is creative and also one of the finest forms of relaxation one can find.

The value of painting comes from heightened observation, seeing subjects everywhere – beauty in Bradford, a wet day in Leeds. The artist always searches for beauty and often in the most unlikely of places, eg Van Gogh's chair and boots, Cezanne's few apples made into a masterpiece, Durer's famous hands –

a picture famous for all time, Lowry's poetic interpretation of grim Lancashire houses and towns.

Many people have said disparaging things about Bradford, - its grim buildings, its sooty atmosphere, its lack of colour and many other such things. Personally, after a lifetime of observing and looking for colour and pattern, each year I find it more and more fascinating from a painting point of view.

I usually come to Bradford in a morning via Valley Road, with a brother of mine. No-one would want to introduce a visitor to Bradford from that direction, but often I have pointed out the possibility of a real painting subject.

One service that the artist can give to the community is to help them see with a new eye the more pleasant aspects of their own environment, or, if not that, an exciting new vision of what might be a very ordinary, everyday scene.

One example that Percy illustrated in a talk in the late 1970s was captured by a discussion of painting in winter. He wrote:

I used to think the winter months were hopeless for painting, until a famous artist living in the Dales, Reg Brundrit, said he thought the winter time was the best time to paint. There was more colour to excite one. The summertime greens of the fields were much easier to be seen – with more colour to stimulate me, of course. Green is in my opinion the most difficult of all colours. Now I've come to the conclusion that what most people would find to be impossible – rain, mist and snow were far more stimulating than the traditional summer scenes.

Some years ago I was up the Dales on a painting trip with a friend when we got into a real rainstorm. We were up at Starbotton, *found a doorway to shelter in and assessed the view. The rain had made the road like a river, the cottage roofs were lit up by reflected light induced by the rain and suddenly we saw a really stimulating subject.*

I remember in 1963 we had a long snow period. I was then retired and I shot out every day painting like mad local cottages which normally were not inspiring but with the snow the landscape was miraculously transformed by subjects galore. Last year of course was a bonanza for snowscenes. I did about 15 – from a car, of course.

Seeing familiar places in a new light or from a different perspective was, then, for Percy an important strength of good painting. He always started optimistically with a sense of anticipation, explaining:

When you come to think of it, it's hard to think of anything less exciting than a box paints to anyone but an artist. A box of paints, a brush or two, some water and a sheet of paper. How simple, but what a box of magic it can be. Whenever I see a blank sheet of paper, I am excited to think of the possibilities that lie ahead. A few washes of colour, a few strokes of the brush and who knows? Your vision and skill may give great pleasure to someone unknown, and, more important, give you great satisfaction, as most creative things do. I've struggled to gain some mastery in painting for some time and enjoyed the struggle. It can be maddening, frustrating, exciting, exhilarating but never boring.

Like anything worthwhile, it needs years of practice, many trials and many daubs before one begins to think 'not so bad'. But always to spur one on is the feeling that one day you will pull off a real winner! There comes eventually a feeling that you are getting somewhere, slowly and painfully. There is nothing so humbling as this job and the greater the artist the more humble he becomes.

This limestone country 'gets into the blood'. To a Southerner the landscape beribboned with grey limestone walls, likened to lines over a billiard table, does not readily appeal. Only when painting the walls does one realise their beauty. Changing in colour almost hourly, they challenge all artists. Reflecting light, they can range in colour from oyster-grey and white, when the sun is absent, to almost cerise when the setting sun caresses them.

He often quoted Sir Winston Churchill on his favourite hobby when he summed up his attitude to painting as 'inexpensive independence, a mobile and perennial pleasure apparatus, new mental food and exercise, an added interest to every common scene, an occupation for every idle hour, an unceasing voyage of entrancing discovery and the most wonderful distraction, one cannot paint and think of anything else' – a pretty good recommendation from such a source, Percy would say.

Early experiences

Percy's start in his life as a painter was, to say the least, inauspicious. As he often said when giving talks about painting, 'Art in my schooldays was a non-event and art teaching was pathetic'.

When he gave a speech at a Speech Day for a local secondary school in 1962, he recalled 'The art we were taught was as primitive as could be. All I could remember in that line was being given a brush like a worn-out toothbrush and taught what I can only describe as blob painting. So I didn't pick up a lot about art at school'. He went on to say ' But I must have got the germ from somewhere, because from schooldays I practised and learnt all I could from every possible source... and I'm still going to school (now the Bradford Arts Club) regularly and I'm still enjoying it'.

His interest was first shown at chapel in his teens when he used to draw ministers and even got some of them to add their signature to his drawings. But he did say many years later that he won his first painting prize at school – a three-penny bit for a painting of flowers that he had to parade round the classes.

Percy Monkman

Marché, Cambrai (1919)

Eglise Saint Gery and ruins, Cambrai (1919)

Percy's first documented serious attempt at art came during six months at the end of the First World War. At the start of 1919 Percy's demobilisation was deferred. This was a period of some boredom, Percy later wrote, but a couple of pen and ink drawings of the centre of Cambrai indicate how he spent at least some of his time. According to his personal catalogue, these were the first pieces of art that he ever produced and exhibited in the Bradford Spring Exhibition of 1924.

The first drawing is a busy market scene with many detailed drawings of people buying, selling and walking by. In contrast, the second one is purely a set of buildings with no human interest, in the form of a large church built around small houses that have been damaged, perhaps by the war.

Completely different, though in the same town centre, both are very carefully drawn with some skill on small sheets of paper (just 7.5"by 6.0"). Together they form an unlikely start to a portfolio of well over 2,000 paintings set in very different surroundings. They show an innate talent for drawing – both buildings and people – before he was exposed to any serious art training or the influences of fellow-artists. Although the subjects differ, the drawings show the same distinct technique and style.

An Extraordinary Bradfordian

Painting and working (1919 to 1952)

In 1920, a year after his return to civilian life, Percy painted his first outdoor work in a local wood at Heaton. This was followed in 1922 by two paintings on holiday in Silverdale (near Morecambe) and a couple of still lives, plus another painting in Heaton. This was to be the pattern of much of his early work in the 1920s. He had a young family and many commitments as an entertainer and hence little opportunity to develop the passion that became obvious later in life.

His main opportunity for painting came on holiday. The catalogue of paintings, that he maintained all his life, can easily be read in the 1920s and 1930s as clear evidence of where he took his holidays: Morecambe, Filey, Grange-over-Sands, Lytham St Annes, Dorset, Grassington, Whitby, Kettlewell — these are the scenes of holidays in the late 1920s and early 1930s and hence where many of his early paintings were completed. In the late 1920s he did not paint much in the Yorkshire Dales and it would have been more accurate to describe him as Percy Monkman, the promising Lancashire artist! Dorset where he did 11 paintings in 1930 in what must have been a fortnight's holiday was an interesting exception, being his only holiday in England south of Yorkshire (or Lancashire) in his whole life.

Compared with the rest of the 1920s, when he painted an average of five works a year, 1929 was a prolific year in terms of output with 36 paintings boosted, it appears, by two holidays — at Lytham St Annes and at Hawes in Wensleydale. For the first time he also painted regularly in what became favourite haunts in Wharfedale. Thereafter, he averaged about 25 paintings a year throughout the 1930s.

Unfortunately, very few examples of his early work survive. He sold relatively few, just six, in the 1920s with many others being offered as gifts to family and friends. One early painting in 1930 of the quayside at Poole in Dorset was bought 45 years later by his friend Roger Suddards who by that time had become something of a collector of Percy's works.

It is difficult to assess pictures in his first 15 years of painting. He did not sell many, but he did in the early 1930s start to exhibit and collect favourable press comments. One important part of his early development that we have not been able to place were the evening classes that we know he attended: his only formal art training. The likeliest time for this might be the early or mid-1920s when he had dabbled with some painting and realised that he needed some training if he were to develop his interest and skills further.

The mid-1930s saw an important stage in his development when he came to be noticed outside Bradford. First, he started to exhibit as part of the newly-formed Yorkshire Group of Artists, for which he became treasurer. Their first exhibition, in Leeds, was opened by Sir William Rothenstein, another Bradfordian who made a national reputation in the arts. He attended Bradford Grammar School and then the Slade School of Art, later becoming the Principal of the Royal College of Art from 1920 to 1935. A press review of the exhibition picked out Percy's 'Canal locks at Bingley' as 'deserving special notice'.

In 1936 Percy had two works selected for an exhibition at the City of Birmingham Art Gallery, the first time he had shown paintings outside Yorkshire. Perhaps the most significant accolade came with Percy winning the first prize four years in a row from 1935 to 1938 at the Westminster Bank's annual art exhibition in London. The story of a local artist doing well on a national stage generated a number of local press notices, which will have raised Percy's profile as an artist, rather than an entertainer, quite significantly.

The momentum in painting that Percy had slowly built in the 1930s slipped back in 1938 and 1939 when his output dropped to just 15 paintings a year. The most likely explanation was that his priority was his growing acting commitments at the Civic Playhouse, and in particular the highly successful production of JB Priestley's *When We Are Married*. In fact this was the start of a drop in painting that lasted several years as a result of the Second World War. We have already seen that Percy was very active in organising concert parties for returning servicemen throughout the war and he also continued to be committed to the Civic Playhouse's programme of plays.

He averaged just six paintings a year during 1939 to 1945. Like his start-up years in the early 1920s, most painting was restricted to holidays that he managed to secure in places such as Grassington, Grange-over-Sands and Austwick. He sold very little over these years. No doubt people had little spare money to spend on such non-essentials.

After the war things picked up slowly but he was still well short of his output in most of the 1930s, with an average of one painting a month. Holidays in Switzerland (1946), Coxwold at the edge of the North Yorkshire Moors (1947) where my parents lived for a few years and the Lake District (1949) stimulated his painting. His visit to Lugano in 1946 was the first time he had painted seriously out of the UK, and perhaps a surprise choice so soon after the end of the war.

However, it would require a major life change for his painting life to become his top priority.

That event was retirement from the bank in 1952, at the age of 60.

Painting in retirement (1953 to 1986)

The prospect of having the whole day for painting, rather than just weekends and holidays, must have been exciting for Percy. From the late 1950s he averaged 50 to 60 paintings a year almost to the end of his life.

He did not, in fact, jump immediately from a full-time job to a life of leisure. He worked on a part-time basis (mornings only) in the accounts department of his brother Frank's firm in Bradford, which doubtless helped to bridge the five-year gap before he received the state pension at 65. Driving in from Ilkley, Frank picked up Percy outside the Half Way House at the bottom of the road in Baildon where Percy lived. They then went in to Bradford together.

For all his life Percy depended on lifts from family and friends. His ability to secure transport played a major role in expanding his painting output. Throughout his retirement he developed friendships with people happy to drive him into the Yorkshire Dales, or occasionally the Bronte country. His drivers included people with a range of reasons to help. For example, Peter Bonney was a commercial traveller who had many clients in the Dales and took Percy to places where he could be left to paint and be picked up two or three hours later. Later Peter moved away from Yorkshire and became a regular buyer of Percy's paintings in the 1960s and 1970s.

The more usual arrangement was that the driver wanted to learn to paint or improve. Percy would offer help in return for the lift. Harry Butterfield, who ran a signwriting company in Bradford, had time on his hands and was a regular driver. He was also prepared to be a chauffeur on a family holiday in 1960 to Ambleside in the Lake District, taking three adults and two boys in his comfortable saloon, which included a hair-raising trip over the Wrynose and Hardknott passes.

Other drivers on these painting outings included Jean Barker, Ian Brown, Ken Feakes, Tony Greenhalgh and Brian Walker. Friendships developed and, whatever the original reason for being the chauffeur, Percy came to rely on the help, and the friend enjoyed the company and the day out. One friend, David Waddington, still alive when this book was written, recalls that Percy was an amusing companion, always optimistic and full of good stories. David also lived in Baildon and took Percy to the arts club in Bradford, maybe twice a week, over many years.

The portfolio of paintings

Percy's reputation as a painter was as a watercolourist. His catalogue indicates that at least 90% of his works were watercolours. However, he did dabble in other media such as oils, gouache and pen and ink drawings throughout his life, but, generally speaking, these were not as successful as watercolours, to which he soon returned.

Temperamentally, he was well suited to watercolour in that it was easy to apply, being a medium for quick expression. Having seen a subject or an angle, he just wanted to get it down on the paper. He often said that, like golf, the fewer strokes the better, as long as they were the right strokes. He admitted to not being patient enough to be a regular painter in oils. Watercolours are also quick to assemble, not involving carrying heavy things nor much in the way of cleaning up.

Most of his watercolours were landscapes, interspersed with some city scenes of Bradford. He did paint still life, especially in his early days, but in terms of sales they were less successful – about 15% of around 50 sold. Perhaps they were not of the same interest to potential buyers or perhaps his style was not distinctive enough or sufficiently well-developed.

He also painted a number of portraits. He rarely entered them in exhibitions, instead often gifting them to the sitters. Hence, they were not really seen as a prominent part of his portfolio.

Without doubt he was seen as a Yorkshire landscape watercolourist. His main subjects were found in the Yorkshire Dales, especially Wharfedale. Core to his work was the painting of just about every hamlet, bridge, village and town on the River Wharfe from Hubberholmein Upper Wharfedale down to Otley and beyond. Buckden, Starbotton, Kettlewell, Littondale (adjoining valley), Conistone, Grassington, Burnsall, Appletreewick, Bolton Abbey, Ilkley, and overlooking the town, Ilkley Moor, Otley and, overlooking the town, Otley Chevin. Each place was painted many times from different perspectives in different lights. Familiar landmarks such as Kilnsey Crag, Barden Tower (both overlooking the River Wharfe), Cow and Calf Rocks (Ilkley Moor) and bridges at Kettlewell, Grassington, Burnsall, Bolton Abbey were all frequently painted. Over one third of his paintings (more than 800) were based on Wharfedale.

He liked to find quiet spots off the beaten track; hamlets such as Linton and Thorpe just outside Grassington, were ideal. Another such spot was High Bradley, a hamlet a few miles west of Wharfedale on the way to Skipton, where he got to know a local farmer and Dales character Sam Throup. Here he painted over 20 watercolours in the 1950s, 1960s and 1970s.

Percy Monkman

Percy's love of Wharfedale is captured in a rare piece of writing from him, below.

Wharfedale

That distinctive gem of English riverside and moorland scenery, Wharfedale has long been and still is the happy hunting-ground of artists. Situated within an hour's run of the textile part of the West Riding, Leeds and Bradford, it has an irresistible call to all nature-lovers, for happily it retains almost unspoilt its natural character, Otley and Ilkley are really the starting points for the visitors to the more picturesque and wilder parts of the valley.

Ideally situated, as most of these abbeys are, near the river, flanked by trees of character and beauty, with a foreground of meadows that build up the atmosphere of tranquillity, and with an ever changing background of heather-flecked hills, Bolton Abbey is almost the perfect subject for an artist. No wonder then that men like Cotham and Turner visited and painted there. No wonder that kings of England have spent the shooting season there with the Duke and Duchess of Devonshire.

Six or seven miles further along the river, and this particular stretch is probably the most beautiful in its richness and variety, and passing the most picturesque of all its villages, Burnsall, with its village green and maypole, and noted for its annual fell race, we arrive at the artists' centre, Grassington.

Source: Percy Monkman (undated)

Further north he only made occasional visits to Wensleydale and just twice in Swaledale, further north still. Given his love of Yorkshire countryside it is surprising that he so rarely went further north than Wharfedale, but the lack of his own car might have been a constraint. Also, to get to Wensleydale and Swaledale, he had to travel through Wharfedale, where you could always stop and paint. Had he had the opportunity in an alternative life, these equally beautiful dales would surely have excited him as much as Wharfedale.

He had another favourite place, Malham, west of Wharfedale. Here, he had several holidays, sometimes staying with his artist friend Constance Pearson, who lived there. The village had many subjects for Percy's paintings – the cove, the tarn, some prominent farm buildings, the bridge, the infant River Aire and two pubs.

Percy found subjects at every corner in places such as Kettlewell, Grassington and Malham, sometimes just turning round to look up the street, having painted the view down the street. They were his ideal places for painting and perfect for holidays because he saw so many painting opportunities.

Another rural area that he frequented as he grew older was the Brontë country. He often painted in and around Oxenhope, home of Joe Pighills, another respected Yorkshire artist friend. Surprisingly he avoided Haworth itself. It was not until 1975 when he was 83 years old that he painted the famous Old Parsonage, home of the Brontë family, in the centre of the village.

He tended to avoid tourist traps, not wishing to go for the obvious subjects, or what he called 'sit-up-and-beg' subjects. For some reason Percy also never visited Saltaire, just three miles away, for a painting subject until very late in his life in 1976 – where Sir Titus Salt built his large mill and model village and now a World Heritage Site attracting many tourists. Another tourist centre that he ignored all his life except on one occasion was York. However he was very fond of the Yorkshire coast, holidaying several times in Filey, Scarborough, Robin Hood's Bay and Whitby. Many paintings resulted from these holidays.

The place that he painted the most often was Baildon, home for all his retirement. Not an obvious centre for painting, it did nevertheless have several different areas of interest. The old village at the top of the hill had many buildings of interest in and around the centre. Baildon was at the edge of the moors with some 18th century buildings in hamlets such as Low Springs and Moorside. He found many opportunities to paint around Dick Hudson's pub and Dobrudden Farm, both a little further on to the moors. At the west end of the village Shipley Glen was a local beauty spot where he sometimes painted. At the other end of Baildon, down by the River Aire and Leeds & Liverpool Canal, he often painted around Esholt, a small village later to be the home of the TV sitcom, *Emmerdale Farm*. Never owning a car, Percy made a virtue of painting in every direction within a couple of miles of home.

In terms of exhibitions and sales he was markedly less successful when painting landscapes outside Yorkshire. He did a few paintings around Warwickshire, where I lived, and some in Sussex, where my brother lived, when he came to visit, but he found it a little difficult to capture the different lighting and stonework of the buildings. Although he was very fond of the Lake District, spending several holidays there, nevertheless he found the greener landscape and the bluey-green slate of the buildings and walls harder to paint than the browner landscape and the light-grey limestone walls of the Dales.

He also painted on his four main holidays abroad (Holland and Germany in 1937, Switzerland in 1946, Italy and Switzerland in 1953 and Paris in 1961), but found the much brighter light a very different painting experience.

Perhaps the different settings just required more practice. After all, it took him a number of years before his Yorkshire paintings developed a distinctive style that led to success.

Just very occasionally he did something to surprise. He often talked with some humour about modern abstract art compared with the traditional representational art that he espoused. In 1971 the *Telegraph & Argus* review of an exhibition commented that *'The move to abstract has gone so far that veteran watercolourist Percy Monkman no less, exhibits a Miro-type painting. It looks to me as though he has his tongue in his cheek but for all that it is a delicious piece of work in the most carefully chosen pale gritty colours.'*

Commissions

As, in the 1950s, Percy became more successful in terms of exhibitions and sales, he started to receive commissions from people who wanted pictures of their homes (or in some cases, their pubs). He was, generally, reluctant to take on such assignments. Although he could charge more, they could sometimes be difficult to turn into satisfactory compositions and occasionally the customers were too specific and constraining about what should be included or excluded. However, during the 1950s and 1960s, he tackled one or two of these each year. In his catalogue he describes them as 'house portraits'.

His most regular customer was Eric Fleming of Holly Hill Farm, Huby (between Otley and Harrogate). He had a large converted farmhouse out in the country and, in 1961, he

Percy Monkman

commissioned three paintings, from different perspectives – the front, side and rear. Percy confessed, in a 1971 talk, that he found the place rather dull. On one occasion he added a couple of cows that had appeared as he painted but, although the owner quite liked the idea, they were apparently the worst cows in the herd and he asked Percy to redraw them to include the best. Also for 13 years from 1962 to 1974 he asked Percy to paint or draw an external or internal view with a Christmas theme for his annual Christmas card. At times Percy struggled to find a new angle.

Occasionally, Percy received unusual or more prestigious commissions. One such request came in 1965 from his brother Gordon in Peterborough, Ontario, Canada. Now an aldermanof the city council, he asked his brother back in Bradford to do a painting of Peterborough Cathedral in England for display in the mayoral office as a way of linking the two Peteroroughs. So Percy made a rare journey south to complete this commission and at the end of the assignment received a very nice 'thank you' letter from both his brother Gordon and the Mayor of Peterborough (Ontario), who pointed out that *'the picture was symbolic of the connection between the two Peteroroughs'*.

The painting below shows his skill at depicting buildings. The soft foliage of the trees in the foreground contrasts well with the darkness and precision of the cathedral to which the eye is drawn. The size of the few figures and the houses to the right emphasise the scale of the cathedral and the cloistered calm of the precinct.

Peterborough Cathedral (1965)

An Extraordinary Bradfordian

Three commissions that had some prestige locally stand out. First, Percy was commissioned in 1964 by Brown Muff & Co, at that time the premier department store in the city, to do a painting of the store that could be used as part of its promotional material for its 150 years of trading. For example, his painting was on the cover of all its restaurant menus.

This is a view of the front of the store, which occupied a prime position between Bank Street and Tyrell Street and opposite the Wool Exchange (now Waterstones). On the right-hand side one can make out the first part of another familiar name for Bradfordians – Greenwood Menswear (a well-known store throughout the North and still going strong, interestingly founded not by the Greenwoods of my immediate family but by the son of an earlier Greenwood who married into the Monkman family – the husband of Percy's father's cousin).

Not perhaps the most promising of subjects for a commission, the painting is well composed. The store is framed to the side and behind by the solid Victorian buildings, which give the centre of Bradford its character, where the building still remains. The reflections in the windows are delicately shaded, set off nicely against the honey-coloured sandstone. The traffic and people at street level give life to the picture but also add scale to the main building. Overall, the painting illustrates Percy's view that you can find beauty in a city like Bradford. Given that Brown Muffs saw the need for and commissioned such a painting and, given what has happened since to the building, it must be the finest pictorial record of what was a famous Bradford landmark.

Brown Muff & Co (1964)

Percy Monkman

Known in its heyday as 'the Harrods of the North', the store lost its way in the 1970s, was bought by Rackhams and then closed in 1995. Today, in 2017 the four storey building is a sorry shell of what it was when Percy painted it. It is largely unoccupied with large 'To Let' posters. Only three of the ground floor corner sites are occupied: by Betfred, Caffe Nero and Nationwide Building Society; the fourth was recently vacated by Kentucky Fried Chicken ('Due to relocation'). The only reminder of its former glory is an original Brown Muff & Co sign over what would have been a goods delivery entrance, with a supporting sign to say that it had been discovered in a 1996 redevelopment of the site. In the painting the sign is prominent over the front corner of the store where there was a special concave window that the picture cannot show but which caught the eye as it distorted the items on display.

The 16-page brochure that Brown Muffs produced for the celebration, incidentally, included a prominent Percy Monkman cityscape as the centre spread – the view of Forster Square in the 1950s that he painted several times and always sold very well.

This picture was also part of a separate commission from Deloittes, the management accountants, who asked Percy in 1977 when 85 years old to reproduce three views of Bradford City centre in the 1950s. As the city centre had been extensively rebuilt in the late 1950s and 1960s (to the anger of many), Percy could only carry out this commission by going back to paintings and drawings made more than 20 years previously.

Perhaps the commission that gave him the greatest satisfaction came in 1974 from his friend Roger Suddards, now a governor of Bradford Grammar School. Roger asked him for two paintings of Clock House, in the grounds of the school, then the lodgings of the headmaster who was about to retire. One painting was to be a gift to the headmaster, the other for the Old Boys' Association. Percy, whose own education stopped before he was 14, would have been flattered to undertake this commission, the more so as both my brother and I had been educated there some 15 years earlier, the first in the Monkman family educated to go on to university.

An Extraordinary Bradfordian

Passion for painting

Percy kept a catalogue of all his paintings from his first in 1919 to his last, which included details of subjects, dates painted, exhibitions and sales (or gifts). It reads almost like a diary of his painting life.

One thing jumps out from this detailed record – his passion to paint. This can be seen in many examples. In September 1964 he came back from a week's painting in Derwentwater where, despite much rain, (remembered by myself as this was the last family holiday I joined) he managed to paint every day (nine paintings in total), Yet, at the age of 72, he went out the day after he returned from the Lake District to paint at Timble in the Washburn Valley, no doubt invited out by one of his drivers.

On his next holiday, in May 1965, he rose very early to capture the early morning light in the Dales. He would do this at least once on most holidays. He was generally a reluctant early riser and this would have required much effort, but he was drawn by the prospect of finding a 'winner' – usually a familiar subject viewed in a new light.

Six years later, in 1971, (now 79 years old) he could be found painting on New Year's Eve near his old home in Heaton. Five years after that (aged 84), he was again painting on New Year's Eve in a car park in Baildon near his home, most likely sitting in a car with his sketch book and paints. December 1978 and January 1979 must have been snowy months because Percy went on to paint 15 snow scenes in Baildon, all within a very short drive (or walking distance) from home.

On 12 August 1977 (the day after his 85th birthday) he completed two paintings in a day. The first was of Kilnsey Crag, a few miles upstream, on the west side of the River Wharfe from Grassington and a regular subject of Percy's possibly because its striking features can be painted from the roadside. The second was a view of Conistone, a small village on the other side of the river, *'in evening light'* according to Percy's notes. His companion might not have expected a second painting, but Percy will have seen the promising evening light across the valley and have been persuasive in suggesting to him that they do a second painting before they spent the hour and a half journey back home.

All these examples from Percy's 70s and early 80s show a man driven by painting landscapes and keen to exploit every opportunity to paint. It is small wonder that in the 1950s, 1960s and 1970s, when he had more time to paint than when he had a 9 to 5 job, he painted year-in, year-out, an average of 50 paintings a year, and in his most prolific year (1967) at the age of 75, over 90 paintings.

Percy Monkman

A press article written when he was 84 years old conveys neatly this driving spirit to paint.

Percy painting outside

t isn't difficult to recognise Percy Monkman. His artist's tools are one clue to his identity, but it is his bow-tie which is the give-away. Now 84, Percy, who is probably one of Bradford's most active artists, lives in a semi-detached house in Baildon, which is cluttered to the doors with paintings.

It would be strange if his home was not packed as painting has been a hobby for more years than he cares to remember. He has absolute determination to paint as often as he can, which is perhaps surprising if you realise the kind of coaching he got at school as a youngster.

'It was pathetic training. I got nothing at all. But I really wanted to paint, so later I joined the Bradford College of Art for evening lessons'.

'Fanatic, dedicated and impulsive' are the words Percy uses to describe himself and his approach to his hobby. He is not sure, though, just which one is most apt. I have been painting all my life. It is definitely an impulse job. It's all or nothing. Once I get started on a scene, I like to finish it.

Source:Telegraph & Argus, 3 August 1977

Bradford Arts Club

Percy joined the Bradford Arts Club in 1924 and remained a member until the end of his life. He was to play many roles, including vice-chairman (for 13 years), chairman (14 years) and president (three years) and was made honorary life member in 1968. However, he was, above all, just a member participating twice or three times a week in its activities over 60 years or so. The programme involved up to four art classes weekly, including a life class on Wednesday evening. At weekends visiting painters often came to share their experience.

After many years using a number of rented rooms, the club managed to buy a property off Oak Lane, just a short distance from Manningham Lane. This gave it a home that allowed it to build up its programme and membership to around 200. It offered space for exhibitions and social events. The next 40 years, which coincided with Percy's main involvement with the club, saw a thriving community of painters. It gave Percy great satisfaction for the club to be in such a healthy state. Owning its own premises compared favourably with many other arts clubs in Yorkshire where he had contacts.

Almost as passionately as he believed in the value of painting, he believed in the value of the arts club as a network of like-minded individuals able and willing to help and learn from each other. He sometimes referred to going to the arts club as 'still being at school'; it was just an opportunity to learn and improve his painting skills.

One feature in the 1950s and 1960s which Percy fully supported as a development opportunity was the Carnegie weekend programme of visiting talks and demonstrations by leading watercolour painters, under the auspices of Leeds University (Carnegie Hall). This enabled Percy to develop friendships with artists with national reputations, such as Donald Bosher, Donald McIntyre, Angus Rands and Edward Wesson.

He was to say about the club in many of his talks that *'In the Arts Club we have members from all walks of life. There are no class or religious distinctions. I don't know of any other body of men so friendly and who mix so easily and where professionals and amateurs help each other without any signs of jealousy.* In 1979 Percy wrote about *'the spirit of comradeship that was fostered and was probably the club's greatest asset'*

It also gave Percy satisfaction that so many members who were his contemporaries had reputations that extended beyond Bradford and sometimes to the national stage. They included Richard Eurich (one of Bradford's most successful and well-regarded artists, appointed Official War Artist in World War Two with the Royal Navy), John F Greenwood (famous for his distinctive wood engravings), Fred Jones (who exhibited at the Royal Academy and the Royal Scottish Academy), Royal Society of British Artists (RBA) and Laurence Scarfe (the Royal Academy, the V&A and Tate Gallery). Further information can be found at the excellent website www.notjusthockney.info/ which applies clear criteria in selecting all artists born or living in the area of Bradford.

Finally, no mention of the Bradford Arts Club can be made without reference to the annual Christmas party, where entertainment was routinely provided by one Percy Monkman and his concert party. In the 1950s the club also had a formal annual dinner at the Victoria Hotel in Bradford, where Percy also provided the after-dinner entertainment.

Yorkshire Watercolour Society

In the early 1980s a new arts society in Yorkshire was formed; the Yorkshire Watercolour Society. The driving force behind it was Ashley Jackson (its first chairman) supported by Stanley Chapman (its first secretary). The vision was to make the society a showcase for the best watercolour artists in the county, ie those who painted and lived in Yorkshire. Its membership was restricted to 50, selected by a small committee and based on submitted works. Percy was one of the ten founder members.

Although Ashley might have been one of the younger members, he had already established his country-wide reputation as a fine watercolour painter, not just in Yorkshire. For example, he had already had been involved in a TV series in 1978 for BBC *Pebble Mill at One*. He had decided since his early 20s to make his living professionally as a 'Yorkshire artist' and had already some very good connections. He was a close friend of LS Lowry from 1969 till his death in 1976. Another very good friend was ex-Barnsley MP Roy Mason (and Cabinet Minister under Harold Wilson) who helped the new society to set up an exhibition at the House of Commons in November 1983, which he (now Lord Mason) opened. Some 41 artists, including Percy, exhibited just one painting each.

Other early exhibitions, in which Percy participated, took place in Leeds and Brighouse (1982) and Harrogate (1983).

The key to this group was the selection process, which created a standard of painting that defined expectations of what it meant to be a member and so helped to project its membership profile. Percy kept copies of newsletters for members, one of which refers to a selection meeting that accepted just three new members from 12 who had applied.

Percy was already 90 years old when the society started. Although he was very pleased to be included, understandably he did not play a very active role. Three weeks before he died, the committee made him the first honorary member of the society, a message passed to him in hospital.

No doubt Percy wondered if the society might survive longer than an earlier similar attempt in the 1930s. He had at that time played a leading role as its treasurer in the formation of the Yorkshire Group of Artists in 1931 (the president was the Bradfordian, Sir William Rothenstein, another eminent artist of his day with a national reputation). That group, too, put on annual exhibitions around the county, but seemed to disappear at the advent of the Second World War and did not re-emerge.

The Yorkshire Watercolour Society did not survive long after the resignation of Ashley Jackson, after serving ten years as chairman. Ashley commented that, after he left, the society discontinued the selection process that was, of course, the key to its purpose of supporting the best watercolour painting in Yorkshire. This backward step led to the society folding, as it had lost its way.

An Extraordinary Bradfordian

Publicity and exhibitions

The Dalesman

One excellent way of reaching his natural audience was *The Dalesman,* a monthly magazine launched in 1939.

Over the years Percy was a regular contributor, building a good relationship with the first editor Harry Scott and then long-term editor, Bill Mitchell. One of his paintings first appeared in 1940 and thereafter he contributed regularly, right until his final years. In the early days his contributions were black and white drawings. In 1945 he submitted a drawing of the Game Cock Inn at Austwick which led to a commission for a series of drawings of inns. Later, when the magazine went into colour, his paintings were reproduced and occasionally featured as the cover.

Percy also contributed articles (three about fellow Yorkshire artist friends, reproduced in Chapter 6) and was the subject of short features such as 'This Month's Artist' and 'My Favourite Yorkshire Story'. On two occasions after his death, others wrote features about Percy after his death: his daughter Dorothy in 1987 and his chauffeur friend Ken Feakes in 1992 (reproduced in Chapter 9).

Percy himself subscribed to *The Dalesman* until the end of his life. He enjoyed the articles about places and people of the Dales and, of course, others saw him as a Yorkshire character and painter of the Dales.

Local exhibitions

A critical activity for Percy that ran alongside his passion for painting was his support of exhibitions and other forms of publicity. Right from the early days, when he came back from the war in Northern France, being able to exhibit his work was an important facet of painting. It was not enough to paint but he had to submit his paintings to public scrutiny. Throughout his life he spent much time in organising works for exhibitions, a task made more difficult with the lack of a car. The work often included managing submissions by his daughter Dorothy as well as his own. Dorothy had been trained at the Bradford School of Art and was a well-respected painter in her own right.

His staple exhibitions were those put on by the Bradford Arts Club (at least one per year) and the annual Spring Exhibition by the Cartwright Hall, Bradford's main art gallery. In the 1930s he regularly exhibited for the Yorkshire Group of Artists and, in the last few years of his life, at the Yorkshire Watercolour Society.

However, Percy always took advantage of other opportunities that came his way in places such as Harrogate, Ilkley and Leeds. He supported annual exhibitions run by other arts clubs in Yorkshire (eg Keighley) and frequently exhibited at commercial galleries in the West Riding.

For Percy, exhibitions needed publicity, especially positive feedback from local art critics. He was an avid collector of press cuttings and little upset him more than being ignored in reviews of exhibitions where many artists were on display. Fortunately, this happened very rarely and his press cuttings books are full of warm words that he generally underlined in red biro.

Percy Monkman

Annual open air summer show at Harrogate

Percy and Dorothy at Harrogate open-air show (1960)

One annual exhibition that he supported over many years in the 1950s and 1960s was the open air summer show at Harrogate in the Valley Gardens that usually lasted two weeks. Unlike most exhibitions where he was only allowed maybe three paintings, this event allowed him to show many more (up to 20 framed and many more unframed paintings). This, of course, made the preparation and organisation much harder, and doubly so, because Percy was almost always accompanied by Dorothy, who usually had her own stall.

All this took up much time in the early summer (usually July) and my brother and I were sometimes enlisted to help out. Fortunately, the Harrogate bus from Bradford passed at the bottom of Percy's road and so he could avoid asking people for lifts, except at the start and the end of the fortnight when he depended on a lift to transport his paintings. However, with the bus journey lasting an hour, each day of the show (mid-morning till early evening) was a long day.

Although all this made the event tiring, it did have some clear advantages over more conventional exhibitions. The paintings on show were a high standard and so there were plenty of visitors and buyers. One feature that Percy liked was the opportunity to chat with people throughout the day about painting. Potential customers could hear his stories and he could share ideas with fellow exhibitors, friends such as Owen Bowen, Angus Rands and Joe Appleyard, the last two being professional artists.

Sales and gifts

Making money from his paintings was never an important objective for Percy. Nevertheless, it was gratifying to sell them, especially when the buyers were clearly pleased with their purchase. He often received 'thank-you' letters from grateful recipients.

He sold nearly 1,400 paintings. This helped fund the cost of art materials and pay for extras, such as family holidays. Many people were repeat customers, perhaps buying the paintings not just for themselves but as gifts.

He was particularly proud of the numbers of countries, where his paintings were hanging. He kept a record of this and ended up with a list of around 30. Some of the overseas buyers were regulars such as a Linda Johnson in the USA and a FW Heap in New Zealand.

One venture that was overtly commercial concerned two 1952 paintings: a view of Forster Square in Bradford, from his office some 100 yards away and a view of City Hall Square. Ten years later, after a complete regeneration of that part of the city centre, the painting had a strong nostalgic air to it (eg the light blue trolley buses). With his friend Roger Suddards he invested in 1,000 high-quality, full-size prints of each painting, which could be sold at a much lower price than the original. Percy gave a few to people who had helped promote his works such as the art critics of the *Telegraph & Argus* and the *Yorkshire Post*. This venture helped to reinforce many people's view that Percy was an artist who specialised in views of Bradford as well as the Dales. In reality, only 3% of his originals were city scenes.

Percy was generous in using his paintings as gifts. He gave away some 15% of his paintings, most often as wedding or Christmas presents or gifts for charity raffles. He was particularly proud of the times when he could make a gift to a celebrity. His gift of a city centre scene to JB Priestley was well publicised (see Chapter 6). He was, for example, pleased to give a picture of Shipley Glen to another famous Bradfordian, Lord Vic Feather, the General Secretary of the Trades Union Congress in the 1960s and 1970s.

Examples of paintings

Four competition winners in the 1930s

The first national recognition of Percy's paintings came in the form of first prize four years running (1935 to 1938) for a competition for employees of The Westminster Bank.

The monthly staff newsletter, *The Westminster*, was generous in its praise. For example, in 1938, Percy's *'many exhibits were all of a very high standard ... and we should have liked to reproduce more of this artist's outstanding work'* and in 1937 the article in *The Westminster* said that *'mention must be made of Mr P. Monkman's watercolours, one of which was awarded first prize ... and no-one who saw the work could possibly be at variance with this decision'*.

Commenting on the 1936 winning entry, the *Telegraph & Argus* (9 November 1936) wrote that the Brontë painting *'is a watercolour with a beautiful feeling rising from the sea of deep blues in the colour of farmsteads set against a strong gold and green lighting of a western sky.'*

The winning entries, published in black and white in the newsletter, are interesting in two ways. First, they are rare examples of Percy's pre-1950 paintings. Second, they represent a wide range of topics. They include Percy's only known attempt at painting a fair (1938), which is quite striking, and a harbour scene (1937), which is also quite unusual for him. The 1935 winner is a very simple composition set against a lowering sky, while the 1936 winner is a conventional Dales hamlet, typical of much of his later work.

The hayrick (1935)

Source: The Royal Bank of Scotland Group plc © 2018

Bronteland hamlet (1936)

Source: The Royal Bank of Scotland Group plc © 2018

Bridlington harbour (1937)

Source: The Royal Bank of Scotland Group plc © 2018

Bingley Fair (1938)

Source: The Royal Bank of Scotland Group plc © 2018

Percy Monkman

Nine post-war paintings

City Rains (1958)

Source: Bradford Museums & Galleries Collections

In 1958, on behalf of Bradford City Council, the Cartwright Hall Gallery bought a Percy Monkman watercolour as part of its permanent collection. Entitled *City Rains,* this was a very interesting choice, because in many ways it was an untypical Percy Monkman. First, it was his only painting of the centre of Leeds. He very rarely ventured into Leeds for anything; yet on this occasion he took his painting tackle. Second, he captured heavy rain, which he rarely attempted because it was difficult to paint in the rain. He was generally much more interested in clouds and the threat of rain. Apart from these superficial differences, it has a different style from the more 'run of the mill' Dales subjects. The rain, the wet pedestrians and the lowering sky all give the painting a vivid dramatic character rarely seen in his work. The buyer for the art gallery has been quite selective and made an unusual but excellent choice.

An Extraordinary Bradfordian

View of Forster Square, Bradford (1952)

Source: Bradford Museums & Galleries Collections

In contrast, this was probably Percy's most well-known painting, because it was the only painting that he had printed – 1,000 copies in 1978. He also painted the view eight times in the 1950s as well as this, painted in 1936.

The view was from the bank offices where he worked all his working life. One bank holiday he was on duty and became bored and decided to paint what he later described as a *'cracking view of Forster Square'*. This became a popular painting, because this familiar city scene was destroyed within ten years by a major new and unpopular re-development in the much criticised 1960s fashion of ruining cities across the north of England. For example, there has not been for many a year any notion of Forster Square being a square. The picture has an optimistic feel, contrasting with today's reality.

As well as the Victorian buildings that were pulled down, many thousands of Bradfordians would also remember affectionately the trolleybus system introduced in 1911 and closed down in 1972. The distinctive light blue livery was a familiar sight on the streets of Bradford. The 'new system' was still called the 'track-less', in the 1950s and 1960s, to distinguish it from the old tram system that it replaced before the First World War.

As well as its nostalgic value, this is a well-composed painting as the eye is swept by the trolley-bus lines into the square with the blue bus in front of the cathedral beyond an effective focal point.

Percy Monkman

Moorside, Baildon (1964)

This is another favourite subject. After Percy retired to Baildon, he often painted interesting corners of the old village which were within walking distance of home, or a short drive in a friend's car. Here is a scene on the edge of Baildon Moors – the remains of the 18th century hamlet Moorside.

Percy was particularly drawn to, and good at, compositions of old buildings set against threatening skies. Here you can almost feel the moors behind the buildings, even if only a small corner of the painting gives a hint. Both their shape and the use of colour give the buildings real interest. The outbuildings in the foreground complement the odd shapes of the cottage beyond with the different pieces that have been built on over the years. The dark walls and pale pink and blue-grey doors contrast with the white wash of the main building. The total effect is to bring the buildings alive with the rainy sky beyond.

An Extraordinary Bradfordian

Canal at Dockfields, Shipley (1967)

Percy frequently stressed that you can find beauty in any landscape. Here is one such example – a semi-industrial scene by the canal at Shipley, a suburb of Bradford that does not really draw the visitors. He was often to say in his talks about painting that *'We are very fortunate to live in a county so prolific in subject matter for artists as Yorkshire. It offers pastoral, moorland, industrial, the coast line, the hills and plains, wonderful variety in river scenes, Wharfedale, limestone country and Brontë atmosphere subjects everywhere, even Shipley!'*

The view down the tow path to the bridge is framed by a mill chimney on the left, most probably disused, and a gasometer on the right against an almost featureless hill topped by some houses and a cloudy sky. The canal is rather murky and the colours in general are quite drab, except for the whitewashed cottage. Yet the picture as a whole has a kind of beauty to it.

Main Street, Grassington (undated)

Of all the many familiar scenes of Wharfedale that he painted, this is perhaps the most popular one, for Percy at least. His personal catalogue shows that he tackled this subject nearly 30 times from different angles and in different light. Here, we have a winter scene where the snow contrasts with the warm colours of the stone and the bare trees. The use of figures walking up and down the street adds life to the composition and takes the eye into the distance.

Here, the painting provides the cover for the *Bradford Pictorial*, a monthly magazine launched in September 1964, which had a relatively short life of three and a half years. Typically, Percy did not ignore the opportunity that it gave for an extra channel for his work and he featured in several editions. Curiously, he was the subject of a pen picture with a photograph on the last page of the final edition in January 1968.

An Extraordinary Bradfordian

Forster Square station in snow, Bradford (1954)

Percy often said that you can find beauty in the unlikeliest places in the city and that painting in winter was the most rewarding time of year. Here we see a painting that combines both points.

The view is looking towards the city centre from the bottom of Snowden Street which runs from the side of the old Theatre Royal in Manningham Lane (the city's first theatre) down to the railway lines alongside Valley Road. The painting shows the tower of the cathedral rising out of the smoke and industrial murk of the city centre.

Using unlikely elements, the composition is again quite striking. The horizontal lines on the right hand side (the roof, the chapel, the goods yards) contrast neatly with the diagonal lines of the railway tracks and rolling stock, lines that are only broken with the steam and smoke rising up into the air. The skyline adds depth with the cathedral tower contrasting with the industrial buildings.

We cannot be sure, but the original is likely to have been painted in more natural colours. However its reproduction here in sepia and white for a double page spread in a magazine reinforces the murkiness of the subject highlighted by the snow on the ground.

Percy Monkman

Kirklands Farm, Baildon (1963)

The two paintings on these pages are of the same subject from slightly different places in contrasting weather, one set back about a hundred yards or so behind the other. Both are typical of Percy's work. It is typical also that he found a subject less from a quarter of a mile from his first post-retirement home in Baildon. They are paintings of an ordinary scene comprising old buildings, fine trees, scrubby fields, a distant hill and interesting cloudy skies, all brought together into an arresting composition.

The first, above, is cast in late afternoon light with browns, yellows and muted blues. It feels warm.

The second (facing) is dominated by snow and wintry light, probably late afternoon as well. By contrast it feels cold and bare.

As a pair they illustrate how well Percy captures different light and different weather conditions to convert an unpromising landscape into attractive paintings.

An Extraordinary Bradfordian

Kirklands Lane in snow, Baildon (1971)

Percy Monkman

Looking to Guiseley, Otley Chevin (1976)

Here is another example of Percy's ability to construct a satisfying composition from very little. The foreground only has a broken fence on the left and a little scrub on the right. The middle ground has some trees and a hint of a building. The background has rolling hills lit to the right by sun breaking through the clouds. The colour tones of brown, yellow, green and grey help to unify the composition. The overall impression is of a landscape brought to life for a moment.

CHAPTER 5

ALSO, A TALENTED CARTOONIST

Throughout his life Percy drew cartoons. In the bank he was known to doodle on backs of envelopes. At the Civic he often liked to watch other actors at rehearsals so that he could draw them. At work or leisure he always looked for opportunities to communicate the humour of situations. From time to time an idea might then develop so that he could offer more finished versions to local newspapers; on many occasions they were published. Over his lifetime they revealed a real talent for visual humour.

Sporting cartoons

In the 1920s and 1930s Percy often had cartoons published in the *Telegraph & Argus* or the *Yorkshire Evening Post* that provided commentary on recent sporting events. Usually they concerned football (mainly about Bradford City), occasionally cricket or rugby union. They might be based on recent matches or issues that were being talked about. Here we give examples of both.

The first provides a commentary about a Bradford City match when they beat Nelson 9-1 (November 1927) which, at the time, was the club's highest ever victory.

For any fan attending, this match would have been a moment to savour – a collector's item, if you like. Bradford City only ever bettered this score once. No wonder Percy refers to it as the 'close of play' score as if it were a cricket match.

Bradford City vs Nelson (November 1927)

Percy Monkman

The second covers an issue that was current at the time about the use of local sporting grounds from the unusual perspective of cleaners working at those grounds. For those not familiar with the grounds, Birch Lane is where Bradford Northern rugby league team played, Elland Road is the home of Leeds United, Park Avenue refers to Bradford Park Avenue and, of course, Valley Parade to Bradford City. The business logic of ground sharing was a continual subject of debate in the inter-war years, but it never came about because of club rivalry.

The cartoon, appearing in the *Yorkshire Evening Post,* neatly captures some of the differences between the clubs. For example, the lady representing Bradford Park Avenue sees herself a cut above the Mrs Mops from the other Bradford clubs. Bradford City supporters traditionally believed that their Park Avenue soccer rivals from across the city thought themselves to be a superior club than their Manningham upstarts, who had even the audacity in 1903 to join the Football League three years before their Park Avenue rivals.

Although Percy's sporting cartoons were almost always about football and Bradford City AFC, he did one cartoon about cricket to celebrate the famous occasion, in 1956, when Yorkshireman Jim Laker (born in Shipley), who played as a spin bowler for England and Surrey CC, broke a world record by taking 19 wickets in a Test Match against Australia at Old Trafford – a feat never since emulated. The cartoon, 'Lakeritis', was published in the *Telegraph & Argus* on 1 August 1956. Percy would only have drawn this because of Jim Laker's local connections. He was always proud when local people made the national stage. Had Surrey-born Tony Lock, Jim Laker's spin bowling partner, been the hero on that day, as he might well have been, Percy would not have been motivated to put pen to paper.

Football gossip (1928)

'Lakeritis' or May fever (August 1958)

The caption ran 'Lakeritis' or 'May Fever. Symptoms: Falling wickets, dropping ashes and Old Trafford sunshine'. (Reference to May Fever is an allusion to England's captain Peter May.)

An Extraordinary Bradfordian

Cartoons of actors

Did drawing cartoons run in the family? Percy's nine-year-old son Harvey drew this caricature of a famous visitor to the house, which was published by the *Telegraph & Argus* in 1932 with the following credit:

The accompanying sketch (right) is the work of Master AP Harvey Monkman of Jesmond Avenue, Bradford, a nine-year old scholar of Lilycroft Council School, Bradford. He is the second son (error, first son or second child) of Mr P Monkman, who is a member of the Bradford Arts Club and from the age of five he has shown a decided bent for caricature and drawing. Lest anybody should be in doubt as to the subject of the sketch, it may be stated that he is Mr JB Priestley, the Bradford novelist.

JB Priestley by Harvey Monkman (1932)

Not only does this show Harvey in a positive light, but it also demonstrates how Percy put himself forward. How many parents have praised their children for being good at drawing but never taken it further? Here Percy, as a proud father, has taken it a step further by contacting the local paper, most probably via someone he had got to know for his own publicity. His son appears in the paper as a consequence, doubtless attracting wider comment for Percy as well.

Unfortunately, there is no record of Harvey ever building on this ability to draw.

Percy Monkman

During 1939 the *Telegraph & Argus* ran a series of Percy's caricatures of prominent people at the Civic Playhouse, at the end of which it ran the following acknowledgement:

This week we conclude Mr Percy Monkman's series of caricatures of Civic Playhouse personalities. My sincere thanks go to Mr Monkman for his collaboration. I have enjoyed the series immensely, and, judging by the many comments I have heard, appreciation has been widespread.

Source : *Telegraph & Argus* (1940)

These caricatures also formed the basis of a 24-page booklet published by the Civic Playhouse in 1939 entitled *Bradford Civic Playhouse Personalities* under the joint authorship of Percy (caricatures) and 'Prompter' (the newspaper's drama critic who provided the 'biographical brevities' of the 22 personalities caricatured).

The cover, featuring JB Priestley as the Playhouse President, is shown at right.

Forty-five years later these caricatures, below, were used to decorate a celebration cake for Percy, to commemorate being given honorary life-membership of the Civic. This shows, on one side of the cake, six caricatures taken from the booklet. (See Chapter 10 for further information.)

Cover of Bradford Civic Playhouse Personalities

Bradford Civic Playhouse Personalities: celebration cake (1974)

An Extraordinary Bradfordian

They Came to a City (1944)

As a supporting, rather than a leading actor in most of the plays in which he was involved, Percy often took advantage of his spare time at rehearsals to draw fellow actors.

One set of caricatures drawn in 1944 must have been much more difficult to complete as it included the whole cast of JB Priestley's play *They Came to a City* on stage – including Percy. Here is the drawing: Percy is on the extreme right of the stage. Not immediately recognisable because he is made up and dressed for his part, the photograph inset in the top right-hand corner shows how he looked on the night.

Other opportunities

Doing cartoons and caricatures was never a regular occupation for Percy in the same way as painting was. However, when the mood took him and he spotted an interesting face or an amusing idea, he set to work. Here we see three different examples taken from three decades.

Light opera

Light opera! (1936)

This is a caricature of Frank Mullings (1881 to 1953) who was a leading English tenor with the British National Opera Company, during the 1910s and 1920s. There is no explanation why Percy drew this unpublished caricature. He did not have any real interest in opera, or even light opera. The likeliest reason is in the exclamation mark at the end of the caption. In other words, Percy was amused by the contrast between the singer's unusual profile and the genre that made his name.

Famous old boy

Alan Bullock (later Sir Alan) was one of the leading historians of the post-war period (he wrote the definitive study of Adolf Hitler) and Master of St. Catherine's College Oxford. A Bradfordian by birth, he was invited back to the city in 1958 to open the annual Spring Exhibition at the Cartwright Hall. One can easily imagine that Percy, who knew Bullock's father, a minister of the Unitarian Chapel in City Hall Square, might have used the time listening to his speech to draw this caricature published on 28 March 1958 in the *Telegraph & Argus*.

Alan Bullock (1958)

An Extraordinary Bradfordian

Christmas greetings

'Blow in the bag' (1967)

Percy always used his paintings or drawings for Christmas cards. In 1967 he sent this topical cartoon, related to the new breathalyser tests introduced by law that year. Note the registration number on the reindeer's sleigh – oh, 'eck, you!'

Percy Monkman

Pair of banking cartoons

Only very rarely did Percy's day job at the bank connect with his extensive leisure interests. One exception came in the form of two excellent cartoons that drew on his knowledge of banks and were published in *The Westminster*, the bank's staff magazine, some 20 years apart. Together they form probably the best cartoons that he ever published.

Firstly, in 1932 the magazine published a cartoon that was a montage of 12 typical bank customers. This reflects a view of the bank as it used to be, a place that people visited almost as a social activity. The style is one of gentle humour, based on observation of some typical customers as they present themselves at the bank counter.

Customers and their Customs (1932)
Source: The Royal Bank of Scotland Group plc © 2018

An Extraordinary Bradfordian

The Friendly Bank (1952)

Source: The Royal Bank of Scotland Group plc © 2018

The second cartoon is quite a contrast. It was published in 1952 to mark his retirement. This one had more of a satirical bite and today feels very modern compared with the bygone days of the first cartoon.

In Percy's day banks were respected institutions, whereas now they have lost much public esteem, as a result of various financial scandals. Yet in this cartoon the slogans hanging in the *Bank des Folies* have messages that clearly resonate with that lost esteem.

Overdrawn? Why worry? We don't! or **Your interest is our interest** might certainly draw knowing laughs from today's audience. Percy had no reputation for satire, but had he learnt over his career that banking had become a different kind of institution, no longer quite as respectable as it was when he joined? Could he on this occasion have deliberately taken his natural gentle humour one step further, given that he had just retired?

The bank itself did not think so, saying with no hint of irony in its introduction to the cartoon: *'which he drew many years ago and which in this friendly bank of ours is just the job for publication today'.*

Percy Monkman

CHAPTER 6

LOYAL COLLECTOR OF LIFE-LONG FRIENDSHIPS

Percy made many friends for life through his artistic interests. They were a fascinating mixture of people from all walks of life, with similar passions for entertaining, acting and painting, often eccentrics and sometimes very well connected in Bradford society. A couple experienced real tragedies. The friendship that in many ways defined Percy was his life-long connection with JB Priestley, his contemporary and Bradford's most celebrated member of the generation that fought in the First World War.

Patterns of friendship

For a gregarious and extrovert character such as Percy, always ready with some humorous story, making friends was not difficult. His leisure time activities all involved contact with like-minded colleagues in the world of entertainment, theatre and painting; even his day job at the bank involved meeting many people every day at the cashier's desk. He was a familiar figure around Bradford, his life rooted in the community.

It is not possible, for several reasons, to do full justice to all his friendships over 93 years, and in this story we cannot avoid being selective about his friends. Apart from JB Priestley and Ferdy Roberts, very few friendships in his later life dated back to the pre-First World War days, for the sad reason that many men his age from Bradford did not survive the war. For example, the two Bradford Pals battalions were decimated at the Battle of the Somme. His later friendship with JB (as he was known) was also lucky in the respect that they both survived fighting in the First World War.

As Percy lived all his life in Bradford, his friends were local. Some, such as Laurence Scarfe and Harry and Joan Tout, did move away, but they would correspond with Percy, who was generally diligent in maintaining the links. However, Percy had no need to correspond with most of his friends, who were local, because he met them regularly, through his artistic activities and so there is little documentary record of their friendship.

The other factor is that, living to 93, Percy outlived many friends and so fewer memories of earlier friendships have been passed down to the current day, compared with some younger friends who survived him. Fortunately, Percy did make many friends who were at least a generation younger and their testament helps to paint a clear picture of his gift for friendship.

After the First World War, Percy's friendships, not surprisingly, revolved around his artistic activities, particularly around the two institutions to which Percy was fully committed – the Civic Playhouse and the Arts Club.

JB Priestley (1894 to 1984)

JB's reputation

When Percy died in 1986, the *Telegraph & Argus* ran the headline *'JB's lifelong friend dies'*. Many people, not just the local press, saw Percy in these terms, an impression reinforced by the press requesting him for a comment whenever JB Priestley was in the news (eg making one of his visits back home). Percy always obliged with some useful quotation or memory about his friend.

It is worth remembering the scale of JB's reputation. In the mid-20th century he was the most well-known man of letters in England, a prolific novelist, playwright, essayist and critic, and arguably the last of his kind. Until he died he was certainly the most famous Bradfordian, to be rivalled two generations later only by David Hockney. He travelled widely and had extensive international contacts. To coin a 21st century term, that JB would have disliked intensely, he was a 'national treasure'.

When JB was made a Freeman of Bradford in 1973 (aged 79) his citation read:

Writer, broadcaster and critic J. B. Priestley (1894-1984) may be best known for his "time plays", such as **An Inspector Calls***, for enduringly popular novels like* **The Good Companions** *and* **Angel Pavement** *and for his wartime broadcasts, the* **Postscripts***. However, he also wrote essays, autobiography, social history and time theory. Priestley was active in politics, although never a member of any party, expressing his concerns (for instance about the nuclear arms race) through commentary and campaigning.*

Born and brought up in Bradford, Priestley used his Yorkshire background in some of his finest works, such as **Bright Day** *and* **When We Are Married***. His connections with the city were later marked by the statue near Central Library and the naming of the J. B. Priestley Library at the University of Bradford, which was he officially opened in 1975. The University awarded him the title of honorary Doctor of Letters in 1970, and he was awarded the freedom of the City of Bradford in 1973 and the Order of Merit in 1977.*

After leaving Bradford after the First World War, JB clearly moved in literary circles well outside Percy's much more parochial existence. Going to Cambridge University straight after the war, he was much better educated. Very interested in books, he was an intellectual; Percy was not. Yet they had several shared interests rooted in their Bradford upbringing that sustained their friendship over their lives. The first was football.

An Extraordinary Bradfordian

Playing football

JB was almost an exact contemporary of Percy's, being born two years later and dying two years earlier. In their formative, teenage years, they lived within a stone's throw from each other in the Toller Lane area. Both were obsessive about football and seemingly quite good at it. JB (usually a right back) had an (unsuccessful) trial with Bradford Park Avenue and played for Bradford Boys and Percy (usually a right winger) had an (unsuccessful) trial with Bradford City, being rejected because of his light build. They both played for Toller Lane Tykes and later Saltburn United (Saltburn Place being the street where JB lived).

Recalling their football-playing days 70 years later, Percy said that JB *'was a solid and very good full-back'* JB replied that *'Percy wasn't too bad either'*, adding *'We used to play all day long. We would go in for dinner and tea, but then it was straight back to the game'*.

Even then, though, Percy saw that JB *'buried his nose in the classics and he could recite whole chunks by heart'*. He *'never saw JB without a book, under his arm or in a pocket. He was never away from the public library and the bookstalls'*.

Below we see a photo of both of them dressed for playing. However, with 15 boys, they do not seem to be part of a formal team. The photo is not dated or annotated but was probably taken around 1903 or 1904. Percy is in the middle row, second from the left, wearing a whitish short. JB is seated at the front in a striped shirt.

Percy and JB Priestley in same football team (1903 or 1904)

Percy Monkman

The theatre and painting

Percy and JB had a strong shared interest in the theatre, specifically in the Bradford Civic Playhouse. JB was a long-term president of this theatre from 1932, when it broke away from the Leeds Civic Theatre, until his death in 1984. Percy joined in 1935. His proudest achievement was playing an important role (Herbert Soppitt, hen-pecked husband) in JB's *When We Are Married*, performed in 1938, the first of 66 performances including several revivals. It was also one of the Civic's most successful productions, playing to packed audiences and giving the theatre much-needed income.

They also had another strong shared interest, in painting. We know about Percy's passion for water colour painting, but JB was also a keen painter, finding it a very relaxing hobby. During his own very busy life he managed to paint more than 500 pictures. Percy was instrumental in encouraging JB to be a Vice-President of Bradford Arts Club in the early 1930s (even though he was living in the South of England), which led to him being President for one year (1934/35). He returned occasionally to open exhibitions on behalf of the Arts Club.

JB's *Lost City*

In the late 1950s JB became very concerned about the destruction of old Victorian buildings in the centre of Bradford, such as the old Kirkgate Market and the traditional Swan Arcade, where he had had an office job in his youth. Favourite places such as a particular pie shop were under threat. He campaigned in the local press against such vandalism, as he saw it.

In 1958 the BBC commissioned JB to make a documentary about his lost city, produced by Richard Cawston, a prominent BBC documentary-maker. The 45-minute film, '*Lost City*', was in effect Priestley's lament that the Bradford he knew no longer existed. It caused much local controversy. Writing in the *Radio Times*, JB claimed that the film was the subject of a complaint before it even started. The Bradford Civic Society protested that even the documentary's title showed bias and hostility. After it was shown, the film created further exchanges of views with some people complaining that it presented the city in a poor light.

Although he agreed with JB about the destruction of the city centre, Percy had his own disappointment with the documentary. He had spent a whole day being filmed in conversation with JB at the Bradford Arts Club and then in '*The Mucky Duck*'– real name '*The Black Swan*' – in Frizinghall where Percy's Arts Club friends often met after painting and drawing sessions. In expectation of a prominent role, he gathered a large family audience to watch the programme only to discover that, when edited, the material involving him lasted less than one minute. It was little consolation that JB admitted that many old friends would be disappointed that *'so much good stuff had to be edited out'*!

An Extraordinary Bradfordian

Percy's meetings with JB

Over the years JB visited Bradford from time to time and usually he would meet up with Percy. For example, he was reported by the *Yorkshire Post* (25 Nov 1957) to have spent the weekend in Bradford, the schedule including an evening dinner at a Bradford hotel with Phyllis Bentley (well-known novelist and literary celebrity from Halifax), lunch with his sister, who still lived in the area, tea with Percy Monkman the artist at his Baildon home and supper with Bingley-born John Braine, author of best-selling *'No Room at the Top'*.

Percy giving JB Priestley painting of City Hall Square (3 April 1978)

Percy and JB Priestley deep in conversation

Sometimes the occasions would be more formal, such as the 40th anniversary of the Civic Playhouse (of which JB was still President) in 1969, the award of the Freedom of Bradford in 1973, an invitation to lunch with the Lord Mayor of Bradford in 1975 and a reunion in 1978 at the Victoria Hotel, which had just named a bar after JB. Each time Percy attended and appeared in the press photographs. On the 1978 occasion Percy presented JB with two watercolours of the old Forster Square and City Hall Square painted from the bank where he worked close by. JB commented in the *Telegraph & Argus* that *'they are very good indeed'*.

I was present at some of the later visits, around the mid-1950s and early 1960s. My strongest memory was that Percy, so often the dominant person in any group of friends or family, very much took a back seat and seemed dominated by this visitor with charisma, an outsize personality and an even stronger sense of humour than Percy himself.

Curiously, JB was very subdued at one of the last meetings of the two old friends, around 1980, at Alveston, near Stratford-upon-Avon where JB lived, less than ten miles from Warwick, where I lived. JB invited us to afternoon tea, but it was the livelier and sprightlier Percy (two years older) who led the conversation. We concluded that JB, then in his mid-80s, was finally feeling the effects of old age.

Percy Monkman

JB's correspondence with Percy

> J. B. PRIESTLEY
> KISSING TREE HOUSE, ALVESTON,
> STRATFORD-ON-AVON, WARWICKSHIRE.
> Stratford-on-Avon 3798
>
> 1st October, 1968.
>
> Dear Percy,
>
> Many thanks for your extremely interesting letter of the 27th and for the photograph and article. I remember your brother Gordon very well but have forgotten the younger pair. I agree that you are extraordinarily lucky to survive the Somme. I am returning the cutting from the Telegraph because, after looking hard at the photograph and digesting the article, I feel that perhaps you might have some further use for it. I have not visited Bradford for some time, otherwise I would have got in touch with you.
>
> With warmest congratulations and all good wishes - and tell your wife that I can still call up from memory quite a clear picture of her as a girl, and a very pretty girl she was too.
>
> Yours ever,
> Jack

Letter from JB Priestley (1 October 1968)

> J. B. PRIESTLEY
> KISSING TREE HOUSE, ALVESTON,
> STRATFORD-ON-AVON, WARWICKSHIRE, CV37 7QT
> Stratford-on-Avon (0789) 3798
>
> 16th December, 1977
>
> Dear Percy,
>
> Many thanks for your letter of the 13th and also for the card with its very spirited painting.
>
> Please accept my sympathy for your family losses. Gordon, of course, I remember quite well. I am afraid that all correspondence between men our age begins to read like funeral notices.
>
> Glad to know how well the painting is going and wish I could have seen it in the Royal Exchange, London, a city I do my best to keep away from these days. I suppose I ought to be writing, but I am not, though I feel I must start something soon.
>
> Incidentally, the Queen awarded me the Order of Merit, so that I can put O.M. after my name.
>
> All good wishes,
> Yours,
> Jack

Letter from JB Priestley (16 December 1977)

Percy kept around 30 letters from JB over the years, usually less than one page and very much to the point. The early ones, up to the Second World War, are addressed as 'Dear Monkman'; thereafter the address reverts to 'Dear Percy'. The topics are usually about imminent visits, or 'thank-yous' for recent visits, or polite declining of invitations to open exhibitions or other plans for 'coming up North'.

A few of the letters have greater interest.

For example, in 1968 JB told Percy *'to tell his* (Percy's) *wife that I can still call up from memory quite a clear picture of her as a girl, and a very pretty girl she was too'*. In reality JB had gone out with Doris when they were young, before she met Percy. The story goes that Doris thought JB was 'ugly' and wore clothes such as corduroys that were too eccentric for her taste.

In 1977, in a short letter with condolences to Percy for the death of Percy's brother Gordon in Canada and a brief update about painting and writing, JB has a nice throwaway line - *'Incidentally, the Queen awarded me the Order of Merit, so that I can put OM after my name'*. This is extremely prestigious, being limited to only 24 living people, such as at different times Margaret Thatcher, Nelson Mandela and Sir David Attenborough.

In 1981 JB wrote to Percy that *'It is good that we are still able to celebrate such an old and warm-hearted friendship'*.

An Extraordinary Bradfordian

Final meeting?

What might have been the last time the two met was an unusual meeting, around 1981 to 1982, recounted by Mike de Greasley, then the recently appointed Treasurer of the Arts Club. In early 2017 he wrote and spoke about a meeting involving Percy, Percy's daughter Dorothy, Nancy Hickson, JB and David Hockney. Mike's words were: *At this time I was between jobs and would often spend a bit of time up at the Art Club doing a bit of drawing and/or painting as well as sitting for others to draw. I remember one lunch time – I had popped out to get us all some fish 'n' chips from the corner chippy and when I returned – Nancy Hickson (then in her late 80s/early 90s) had arrived all excited. She often talked of Percy and of David Hockney. It was whilst we were all tucking into our fish 'n' chips that George Jeakins (President before Percy) arrived with your mum, grandfather and JB – soon to be followed by Hockney. They all sat about a drop leaf table with barley twist legs and entered into discussion at the back of the long clubhouse room. I was sitting for others to draw and after the group's conversation they spent some time doing a sketch – even Hockney and JB. Afterwards, your grandfather passed me the unsigned portrait sketch he did of me, which I still have to this day.*

Having succeeded Percy in 1980, Nancy Hickson was at that time the President of the Arts Club and had known David Hockney for many years, since his student days. We also know that JB and Hockney knew each other before this meeting because Hockney had done a drawing of JB some years before, but this is the only time the three of them met. Hockney left Bradford around the age of 20 for the Royal College of Art in London and, to Percy's disappointment, never had any connection with his native city's arts club.

JB's death

Percy's final contact with JB's life was via a BBC Radio Leeds programme in 1984. Arranged to celebrate JB's 90th birthday in September, it became a memorial programme to him, as he died in August. The programme involved interviews with Percy and the famous northern writer Stan Barstow. Percy recalled their days playing football and then their shared interests of theatre and painting.

When JB died in August 1984, the Yorkshire Post ran a full-page feature entitled *JB Priestley: Tributes to a Yorkshire legend* which had articles by authors Melvyn Bragg, John Braine, Stan Barstow and Jack Higgins, followed by an article by Percy with his memories of JB. Unfortunately, Percy did not survive to attend the unveiling of a JB statue in front of Bradford Central Library on 31 October 1986 (he had died six months earlier), although he still received an invitation to the event and the Lord Mayor's luncheon that followed.

In reply to Percy's letter of condolence to Jacquetta Hawkes, JB's wife, she said that *'Jack, such a bad correspondent always liked to think of you as a friend. He enjoyed your painting, and admired it, too'.* Two and a half years later, when Percy died, she wrote: *'Jack always felt a close friend even when age meant they met only seldom'.*

JB's friendship

In conclusion, the contact between the two was sometimes spasmodic. They moved mostly in quite different circles, but their lives did cross at many important points. JB was a constant reference point for most of the things in life that mattered to Percy. His friendship with JB was important for him on a number of levels.

First, he was proud that a boyhood friend who lived nearby and with whom he played football achieved such a national and international reputation. Second, they shared a strong interest in the theatre. JB wrote the play that gave Percy the actor the greatest satisfaction and the Civic Playhouse (of which JB was President for more than 50 years) its greatest success. Third, they shared another strong interest in painting. Although he painted much less than Percy, JB often articulated important thoughts about painting for Percy such as when he produced a definition of watercolour painting, which Percy used many times in his talks to art societies and others. JB certainly took painting seriously, but he deferred to Percy's greater experience and expertise, clearly admiring Percy the painter.

An Extraordinary Bradfordian

Tommy Crosby – friend from the First World War

During the First World War Percy and Tommy Crosby must clearly have been close friends, working together on their scripts and comedy acts and at a formative time in their lives well away from home. It is surprising in view of Percy's other long-term friendships that there are only two records of them meeting up after the war and indeed little evidence of any contact. Percy did very occasionally mention Tommy Crosby, and one year around Christmas perhaps in the 1960s he rang him up in Liverpool out of the blue for a chat. Tommy had been the co-author of some of Percy's sketches, especially *The Disorderly Room*. He was a Scouser, like many of Percy's friends in the army, and Percy occasionally referred in later life to having to face as 'a Yorkie' the weight of Scouse humour. One entry in Percy's art catalogue shows that he sent Tommy Crosby a painting as a wedding gift in 1926, although we have no record of whether he attended the wedding.

There is one record of a meeting in June 1931 when Percy travelled with his parents to Liverpool to see them off on a 'once-in-a-lifetime' trip sailing on the Duchess of Athol to Canada to visit their son Gordon. He used the opportunity to meet up with Tommy. There is a photograph of that day. Until then this was also probably Percy's only visit to Merseyside and the nearest he ever got himself to visiting Canada.

The only other meeting of which there is a record was in October 1977, when it seems that Percy dropped in to see him in Liverpool with at least a couple of female friends. This was most unusual as he hardly ever visited Liverpool and there is no obvious reason for him to do so on this occasion. However, Tommy wrote to him a day or two later, saying: *Having just recovered from the shock of your visit to ENGLAND (sic) and the pleasure of having a few words with you... Well, apart from losing a few strands of your hair, you haven't changed and having such a bevy of feminine beauty escorting you, I am pleased to note you still are a competent picker. I really was thrilled to have a few minutes with you. Look after yourself for, as you know, there are only a few of us left.*

As well as these meetings they exchanged Christmas cards. Their last contact was a letter from Tommy's wife in December 1981, prompted by Percy's annual card, to say that Tommy had died on 29 November. She wrote *'The card is beautiful but there is no Tom to cherish it'.*

Percy Monkman

Yorkshire artists – Percy's contemporaries

Like-minded obsessives

Percy sought friendship with other artists, especially if he looked up to them as being better or more experienced. What could he learn from them?

During the 1920s and 1930s Percy became friendly with a number of artists who shared his passion for painting the Yorkshire Dales. They were people whose artistic talents he respected and learnt from. He frequently talked about them, especially with his daughter Dorothy, who shared his love of painting.

They were all highly individual, if not eccentric, and with one exception lived in Dales villages where painting opportunities were on the doorstep.

John S Atherton (1877 to 1943)

Fifteen years older than Percy and with a solid reputation from exhibiting at the Royal Academy, the Royal Institute of Watercolour Painters and the Royal Society of Arts, John Atherton was one such friend, whom Percy got to know in the 1930s. Here is an extract from an article Percy wrote in *The Dalesman* magazine in August 1977 about two artist friends; John Atherton was the first subject.

I was fortunate to meet him at a formative period in my lifetime as a young, struggling amateur, over forty years ago.

My first meeting with him was very fortuitous. Wandering up Main Street in Grassington, I saw a gentleman walking around with what looked to be a portfolio under his arm. Instinctively I sensed he might be an artist, though nothing in his appearance suggested that. However I approached him and found I was right.

The outcome was that he invited us to his studio, which was in a wooden bungalow tucked away near a farmhouse facing Grass Woods. This turned out to be the start of a life-time friendship. I'd heard of him and seen many of his paintings, as a member of a famous group of Yorkshire artists, known as 'The Wharfedale Group'.

From then on, whenever I visited Grassington (which was regularly and frequently), he invited me up to his studio, after each painting holiday, and went through my paintings, one by one, putting them in a mount. He then gave me a kindly but thorough criticism which I appreciated fully. Mrs Atherton who was always present then regaled us with tea and home-made scones. She was the ideal wife for an artist. No histrionics if he turned up late for meals, but always the right meal for the day available (Note: Percy clearly valued this with his own wife, Doris!)

It was very gratifying after many years of visits and criticisms when he said 'Well I think you've some progress since you first came here. You used to get about one in ten right, now I think you've got it down to one in three!'

A short time before John died, he remarked 'Well, I've had a wonderful life and if I want to go to some heavenly place I just want to go on painting, or if I come back to earth, there's now't I want to do better than this job!'.

John S Atherton was a quiet, kindly and happy man who had found his true vacation in art.

Source: *The Dalesman* (1977)

An Extraordinary Bradfordian

Jimmy Arundel (1875 to 1960)

The second subject in *The Dalesman* article was Jimmy Arundel. Seventeen years older than Percy, he was another friend who came from the inter-war years. Percy wrote about him as follows:

He was one of the earliest members of the Arts Club which was formed in 1902. Jimmy joined in `1905. He was a lively, volatile character, red of face, red of hair, small in stature. But as 'tough as they make 'em'. He always spoke with a broad Bradford accent whether he was in distinguished company or at his local pub.

By nature he was adventurous, intrepid and resolute. In his teens he ran away to America with a friend working their passages. They got as far as Philadelphia, where they did odd jobs. After a while his father sent him money for his return journey. In his early years he became a notable weightlifter. In 1907 he was part of a team that built the first unattended lighthouse in the world at Platte Fougère, near Guernsey.

This preceded his professional business, which included painting and decorating lighthouses, railway stations and government properties. This may have induced the broad vital technique he later developed in his paintings.

Jimmy did not take up painting seriously until he was turned 50. In the years following he exhibited in most Yorkshire galleries, also in the RA and the Paris Salon. In that period he also joined the Chelsea Arts Club. He contributed work to The Dalesman.

In 1959 the Cartwright Hall, Bradford held a retrospective exhibition of his paintings. During this period he painted frequently in France and was particularly fond of the Dordogne region where he must have caused a great impression. He was honoured, becoming an honorary mayor of the town.

He painted in a vibrant, colourful, expressionistic style, with strong reds and hot tones. In winter he concerned himself with 'still life' pictures of exotic birds and flowers, often painting well into the night.

I remember him once exhorting me to 'drink a bottle of Burgundy and let thisself go, lad.'

Despite his blunt speech Jimmy was an avid reader and a real bookworm. He was very well read on all the French Impressionists, particularly Gauguin. It was a joy to go round an exhibition with him, and listen and enjoy his pungent and well-informed comments and criticisms. He was also a great favourite at the life classes in the Arts Club, where he stimulated and was always helpful.

He enjoyed a very full and rewarding life. Like many artists he found in art much fulfilment and an ideal way of life.

Source: *The Dalesman* (1977)

Percy Monkman

Jacob Kramer (1892 to 1962)

John Atherton and Jimmy Arundel were both at least 15 years older than Percy. He wrote a third article a year later for *The Dalesman* about another artist friend who was born the same year as himself.

Jacob made a great impact as an artist. He was also an unforgettable character. He arrived in Leeds with his parents at the age of eight in 1900.

The Kramer family, emigres from the Ukraine, settled readily into the Jewish community of Leeds. They were a family with a background of culture in the fields of art and music.

Jacob's training began at the Leeds School of Art. Then followed a period at the Slade School, the mecca of 'up and coming' artists.

During the 1914-18 war Kramer served in the army as a soldier until it was discovered that he was familiar with four European languages. He was made an interpreter and later became a war artist.

He set up a studio in Preston Cottage, Little Woodhouse, Leeds and this became the meeting place of celebrities from the world of music, the arts, ballet, the stage and literature. He conceived and formed the Yorkshire Luncheon Club in Leeds, and the lucky ones who managed to get tickets will long remember the meetings with fervent nostalgia.

Jacob loved good company and conversation, excellent food and drink. His guests not only included celebrities in diverse forms of art, but quite humble acquaintances. All were welcome. Basically he was a humble man. He enjoyed his countless friends, and he had many from all walks of life. Probably his greatest joy was convivial company and he could talk 'till the cows came home' on his favourite subjects, ie art, music and even sport, including football which he patronised.

One aspect of his life that endeared him to many local artists was his readiness to help them in a practical way. For many years he arranged one-man shows at the Jubilee Hotel on the Headrow in Leeds. I felt honoured to be asked to exhibit there on one occasion.

Source: *The Dalesman* (1978)

An Extraordinary Bradfordian

Fred Lawson (1888 to 1968)

Another friend from the same era, Fred Lawson, lived in Castle Bolton in Wensleydale. Percy wrote this piece about him.

From an early age when I was a budding water colourist, I never ceased to admire the great quality in his pictures. He always impressed me by the magic that seemed to flow effortlessly from his brush. There was always a feeling that he was a natural painter. One never sensed any sense of affectation or gimmickry in his work. The only trend he followed was his own, which was totally sincere and enduring. His talent was individual and unique.

He also had the ability to find his subjects in very mundane objects, ie an odd shelf, a fireplace, a few steps etc and by his special touch of magic transfers them into things of beauty – the hallmarks of a true artist. Inherently modest he fought shy of publicity, though ever ready to help less gifted amateurs. One remark of his that I never forgot was 'I'd rather see an amateur's spontaneous attempt than some boring "potboilers" by professionals.

I particularly remember one visit to Castle Bolton by my own society (the Bradford Arts Club) As usual our members spread around the village and quite voluntarily, Fred went round to them individually giving valuable advice and criticism, which was greatly appreciated.

I am proud to own some of his paintings, which are as fresh today as when I acquired them some fifty years ago.

'By his work shall you know the man'; and it is a lasting pleasure to me to have his paintings around, and particularly to remember Fred as a friend and one who throughout the years has remained one of my favourite artists.

Source: *Telegraph and Argus* (1974)

Constance Pearson (1886 to 1970)

Constance became a very well-known Dales artist. Born in Leeds and trained at the Leeds School of Art, she moved to High Barn Cottage, Malham, where she lived the rest of her life. Both her daughter (Philippa Holmes who became friendly with Percy's daughter Dorothy) and then her granddaughter (Katharine Holmes) who now lives at High Barn Cottage followed in her footsteps.

In June 2011 *The Guardian* published an interview with Katherine about her family of artists on the occasion of an exhibition of her works. Katharine recalled that '*When I was a child, I vividly remember going to see my grandmother in the bedroom upstairs. It was full of paintings, and an easel I still have. It was her bedroom-cum-studio. There was always something on the easel, paintings hung up all over. She used to let me play in there, and squeeze tubes of paint out.*'

An essay in the exhibition catalogue described Constance, who had always sought uninhabited rural scenes for her subjects, becoming a familiar figure in Malham, hungry to paint: '*Tramping about in all weathers, her hat bound to her head with a scarf on windy days. She endured rain and snow traipsing out to Malham Cove or Gordale Scar*'

One of my earliest holiday memories was staying there over one May bank holiday week of 1954 and, indeed, on one very wet day Constance taking our family out to Malham Tarn.

On the many times when Percy visited Malham to paint, he would call in at High Barn Cottage, if at all possible.

Percy Monkman

Friends from Bradford Civic Concert Party

When Percy joined the Civic Playhouse in 1935, he made a new group of friends who were regularly acting and putting on plays. The booklet of 23 caricatures that he produced with the drama critic of the *Telegraph & Argus*, *Bradford Civic Playhouse Personalities* lists many of these new friends.

These friendships were strengthened in 1940 when the Civic formed a concert party that performed several times a week across Yorkshire. Many names appear on the programmes time and again. Since this concert party lasted for over 20 years there were almost two generations of performers with Percy and one or two others who straddled both.

Early names and their billings included Barbara Cheetham (a song and a smile), Muriel Greenwood (comedienne), Olive Kitchen (soprano), Bernard Muff (baritone), Roger Read (pianist), Mona Salter (accompanist), Edwin Smith (baritone and entertainer), Henry Stead (raconteur), Ossie Ward (comedian and compère), Bernard Wilson (compère) and others such as Edward Barker, Jean Oldfield, Arthur Tetley, Roni and Bill Vine, Mary Whitehouse and Newton Wood. After the war further names could be added, including Geoffrey Bryson, Teddy Nathanson, Rita Scully and Audrey Woodrow.

One couple with whom Percy became very friendly from his early days at the Civic were Harry and Joan Tout. The friendship lasting for the rest of their lives, Harry first appeared as an actor in plays with Percy and then he and his wife appeared regularly in the concert party performances, usually as a singing duet (tenor and soprano). As well as their time together rehearsing and performing, they often dropped in at Percy's home in the 1950s and 1960s. They were lively and entertaining company, as likely to burst into song off stage as on stage.

When Percy died, Harry wrote these words to Percy's daughter Dorothy about their last meeting (by this time Joan had already died): *I was so very glad that I was able to see and eventually get through to Percy. I first went to the hospital on the Friday afternoon but couldn't get through to him. The nurse suggested Sunday morning, I went about eleven and he did recognise me and I even managed a response to 'I'm shy, Mary Ellen, I'm shy'. The nurse was tickled pink that Percy attempted to join in. I have always considered it a great privilege to have your father as a friend and have so many, many, happy memories to look back on with Joan and Percy.*

Concert party friends Harry and Joan Tout (3 January 1962)

An Extraordinary Bradfordian

Friends from Bradford Arts Club in the 1950s and 1960s

From 1924, for over sixty years, Percy spent two to three evenings a week at the Bradford Arts Club. Not only did he participate as a member, he was also heavily involved in organising the programme of events. So he developed friendships with a large number of members. However, because they were local and he saw them regularly, very little documentation about his main Arts Club friends exists.

It is only feasible here to single out a handful from a long list, although others have been mentioned elsewhere in this chapter. During the 1950s and 1960s Percy was friendly with the Horrocks family. Alfred was the vice-chairman when Percy was chairman and so for those 14 years the two of them worked together in leading the club. Alfred and his wife Mabel held a Christmas Eve party every year, which was one of the rare occasions in my lifetime when Percy and Doris went out socially as a couple.

Before then, when Percy had been vice-chairman, his friend Bill Briggs was chairman – a partnership that lasted 13 years. Bill painted the only portrait of Percy, which he gave him and which is used as the cover of this book.

Another close friend for many years was Charlie Gill, who was completely devoted to the club. When Percy was president, he paid tribute to Charlie in a short speech:

It seems almost an impossibility to discuss the history of the Bradford Arts Club without some reference being made to Mr Charles Gill, or Charlie. He is and always will be a vital ingrained part of the club. Even when not visibly in attendance there is always a succession of his posters of current events on display on the noticeboard, infinitely varied with expertise. On a recent display of some of them one admired his great versatility in the art of lettering and layout.

Older members will remember the cards of invitations to special events and Christmas greetings, many of them done by hand.

As one of our oldest members and now Vice-President, he has worked unceasingly on many projects for the good of the club, not the least keeping a watchful eye on the building at all times. His living quite near Mansfield Road has been of great value to us, keeping an eye on work being done, receiving and despatching paintings etc. On our annual outings, besides painting, he has produced a photographic collection of members on those trips.

Percy Monkman

The tragic story of Iris (1930 to current day), and her mother Trudi

One Arts Club friendship sticks out for leading to a shocking story in which Percy became involved, although the circumstances were totally outside his control. After the Second World War he became friendly with Trudi Boetschi, a Swiss lady whose husband Hans had moved to Bradford from Basel as a director of a Swiss chemical company (Sandoz as it was), based at Apperley Bridge, between Bradford and Leeds. Trudi was a talented artist and had joined the Bradford Arts Club, where she met Percy. They knew each other for several years when tragedy struck in 1951.

Trudi's husband committed suicide by shooting himself two days after their 14 year old daughter, Iris, blurted out over dinner, in the presence of her mother and two of her father's colleagues, that her father was sexually assaulting her on a regular basis. Her father had been away abroad and to her horror was due back the following day.

This incest had been taking place for over four years. He had threatened to kill her if she ever revealed his secret. This was a devastating event, the more so since incest at that time was a strong taboo subject, certainly in the middle class circles in which her parents lived, both in Switzerland and Bradford.

Iris was sent away to a Swiss finishing school and Percy offered sanctuary for Trudi in his new home at Kirklands Villas, Baildon for around six months in summer 1953. This turned out to be an awkward time for Percy and Doris for another reason.

Shortly after Trudi moved in, Percy and Doris received further devastating news, that their daughter Dorothy's marriage had broken down and that she and her two sons had no alternative but to move back in with her parents. I remember very clearly 'Auntie Trudi' as we called her. She decorated, with still life paintings, in a most imaginative way, Swiss-style, a set of wooden panels in ceiling-to-floor built-in cupboards in the kitchen/dining room which, to this day, are still displayed.

Eventually Trudi returned to Basel and Iris finished her schooling. However the whole episode marked their lives for ever. Trudi and Iris had a very difficult relationship. Iris blamed her mother for being silent about what had happened and lacking any understanding of how her daughter suffered. Iris's trauma has remained with her all her life.

With little love and comfort from her mother, who found escape from her own problems in alcohol, Iris spent 35 years struggling to recover and lead a normal life. She married young at 20 but she was beaten by her husband, who was awarded custody of their daughter when she divorced him. She spent time in a psychiatric hospital after the marriage ended. Eventually, with the help of a skillful counsellor and with loving support from her second husband, John Galey, she was able to overcome the many emotional problems that plagued her for so long. John and Iris emigrated to New Zealand with their daughter, the second for Iris. This marriage lasted much longer but eventually broke down. Iris' relationships with both of her daughters were also badly damaged as the result of her trauma.

In the 1980s, as a way of overcoming her childhood trauma, Iris wrote a book telling the story of what happened. Published in 1986, *I Couldn't Cry When Daddy Died* became a best seller in New Zealand and in many countries in Europe. This is a harrowing and searingly honest account of what happened, of the severe emotional and psychological damage on Iris and of its impact on all her relationships with family and friends.

It was one of the first publications to break the taboos of incest. Interestingly, it coincided with the publication in the UK of the 1998 *Report of the inquiry into child abuse in Cleveland* after media publicity about a sudden increase in diagnoses of child sexual abuse at Middlesbrough General Hospital in early 1987. Iris gave many talks about her experiences and wrote further books (including one on the impact of religious fundamentalism on people's lives, triggered by her second husband's beliefs). She also took a degree in Auckland in psychotherapy.

Eventually, in her 60s, Iris returned to Basel and found real peace and happiness in a third marriage at the age of 76.

Growing up in Bradford and Basel, Iris yearned for a normal family life. Why was her father such a bully and so mean to her? Why was her mother so indifferent and so critical of her so often over the most trivial of things, yet occasionally affectionate and loving? Why did her parents not care for each other? Why was her family so dysfunctional? In contrast, she watched enviously how others seemed to live normal happy family lives free of such trauma. In her diary she writes, as a 12-year-old in 1948, about Uncle Percy, who represents such normality:

Still the same. Dreary, awful, frightening life. Mummy is scared of Daddy. Mum becomes famous. She goes to an art club, exhibits and is even in the newspaper with photos of her pictures, She did one of the Bradford Town Hall with all the electric poles and wires in front. It's black and white charcoal. Very good. She does flowers in vases with brass candlesticks, in oil, all with the highlights and shadows. Marvellous. I don't know how she does it...

Uncle Percy is a Dales painter. He's a new friend, banker, painter, actor. He takes us to the Civic Playhouse and we all see a funny play. We have a big party on New Year's Eve and Swiss people from the firm come and friends from the arts club and we all play games. Uncle Percy does a few sketches, acts the 'lady in the bath'. We all laugh and have a wonderful time and I'm amazed it can be like this and sorry it can't always be.

At the time Percy certainly knew nothing of the horrors that were taking place and almost certainly had no hint of the young girl's unhappiness. The full truth only emerged years later when, in the early 1980s, Iris invited him to comment on a draft of her book.

Throughout all this time and until the end of their lives Percy maintained contact with both Trudi and Iris. Trudi sent Christmas presents of Swiss chocolates year after year and occasionally wrote. Iris was also a regular correspondent and clearly looked back very fondly to the days when her 'Uncle Percy' was a familiar figure and was forever associated in her mind with a homely, friendly Yorkshire life so different from her own.

Today, Iris remembers two amusing points about Uncle Percy. First, as in the diary extract above, he performed an amusing and entirely innocent routine called *'Lady in the Bath'* where he pretended to do a striptease about a lady taking a bath which did not work. Everyone, adults and children, found it extremely funny. Second, he had an amusing habit of being able to close one eye by letting his eyelid drop without creasing it while keeping the other eye open. It was a trick he often used to entertain children.

Percy Monkman

Percy's daughter Dorothy sent Iris a tape of a BBC Radio Leeds interview that Percy had made in 1983. She replied *'I adored the tape. The songs and Percy's voice and all the lovely memories. So old-time England. I don't know what I'd have done without you all.'* A little later when Percy died, she wrote to Dorothy: *'You and your lovely mother and father were such a meaningful, enriching part of my childhood and I am deeply grateful to you.'* Three years later on, in another letter she wrote: *'I do thank you for the many lovely memories I have thanks to Yorkshire. You and your parents were a big part of the few flimsy roots I've got'*.

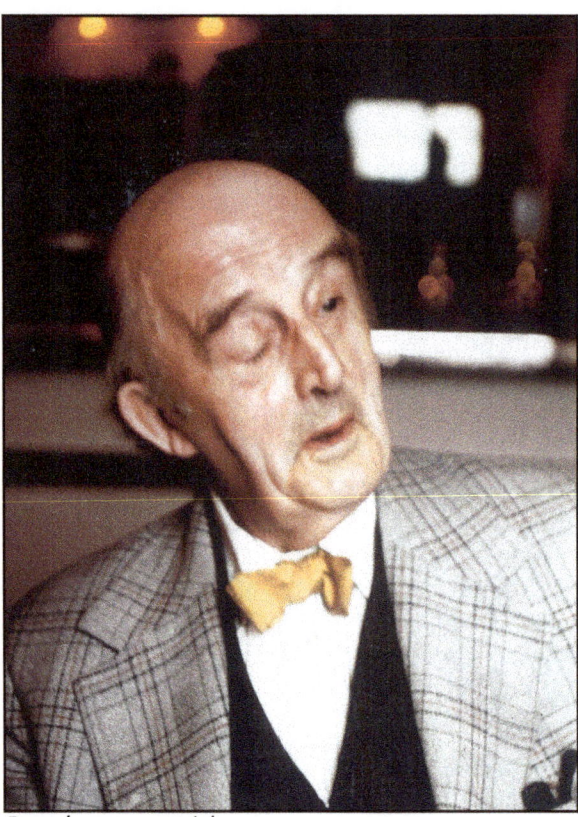

Percy's one-eye trick

Roger Suddards (1930 to 1995)

One of his last friends to see Percy alive, in Shipley Hospital in 1986, was Roger Suddards.

Born in 1930, he was a generation and a half younger than Percy, who got to know him in the 1960s through music hall events at the Bradford Civic Playhouse.

His first event involving Percy seems to be a Music Hall that ran for the week 8 to 13 January 1962 (including a Saturday matinee) at the Bradford Civic Playhouse. Roger was the director for this set of performances, which involved using most, if not all, of Percy's friends who had worked together over the 1940s and 1950s in similar programmes. In 1958 Roger had stood in as compère for a similar event on one night, but in 1962 he was the producer for the whole show.

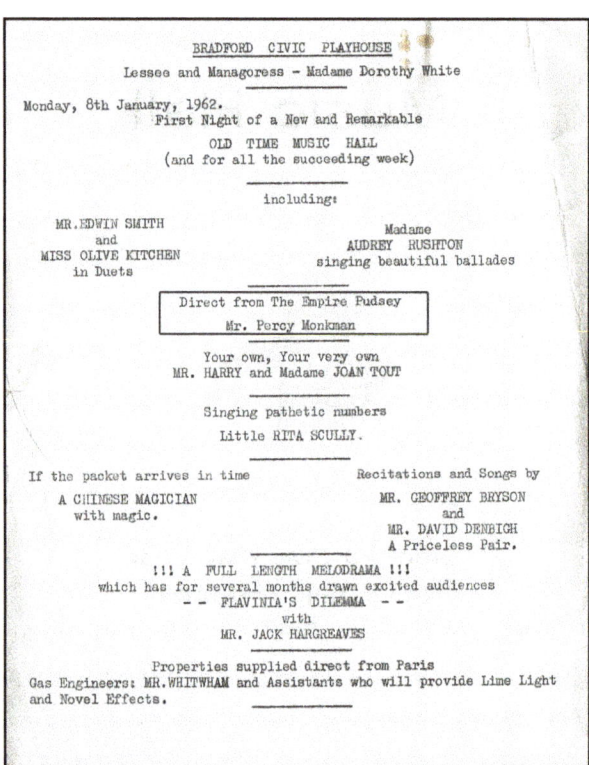

Music Hall, Bradford Civic Playhouse (8 to 13 January, 1962)

An Extraordinary Bradfordian

Roger also wrote the programme with great gusto, including many 'tongue in cheek' references, Percy being billed, for example, as 'Direct from the Empire Pudsey'. It is a pity that the presentation of the programme does not do justice to the humour and camaraderie that comes across from the words.

Roger put on similar shows in September 1968 and July 1969 with largely the same cast, including Percy (aged nearly 77), described in the 1969 programme as *'Our sprightly Mr Percy Monkman'*.

On 9 November 1974 Roger was also the chairman of a special event celebrating Percy being made an Honorary Life Member of Bradford Civic Playhouse, where he formally represented the Playhouse by conferring the award on Percy.

Although Roger's first love was the theatre, his father made him qualify as a solicitor. He practised law at Hammond Suddards, which became the second largest provincial firm of solicitors in the UK. He enjoyed an international reputation in town and country planning law, becoming one of only 11 English Heritage Commissioners. Moreover, as a 'mover and shaker', he was also extremely well connected in Bradford circles, being for example, Chairman of the Council of Bradford Grammar School (1987 to 1992) and Vice-Chancellor of Bradford University.

He found fame nationally for the much-praised administration of the Bradford Disaster Fund, set up after the Bradford City AFC fire disaster on 11 May 1985. Immediately made the first trustee, he was responsible for what everybody saw to be a very efficient and fair system for distributing funds of over £4.25m, for which he was awarded the CBE. The Bradford City fire was quickly followed by other disasters such as the Herald of Free Enterprise ferry (1987) and The Marchioness boat on the Thames (1989). Roger was asked to Downing Street to talk to Prime Minister Margaret Thatcher about his idea of creating multi-skilled emergency units to deal with disasters by land, sea and air.

With all his connections, it is no surprise that Roger was an organiser of the programme of commemoration of JB Priestley's life on 4 November 1984. Then in his 93rd year Percy was, of course, invited and he attended. After Percy's death Roger wrote a typically punchy foreword for Peter Holdsworth's 1994 book *The Rebel Tyke* about Bradford and JB Priestley.

Although Roger had no formal connections to the painting world, he seemed to have a strong interest in pictures. He was the most regular customer for Percy's works. From the mid-1950s to the early 1980s he bought his paintings – some 30 in total, according to Percy's records. Buying one or two pictures year by year is certainly the mark of a serious collector.

Bronwen Nixon and her tragic end (1919-1986)

In the 1950s Percy became friendly with Bronwen Nixon, a member of Bradford Arts Club. In 1966 she moved away from Bradford to run a hotel in the Lake District. Twenty years later her life came to a brutal end, three months before Percy's own death.

A catering lecturer by background, Bronwen, born In Ilkley, was later resident of Manningham where she became well-known for lavish Elizabethan banquets at 15th century Bolling Hall in Bradford, which Percy and Dorothy attended at least once. Bronwen then settled in the Lake District and built up a national reputation at her Rothay Manor Hotel just outside Ambleside in the Lake District. She won several awards as a hotelier and restaurateur, appearing year after year in Egon Ronay's *Good Food Guide* and in 1979 won a national competition for the Best Afternoon Tea. She also presented a series on catering on BBC's Radio 4.

In the late 1970s and early 1980s the only holidays that Percy and daughter Dorothy took were the several occasions when they stayed out of season as Bronwen's guests at Rothay Manor. The hotel, just outside Ambleside, was well situated for subjects for watercolours, Percy's main criterion for a good holiday.

Then in January 1986, Bronwen was savagely strangled at her hotel by a burglar who broke into her rooms. After a feature about the crime on the BBC Crimewatch programme the murderer was caught and eventually convicted and given a life sentence. Very shortly after that awful event, Percy was moved into Shipley Hospital where three months later he died.

Ashley Jackson (1940 to current day)

Percy made new friendships throughout his life. One of the last was with Ashley Jackson, a watercolour painter from Barnsley with a rising reputation when Percy met him in the early 1970s. Nearly fifty years younger, Ashley and Percy shared the same obsession with painting. Percy would also have admired Ashley's aim of making a living from this passion.

After the First World War, Percy might have contemplated becoming a professional entertainer, although opting for continuing his bank job with its stability and promise of a pension. However, his painting had developed more slowly as a result of his other time-consuming activities on the stage, and so he never really seriously thought of being a professional painter. Ashley's career illustrates what a difficult challenge this was, especially for someone living in a working class area that might not be a natural home for a talented and ambitious artist.

The story of Ashley's life is covered in a 2010 biography by Chris Bond entitled *Ashley Jackson: An Artist's Life*. This describes what was involved in making a living from painting, notwithstanding Ashley's natural talent and commitment. *'Art is a hard, hard game'* commented Ashley when asked about the challenge. It meant major sacrifices (eg no family holidays for many years) and occasionally required serious risk taking (eg staking his home on several occasions when he had to invest in his career).

The main barrier for a provincial artist, especially one like Ashley who styled himself as 'Yorkshire artist', is the London art establishment. Ashley had his fair share of rejection. On one occasion, the biography recounts that *'He didn't take kindly to being*

An Extraordinary Bradfordian

told by an RI member (Royal Institute of Water Colour Painters) that he had been a "whisker away from being invited to join". I told him where to stick it. I don't need letters after my name to show people that I'm any good. The only thing that matters is "Can I do the job?"'. And as long as the public are buying my works then I'm happy to let them be the judges.

Ashley had learnt that *'You can't fight this establishment. You have to go round them'*. For example, he had found new ways of reaching out to a wide audience through TV series about painting that started with Pebble Mill at One (BBC1) in the late 1970s and included Yorkshire TV's *A Brush With Ashley,* which ran for over nine years in the 1990s. In the 1980s, Ashley was also a regular TV celebrity in the USA with his *Ashley Jackson's World of Art* series for the Public Broadcasting Service (PBS).

Chris Bond's book refers to Percy in Ashley's mention of the Yorkshire Watercolour Society that he was instrumental in setting up in the early 1980s:

Stanley Chapman co-founded the now defunct Yorkshire Watercolour Society with Ashley. And it was Chapman who introduced him to Joe Pighills, 'a brilliant 'half-deaf' Dales artist', Percy Monkman, a 'lovely Capo di Monte type' fella from Bradford' and Tom Sykes from Otley. I would go out painting with all these codgers and they took me under their wing, because I was a young artist starting out. They were very well placed amateurs in watercolour painting. We all used to swap works.

Source: *Ashley Jackson: An Artist's Life* © Chris Bond, 2010

Percy's personal catalogue showed that he swapped his December 1973 painting of the 'Road to Dick Hudson's' (a famous pub and familiar landmark on the edge of the moor near Percy's adopted home of Baildon) with one 1975 Ashley Jackson painting of a back street in his adopted home of Holmfirth set against the Pennine moors, a painting that hangs proudly today in this author's lounge. Each painting is typical of its painter – in its choice of subject and its treatment.

Although they were a generation and a half apart, Ashley and Percy shared the obsession about painting in watercolours that led them to paint outdoors at every opportunity and capture the atmosphere of Yorkshire scenes, typically brooding skies and moorland. They also shared other key values – the commitment to self-improvement, the importance of promoting one's work and antipathy to many of the fashions of the art world. The need and desire to make a living out of painting drove Ashley to higher levels of achievement than Percy reached as a painter – a highly successful professional and a seriously good amateur, sharing very similar views of their art.

Other friends

Joe Appleyard (1908 to 1960)

Joe was another Yorkshire artist, but one who specialised in painting horses and hunting scenes, rather than landscapes of the Dales. Born and brought up in Leeds, he managed to make a living from painting largely from commissions. He exhibited across the whole of Yorkshire, which is how Percy came to know him.

In 1960 Joe was tragically killed when he fell from a bus at Lawnswood roundabout on his way to Kettlewell. Percy attended the funeral.

John F Greenwood (1885 to 1954)

A watercolour artist, wood engraver and printmaker, John studied at Bradford School of Art and at the Royal College of Art (RCA). For most of his life he lived at Ilkley and he died there. He is best remembered for his distinctive wood engravings, which Percy always admired. In 1952 he published 'The Dales are Mine', which tells his story.

In autumn of 1937 John and Percy held a two-man exhibition at a gallery in Leeds.

Ivy Lewis (age unknown)

A regular correspondent to Percy and an occasional visitor to his home was Ivy Lewis, a widow from Swansea. In the 1930s her husband Elvet moved to Bradford as a pastor at Girlington Congregational Church. They quickly made friends with Percy and Doris. However, they soon moved back to South Wales. Her husband died relatively young, leaving her to bring up their only son Peter with little financial support.

The Welsh lilt to Ivy's voice made her stand out from almost all of Percy's other friends who, of course, had strong Yorkshire accents.

Joe Pighills (1902 to 1984)

Another well-known Yorkshire artist that Percy became friends with was painter and printmaker Joe Pighills. Joe was born in Oxenhope, near Haworth, where he lived for all of his life in the same row of cottages on the edge of the moor.

He was another eccentric character who was driven by watercolour painting, and another friend who Percy would drop in to see when he was painting in Bronte country.

An Extraordinary Bradfordian

Clem Pulman (date of birth unknown, died 1980)

Not very much is known about this friend from the 1930s and 1940s, except that Percy sometimes mentioned him in later life after Clem, who was an actor and writer, had moved out of the area. Judging by the unusual photograph taken of Percy's young family (see Chapter 8), he also took a serious interest in photography.

A Civic Theatre programme from 1935 included a short piece about him: *He created the Playhouse design and does the posters you see where you book. He writes, draws, photographs and reads more than is good for him and criticises more than is good for us.* He was already a regular member of the cast when Percy joined the Civic Playhouse in 1935, occasionally producing plays and directing the Civic's drama class. He published five books, including short stories and sketches of people and places, although it is not easy to identify a strong common thread from his work.

He certainly discussed a collaboration with Percy for a book on the West Riding of Yorkshire, asking Percy to illustrate it. Percy has left behind a set of 23 small black and white drawings of both urban and rural scenes, which are all in a common style. The drawings are clearly referenced to what must have been a full draft of the book, but there is no record of the book having ever been published. From Percy's viewpoint this was a serious piece of work that never seems to have seen the light of day.

After the Second World War, Clem seems to have left the Bradford area and moved up to Aberdeen where he became a secondary school drama teacher. The last contact was from his wife in Aberdeen informing Percy of his death.

The caricature of Clem, left, is typical of many that Percy drew in his years at the Civic Playhouse.

Clem Pulman by Percy

Laurence Scarfe (1914 to 1993)

Laurence was born in Idle, Bradford, and studied art at the Royal College of Art. He left Bradford in the late 1930s to live in a flat in Chelsea and after the war moved to Brighton.

He struggled in his 20s but gradually built a reputation as a painter, muralist and illustrator. He was an elected member of the Society of Mural Painters and a Fellow of the Society of Industrial Artists. He exhibited at the Royal Academy, Royal Society of British Artists. The V&A, Tate Gallery, Imperial War Museum and Brighton Art Gallery hold his work.

A generation younger than Percy, Laurence was the friend who was the closest match to the Bohemian image of an artist. He dressed unconventionally, had a sharp wit and was an amusing conversationalist.

Percy and Laurence corresponded from time to time. In 1978 Laurence wrote: *The years slip by at such a rate that it's always later than one thinks... next August I shall give up full-time lecturing, but would not mind one day per week with the boys and girls. They are so earnest! I could tell them a thing or two not in the curriculum – except they wouldn't believe me!*

CHAPTER 7
LONG-SUFFERING BRADFORD CITY FAN

No biography about Percy Monkman could ignore his life-long support for Bradford City AFC. He was born within a mile of City's ground at Valley Parade, just off Manningham Lane. A keen player himself, he was a boy when the team first joined the Football League in 1903. The pre-war era turned out to be a golden time for the club. Naturally interested in sport, Percy could scarcely fail to support his successful local team, and continued to do so all his life through the many subsequent periods of mediocrity and occasional successes.

Playing football

Bradford YMCA (13 February 1909)

As the stories of his early friendship with JB Priestley show, Percy was obsessed with playing football. He played up to 20-a-side with friends on the Belle Vue School playing fields on Scotchman Road near to where he lived. He did from time to time mention that he broke his leg playing football, which made him more nervous about playing. However, we have no written record of when, or whether, it happened.

Here we have a photo dated 13 February 1909 when Percy aged 16 played right-wing for the Bradford YMCA side which beat Yorkshire YMCA 5-2.

Percy is the first player (in white) on the left standing up in the back row.

Bradford City's golden era

Percy's childhood coincided with the rise of organised competitive sport, including football, cricket, rugby union and rugby league.

In the 1890s association football (soccer) began to supplant rugby football which until then had been the predominant sport in the West Riding. Playing at Valley Parade, Manningham RFC was a strong rugby team and a close rival to Bradford FC, which had established itself at the newly-built Horton Park ground across the city. The club became known as Bradford Park Avenue.

However, a group of local businessmen started to put together a case for Bradford to have its own soccer team. Within few months it had persuaded the rugby committee at Manningham RFC to allow a team to play soccer there and, a few months later, against all the odds, this group then persuaded the Football League to admit Bradford City AFC to replace Doncaster Rovers in the Second Division, despite having not yet assembled a team.

So, without ever playing one game of competitive soccer, the new club kicked off the 1903/04 season as a professional team in the Football League – a quite remarkable start.

Five years later they won promotion to the First Division and then, at the end of the 1910/11, they won the FA Cup, beating Newcastle United 1-0 at a replay at Maine Road, Manchester after drawing the first game at Crystal Palace in London. Percy saw that historic game. This remains Bradford City's only honour.

Interestingly, the FA Cup itself had been redesigned the previous year to replace the original trophy, which had been stolen while on display in Birmingham. The new version was made by Fattorinis, well-known jeweller from Bradford, and now had been won by the local team. Moreover, JE Fattorini had been one of the innovative promoters who had, eight years earlier, pushed so energetically for Bradford City to join the Football League.

An Extraordinary Bradfordian

The inter-war years

As with many professional teams, the First World War took its toll on Bradford City. For example, the goalscorer in the 1911 Cup final lost his life in action. After two seasons the team was relegated to the Second Division.

It suffered a second relegation five years later into Third Division (North), and at the end of 1927/28 it came close to liquidation. It quickly recovered from this blow, being promoted the next season back into the Second Division. It stayed here until another relegation at the end of 1936/37. The serious threat of liquidation was faced and overcome at least half a dozen times in its next 80 years and, in the 1999/2000 season finally returned to the top league.

There was a continuing debate, which included Bradford Northern, the Rugby League team, not just about the lack of finances but about the wisdom of the city having two professional teams and the ideal location for a shared ground. However nothing changed. Gradually, both team and fans became resigned to underachievement.

We do not have much information about Percy's active support of the team over this period. Information that we have about his entertainment and acting must have curtailed his attendance on many Saturdays. However, we do have many cartoons from matches of this period which he clearly attended. The matches he selected were highly suitable, such as a 9-1 victory against Nelson in promotion season 1927/28. He might well have had to attend many uninspiring games before such a game came along, or else he was just extremely lucky.

The post-war years

After the Second World War the club had little ambition and little investment. It remained in the doldrums, 'yo-yoing' between the Third and Fourth Divisions with little prospect of any real success. For such a large city, the club underachieved on a massive scale.

Percy had a regular season ticket until around 1970. When my brother and I were boys, he encouraged us to attend and we used to sit with him in the main stand before, a little older, we were allowed to go with our own friends in the main standing areas. Football and how our team was doing was always a regular topic of conversation with him right until his death.

Although this period had many frustrations and tested all our patience and enthusiasm, we did enjoy some times when the team's fortune picked up. For example in the late 1950s and early 1960s we had a succession of three centre forwards who scored heavily. In 1959/60 we soundly beat First Division Everton 3-0 in the third round of the FA Cup and then drew with First Division Champions Burnley 2-2 in the fifth round, conceding a final goal five minutes from the end at a packed Valley Parade (over 26,000 attendance).

However, as ever, the club sold these local stars as soon as they became successful. The prospect of long-term success seemed as far away as ever. At times the club seemed to be in permanent depression, no time more so than when they suffered 7-1 defeats in two matches in a row in 1965.

The Bradford City fire disaster

Percy's final visit to Valley Parade was the saddest of hundreds that he made in his life. This occurred the day after the tragedy of the Bradford City fire on 11 May 1985 when 56 people lost their lives and 250 suffered injuries. In terms of loss of lives this was, at the time in the UK, the second worst stadium disaster and the second worst peace-time fire disaster in the 20th century. Like the Grenfell Tower fire in 2017, it attracted national headlines for several weeks. It stunned the city of Bradford.

Although he had not been a regular visitor for at least ten years, Percy had been invited by a friend, Brian Walker, to go to that fateful match against Lincoln City to celebrate City's promotion to Division 3, just a year before Percy died. Fortunately he turned down that invitation. Had he gone, he would have undoubtedly found a seat in the main stand near to where he used to have a season ticket, which was also very close to where the fire started. He would have stood little chance of survival.

As it was, Brian took him to the ground the next day to survey the wreckage of the main stand and a *Sunday Times* photographer took the picture of the pair of them surveying the mementoes that fans had placed against the wall of the burnt-out stand. That picture was published in the next edition, on Sunday 19 May. Shortly after, Percy wrote to the paper to ask for a copy of that photograph; they never replied. However, 32 years later the *Sunday Times* found the picture! They also unearthed the whole series of unpublished photos taken by the photographer on the day, one of which is also shown here.

Here Percy is standing with Brian looking at the devastation of the burn-out stand and all the flowers and cards that had been left by well-wishers. Like all Bradfordians, fans or not, Percy was shocked; he was also highly relieved that he declined the invitation to attend.

Bouquets, wreaths, scarves at Bradford City AFC (The Sunday Times, 19 May 1985)

Source: The Times – News Syndication (2017)

As they started to walk away, Percy must have realised that not only would he never attend another game, but also must have feared that the club might never rise up from the ashes of this fire. The club that had been created 10 years after his birth and then won the FA Cup for the only time just eight years later might well now be dying in such a devastating way before his own death.

No return to Valley Parade. (unpublished)

Source: The Times – News Syndication (2017)

An Extraordinary Bradfordian

Nearly a year later after the fire Percy died. He would have been oblivious to the club's recovery from the disaster and to the many switches of fortune over the next 30 years, starting with gradual recovery (1987 and later), then promotion to the Premier League (1999), followed by relegation and two financial collapses in the 2000s and then another gradual recovery (2011 to present-day).

Other sports

Although soccer was Percy's main sport, he took a strong interest in other sports, mainly cricket, golf and rugby union.

For at least two years after the First World War, he played in a local cricket team, Toller Lane Cricket Club. Not affiliated to any league, it nevertheless had a published fixture list with 10 to 15 matches. No record of any game survives, nor any mention of Percy's contribution, although, as 'a committee member', according to the fixture list, he was presumably more or less guaranteed a place. He would watch occasional Yorkshire county games at the Bradford Park Avenue ground. There is also a scorecard that survives of the third day of the 1934 Test Match at Headingley when Bradman famously scored 304 against England.

He played golf once or twice. A card survives of a round at Filey. Again, golf took too much time for him, not surprisingly given his other commitments. But he followed the big tournaments (eg the Open and the Ryder Cup).

Never a player, he must have been a rugby union spectator in the 1920s, as he published 15 individual caricatures of a Bradford team. In the television era he watched international rugby union, although he was bored by teams that relied just on the kicking game.

Finally, Percy regularly obtained the *Yorkshire Sports.* Published every Saturday teatime on an iconic pink newsprint by the *Telegraph & Argus,* this special edition newspaper contained all the days' results and articles about all the local teams and sportsmen. Launched in 1900 and closed down in 1981, the *Yorkshire Sports* had a very similar age to Percy himself. Equally regularly every Monday, Percy mailed it to his brother Gordon in Canada. In return he received a copy of *Time Magazine,* but Percy never seemed to take much interest in it.

CHAPTER 8

COMMITTED FAMILY MAN

Percy's family mattered much to him. He was, undoubtedly, head of the whole family all his adult life. He enjoyed very good health and was indebted to his wife Doris for her unfailing support. His achievements contrast strongly with those of his three brothers (a fourth dying as a young man), who were all successful businessmen in the wool trade. Although largely happy, Percy's family life, however, did have several very sad episodes, which left their mark.

The Monkman family

The Monkman family was large. Percy was the eldest of five boys; there followed Gordon (born in 1894 and died at 83 years old), Harry (born in 1896 and died at 80), Stanley (born in 1901 and died at 28) and Frank (born in 1904 and died at 70).

Stanley died young from leukaemia just months after getting married. Between them the other four brothers had nine children.

Note: Percy wears the bow tie, but his brothers wear conventional ties, symbolising perhaps how their lives differed.

Percy's parents and brothers (1920).
Back row: Harry (son no 3), Frank (son no 5), Gordon (son no 2)
Front row: Stanley (son no 4), Edwin (father), Martha (mother), Percy (son no 1)

Percy Monkman

Percy with his wife and children (1934)

Percy standing, Doris seated, Colin (left), Harvey (middle) and Dorothy (right)

Married to Doris Northrop (born in 1894 and died at 79), Percy had three children, Dorothy (born in 1920 and died at 80), Harvey (born in 1922 and died at 55) and Colin (born in 1923 and died at 72). Percy and Doris had four grandchildren: daughter Dorothy had two boys, Martin and Adrian, son Harvey had a girl, Avril, and a boy, Andrew, but son Colin had no children. Percy had seven great-grandchildren, all born in his lifetime.

These two family photographs provide quite a contrast. One is conventional and the other quite unconventional.

The first is taken by a professional photographer just before Gordon's emigration to Canada. The figures are all dressed formally, the men in three-piece suits and the mother in her best (and only?) outfit. They face directly into the camera with the front row seated and the back row standing. The lighting is clear in sepia and white. Overall, it makes for a formidable-looking family.

The second (14 years later) is taken by Percy's actor friend, Clem Pulman, who dabbled in professional photography. Although still artificial, the composition is much more artistic, with faces looking in different directions. Here, the lighting is muted to the extent that faces are not fully visible. Only Percy stands, facing away behind his seated wife and children. It is ironical that in this much less conventional composition Percy unusually wears a conventional tie!

An Extraordinary Bradfordian

Without doubt, for all his life Percy was the head of the family, not just by virtue of being the eldest son, but because he lived longer than all his brothers and, indeed, than any of the next generation. He was the only one of the five brothers who outlived his wife; he also lived longer than any of the Monkman in-laws and all the friends listed in this story. A rare letter from his old World War 1 friend Tommy Crosby, in 1976, shortly before he died indicated that Percy also outlived all his concert party friends in 'The Archies'.

In fact, he was and remains, at 93 years of age, the oldest ever member of the family as far as our extensive family history records go back (into the 18th century and earlier in the case of some branches).

Growing up

Percy's parents had hard lives, both as they were growing up themselves and then bringing up a family of five boys. They provided an interesting contrast. Edwin, the parent from a large family, was, according to Percy's daughter, Dorothy, taciturn and undemonstrative, whereas Martha, who had been orphaned as a girl, was much livelier and had a good sense of humour. Their lives were focused on the five boys, the greengrocer's shop and the chapel (first, the Congregational Church at Greenfield in Manningham and then the one in Girlington just off Toller Lane). They had little by way of a social life outside these priorities.

Percy's mother was a strong character. Not only did she bring up a family of five boys, who at times must have made a great deal of work for her, but she also worked in her husband's greengrocery, filleting fish and serving customers. Dorothy thought that she had a 'good business head', playing an active role in running the shop and dealing with the customers.

Martha was not at all interested in material possessions or clothes for herself. The only time her granddaughter could recall her wearing a new outfit was for the couple's visit in 1931 to see Gordon in Canada. On this occasion her daughter-in-law Maud (Harry's wife) bought her a fur stole and a new dark blue outfit.

Their home was, in Dorothy's view, not particularly comfortable. It was furnished in a spartan way. She mentioned a horse-hair sofa that was 'prickly' to sit on. The main room was a kitchen/living room. Cooking was done over an open fire. Dorothy remembered her grandmother cooking sheep's head broth. It was ready to eat, her grandmother said, when the head dropped off and the teeth fell out!

There was a parlour (the 'front room') but that was rarely used, only when a family member paid a social call.

Percy Monkman

Non-conformist background

The Monkman family were brought up as non-conformists, their lives closely bound to Girlington Congregational Church in Little Lane, only a couple minutes' walk from where they lived. Percy's father sang in church choirs for over 60 years. His mother Martha was involved in church work all her life, firstly at Greenfield Congregational Church in Manningham and, when they moved up the road to Toller Lane, then at Girlington Congregational Church (colloquially, 'Congs'). It was the church's social events that first gave young Percy the opportunity to entertain audiences.

Although the family was poor and the boys only had a basic education, their parents influenced them with positive values about living that helped them to be self-starters. Martha was a strong believer in *'counting your blessings'*. Percy's daughter Dorothy remembered that her grandmother seemed to have a saying, often with a Biblical overtone, to fit every situation, which she used in conversation to reinforce the right behaviour. For example, she often said *'Always tell the truth'*.

At the family celebration of Percy and Doris' golden wedding in 1968, Percy acknowledged their influence in his short speech.

We bring up a family of which we are proud – no delinquents, no hippies – and really we've not done too badly. I'm truly happy that we've all been pretty successful from a scholastically poor start. If Mother and Father saw us gathered here together this evening, they would be delighted.

Something I think about often and I must say it – we have a great deal to thank our parents for – and there would be a better world if more families were brought up today as were, pretty strictly with a sound foundation of Christian knowledge – we may not have lived up to this, but it has had a profound effect on all of us, and to the good.

Percy himself was involved in the local church from 1912 when the family moved up from Manningham to Toller Lane. He started as a Sunday School teacher for a few months but stopped when he became as entertainer on the grounds that pupils could not take him seriously when he had amused them on stage the day before.

In 1929 he was pressed, a little reluctantly, into being the Church Treasurer, a role that no doubt used his book-keeping knowledge from working in the bank. He remained in this role for seven years: the Church's management committee accepted his resignation at the start of 1937.

When Percy and Doris moved to Baildon in 1952, they gradually lost the link with the church in Little Lane and never re-established a long-term link with a more local church. However, in the 1960s Percy sometimes attended the Congregational Church in nearby Shipley.

In my early life Percy's strong non-conformist roots were not obvious to me. For example, I never remember attending a church service with him, except for a wedding or a funeral, and even then it would not be at a Congregational Church. He was, however, happy that my brother and I attended Sunday School (Church of England).

Percy's own children were not regular church-goers and the strong non-conformist family tradition gradually petered out, reflecting more general trends towards a secular society.

A largely healthy lifestyle

When Percy retired, I was just six years old. So as a child, teenager then adult, I realised that he seemed quite different from other retired people. The difference was that he had a clear sense of purpose about each day – no sitting around watching the TV or reading the papers or not knowing how best to occupy the day. He was obsessed, largely, at that stage of his life, with painting – finishing yesterday's painting, organising the next outing, planning exhibitions, getting pictures framed and so on. He routinely ignored regular advice to slow down and take things easy. Gradually I realised that it was this obsession that kept him alive – an invaluable model for living one's life.

There is no doubt that this was indeed a healthy lifestyle. He was hardly ever poorly, except for an occasional cold. Even when the end came in his 94th year, he declined in only a few weeks from his normal healthy state after a chest infection. He had just reached the natural end of his life.

With one exception he looked after himself. No doubt influenced by his strictly teetotal mother, he drank little alcohol. Although he liked pubs as sociable places, he would not drink more than half a pint of beer on the odd occasions he went. At home he might offer visitors a small whisky and at Christmas a bottle of red wine might appear with the dinner.

The one exception to this generally healthy lifestyle was his regular pipe-smoking and the occasional cigar at special events. He usually had a pipe in his hand, filled with with his favourite Bruno No 2. The pipe became an extension of his personality, just like his trademark bow-tie. (Not the easiest person to buy for, Percy was often given bow-ties and tobacco as presents, but woe betide anyone who bought him a 'made-up' bow-tie rather than one you tied yourself, or chose a tobacco brand other than his favourite.)

There was also one untypical episode in his life when things were not working out. In late 1936/early 1937 he had what he called a *'bit of a nervous breakdown'* which seemed to last a few months. This was almost certainly why he resigned from being the Church Treasurer at the start of 1937, on grounds of ill-health. It also led him to take a trip abroad for one to two weeks with one or more male friends (names never discovered in his papers). He chose to go to Holland (Rotterdam) and Germany (Hamburg, Berlin and Dresden). With hindsight Nazi Germany seems a rather strange choice at that time, given that, apart from his wartime experiences in Northern France, he had never been abroad. However, he had studied German at evening classes in 1926 and might have wanted to practise it. Three postcards to his wife give no indication of the rise of Nazism.

In view of the hectic lifestyle he lived outside work one might imagine that the sheer scale of his activity might have just got out of control. The truth is different. Surprisingly, it was his day job that caused the problem, because the responsibility of accounting for money got on top of him and, for a while, he just could not do his job.

Percy Monkman

A supportive wife

As the scale of creative energy and sheer volume of activity unfolds in this story, one realises the role Percy's wife Doris must have played. Percy and Doris shared their life for over 55 years, until Doris died on 9 April 1974.

Throughout their married life, the evenings and weekends Percy routinely devoted to entertainment, acting and painting can only emphasise how much he depended on Doris for managing the home and providing stability for the family.

Christmas 1923 was a case in point. They had three young children: aged three and a half, eighteen months old with the third just six months old. Percy ran a children's party on 22 December in central Bradford. He then agreed to do an event on Christmas Day for a Sunday school in Pudsey, on the border with Leeds, a few miles away, which the organiser helpfully indicated involved catching a bus from central Bradford to Leeds at 6pm, returning at 9.15pm (He still had an extra three miles from home to central Bradford and back). To cap it all, he did another church-based event at nearby Allerton on Boxing Day. Fees of one and half guineas in each case might have helped sugar the pill for Doris when money would be tight, but that kind of schedule would have put some strain on a young family.

There are many such instances right through until when Percy retired, after which he had many more hours in the day for his outside interests. During his working life, he might, for example, need three weeks of rehearsals plus a week of performances for each play or he might be out night after night in the winter doing entertainments as in the Second World War, not to mention needing time for developing new material. Finally, supporting the Bradford Arts Club took up two to three evenings a week throughout his adult life.

Percy commented in a talk about his Second Word War experiences as an entertainer that *'My wife must have been a saint to put up with it'*. In truth Doris was extremely tolerant, placid, gentle and kind-hearted, happy to let Percy take the limelight and happy too that this gave him personal fulfilment. She had little ambition of her own, only wanting her family to do well for themselves. No doubt as the three children were growing up, she benefitted from the support of other close family members who all lived in the vicinity. For example, daughter Dorothy remembered her grandmother (Percy's mother) living nearby and being a regular visitor. She wrote later that her grandmother used to say, *'I am making up for Percy'*, knowing that he was out most evenings.

This is perhaps a lifestyle that not many wives today would tolerate, even if in an earlier generation it might have been the norm. Without such loyal support Percy could not have achieved so much. Percy and Doris were able to celebrate 50 years of marriage with Percy's brothers Harry, Gordon and Frank In the picture of the event, facing, Percy still has his bow-tie, his brothers their conventional ties!

An Extraordinary Bradfordian

Golden wedding for Percy and Doris with Percy's three brothers Harry, Gordon and Frank (left to right)

Differences from his brothers

Having three brothers who also reached retirement age provides a very interesting contrast in terms of achievement. Gordon, Harry and Frank were by any account successful self-made businessmen who achieved much, despite only receiving the same basic education as Percy.

We should acknowledge that Percy, Gordon and Harry were indeed all fortunate to survive the war, (Stanley and Frank were both too young to serve). Gordon and Harry both joined the 16th West Yorkshire Regiment, also known as the Bradford Pals. Gordon went first to Egypt, then, in 1916, to Northern France where he survived the Battle of the Somme. He applied for a commission in the infantry and in 1918 he earned the Military Cross for leading his platoon against an enemy machine gun post, compelling 100 German soldiers to surrender, in one of the last battles of the war. Harry also fought in the Battle of the Somme and suffered from shell-shock, now defined as post-traumatic stress syndrome.

Gordon and Harry survived, against all the odds, (as indeed did their first cousin Herbert Monkman, who also joined the Pals). To put their survival into context, the Bradford Pals lost 1,770 men out of 2,000. There can have been very few families in Bradford, and probably few in the whole country, that had three boys doing military service in the First World War who all survived and then lived into their eighties.

Percy, of course, found a very different route for survival during the war.

Gordon emigrated to Canada in 1920 and became a general manager of a textile company, originally based in Bradford, that had developed a Canadian operation. He became a pillar of the local community, entering local politics and becoming an alderman on the City Council for Peterborough in Ontario (a city of approx. 100,000 population). Like all the Monkman brothers, he was interested in sport, especially golf, soccer, badminton and cricket.

Harry worked initially in a wool business in Bradford, before entering into a partnership with a cloth manufacturer. After the Second World War he lived a comfortable life. He was a keen sportsman and, especially, a keen golfer.

Frank was perhaps the most successful. In the early 1920s he set up a scout troop linked to Girlington Congs. After he married in 1928, he emigrated to New Zealand, but returned home after eight years. On his return, he founded and managed a company in the wool trade ('merchants and processors of speciality fibres'), employing up to 100 people. He played golf, was a member of the Lions and was a Freemason. He lived a very prosperous lifestyle with expensive holidays abroad and living in relative luxury in Ilkley. In the late 1950s and early 1960s he and his wife Dorothy organised a large family party for all the Monkmans every Boxing Day that reinforced the sense of prosperity that he enjoyed.

Although Percy was not as wealthy as his brothers, he lived quite a comfortable life, any extra income being used to fund his painting. The real contrast was that he had a steady job, with no risks of redundancy at a time, say in the 1920s, when unemployment was high. Moreover, he had the prospect of a regular pension. In comparison, his brothers had to be risk-takers, experiencing some difficult times in the 1920s and 1930s before they enjoyed success and prosperity

The differences do not stop there. As we have seen, Percy led a remarkable life full of creativity and energy. Never focused on making money, he developed his personality in many ways that led to public recognition. By contrast, though successful in a conventional way, the two brothers who remained in Bradford seemed one-dimensional. For example, Harry and Frank could easily have been the source of Monty Python's famous 'Four Yorkshiremen' sketch, each out-doing the other on reminiscences of their childhood poverty now that they were self-made successes. Gordon, whom we saw on occasional visits back to the UK, had a gentler disposition than Harry and Frank, although he did commit the cardinal sin of being the only Monkman to support Bradford Park Avenue, the city's other professional football team, rather than Bradford City, the local team in Manningham.

When Harry died in 1976, Gordon's son and wife, Cyril and Lois, happened to be in England. They asked Percy to contribute to an audio tape to take back to their family in Canada. On behalf of the Yorkshire Monkmans and for the benefit of the Canadian Monkmans Percy spoke about Harry's funeral and his life. He finished by saying that he always thought that the family had done well considering their humble background and lack of schooling and *'should, as Mother always said, count their blessings'* and signed himself off as *'Patriarchally, Percy'*! A year later, Gordon died. Percy was to live another nine years, outliving all his brothers.

Percy earned the right to be the head of family not just because he was the first-born, but because he had rather different values and attitudes to life, reflected in a very unconventional lifestyle outside work. Although his brothers were all successful self-made businessmen in the wool trade, Percy's social and artistic achievements set him apart.

An Extraordinary Bradfordian

He had the public persona and made the speeches and the jokes. He was the life and soul of the party.

Some very sad episodes

Not everything worked out in Percy's family's life. He experienced several heavy family setbacks.

Sudden death of brother Stanley

The Monkman family had been fortunate to survive the First World War intact, with the three eldest boys all returning from the Somme, against overwhelming odds. However, at the end of 1928, they had some devastating news right out of the blue. The fourth brother, Stanley, suddenly fell ill at the age of 28, six months after he had married Laura Bowes. He died within two weeks.

After the funeral Percy wrote an 18-page letter to Gordon in Canada, explaining in detail how the illness happened, the treatment sought, the death and the funeral. There is no evidence of such a letter to Frank, then living in New Zealand, but Percy refers to an exchange of cables with him.

Stanley had leukaemia that was not diagnosed until it was far too advanced. It appears that he had been looking unwell for some time, but not sufficiently so for doctors to be called. The family was desperate to find a cure. With brothers Gordon and Frank both abroad, it fell on Percy, supported by Harry, to look for help. They contacted a specialist ('the greatest bacteriologist in Yorkshire' according to Percy). He attempted some painful treatment, described by Percy, that sounds like radiotherapy, but it did not work. The specialist said that *'the case was hopeless from the first'* and also that he had known of only five such cases in 30 years of medical practice. They sought advice from the Christian Science Church but again that was too late. Bizarrely, from today's viewpoint, Laura's uncle, who was a company director, bought three bottles of champagne and one of brandy, probably as a way of dulling the pain, but Stanley was too sick to take this medicine.

The shock of the tragedy hit the whole family, especially Percy's mother and Stanley's young widow. They could not understand why the death had occurred. Laura never remarried but remained in the area, keeping in touch with Percy mainly through the exchange of Christmas cards, which she kept all her life.

Breakdown of daughter Dorothy's marriage

The episode that perhaps caused the greatest anxiety and had the biggest impact on Percy's own life was the break-up of his daughter's marriage to Reg Greenwood in 1953, 12 years after they married. Reg was a Cambridge-educated teacher who suddenly announced to his wife that he was leaving her for another woman who had just given birth to a baby girl. Dorothy, my brother and I had to leave our home, only recently set up near Coventry, just after Reg had changed jobs. Dorothy felt that she had no choice but to return to her parents' home in Baildon, just outside Bradford, where Percy had moved, on retirement in 1952.

This changed everything. Percy and Doris had to provide financial and emotional support to Dorothy, my brother and myself, support that lasted until we went to university. At a practical level Percy in particular took on a parental role in bringing up the two of us. Dorothy never really recovered from the marriage breakdown and never met a new partner. My brother and I also found the new life difficult to understand because nobody took time to explain to us what had happened and why our father lived in London (he was teaching there). In the 1950s family breakdowns seemed very rare, compared with today.

In addition to a father's natural distress in such a situation, the blow to Percy had an extra dimension. He had been very supportive of Reg in the Second World War. Reg was a conscientious objector who appealed against military service and was allocated to a wartime occupation of market gardening. Moreover, Reg's own father had been a career soldier who ran away from home to fight in the Boer War and could not accept that his only son was a pacifist. This led to a major fallout as a result of which they had no contact for around ten years. Percy who, as we have seen in the First World War joined the army as a paramedic rather than a soldier possibly because of his own pacifist sympathies, supported Reg. He also admired his achievement in getting to Cambridge University from a working class background. Percy was entitled to feel very disappointed with this sad outcome for his daughter, that changed their lives so dramatically.

Illness of wife Doris

A couple of years later, in 1955, Doris had a nasty fall and broke her thigh. She took around 18 months to recover. However she was now permanently lame, which restricted Percy's life. Any holidays had to be carefully planned and less ambitious than in the previous ten years, when they had, at last, enjoyed a couple of foreign holidays for the first time in their lives.

This experience, however, was nowhere near as traumatic for Percy as the realisation, in the late 1960s, that Doris was developing dementia. For about five to six years Doris' health declined sadly as she lost her faculties. At the time it certainly was not described as Alzheimer's, a term that came to be used much later, nor, from memory, was it even described as dementia, but that was her condition. There was never any question of Doris being put into a nursing home, but her condition severely strained the family support system. Dorothy bore the brunt as the main carer, but Percy struggled manfully to help, yet wanting to continue with his active social life. The end came mercifully in April 1974 when Doris died, aged 79 years.

Percy was to live for another 12 years. He and Dorothy sold their separate homes and lived in a new shared home a couple of miles away higher up in Baildon by the edge of the moors.

Early death of son Harvey and grandson Andrew

Percy was to cope with two further personal tragedies that, thankfully, Doris did not have to suffer. Firstly, his son Harvey died of a second heart attack in 1977, aged 55, after a first one five years before – the sad experience of the child predeceasing the parent. Secondly, his youngest grandson Andrew, (Harvey's son), then aged 28, died on New Year's Day in 1982 in a terrible accident, falling off a bridge into the river at Grassington in Wharfedale, until then a favourite spot for Percy the artist, which he had painted at least three times in the 1940s and 1950s.

Percy Monkman

CHAPTER 9

TEN PERSPECTIVES OF PERCY

During his lifetime and after his death many people felt moved to write about Percy, his unique combination of talents and his unusual life. To understand how people responded to him and how he touched their lives even if not the closest of friends, here is a selection of such profiles and tributes.

Article in *Telegraph & Argus* by Robert Arnott (December 1932)

This feature about Percy, when he was just over 40, gives a fascinating insight into his impact as a 'humorous entertainer'. It contrasts neatly with the final press feature (later in this chapter), by another reporter from the same paper, about Percy the watercolour painter, written 50 years later, when he was approaching 90.

An evergreen of Bradford

By sheer accident I made a remarkable discovery last night. Dropping in at the Salem Congregational School, Oak Lane, I found a large audience laughing uproariously at the original version of a military burlesque sketch which ran during the War for 200 performances just behind the front lines.

As amusing as ever in the part of the commanding officer was Percy Monkman, part-author of the sketch, who will be remembered fondly by thousands of Tommies as a member of 'The Encores' Concert Party, attached to the Royal Army Medical Corps.

Somewhere in France five Generals watched a presentation of this sketch, 'The Disorderly Room,' at one sitting. It is thought that Prince Arthur of Connaught was present at another performance (grandson of Queen Victoria).

The more I talk to Percy Monkman and the more I hear about him from other people, the more interesting a personality he becomes. I knew, of course, that he spent most of his time amongst heaps of cash in a Bradford bank, and that occasionally he attacked little pieces of canvas with a paint-brush, But it was not until last night that I learned how by the skin of his teeth, he missed appearing in a pantomime' Aladdin' which was produced by Leslie Henson at the Lille Opera House at Christmas 1918.

The facts as I know them are these. Mr Monkman's concert party 'The Encores' were performing three days a week in a certain theatre in France and for the remaining three days the boards were occupied by Leslie Henson's party which was, I believe known as 'The Gaieties'.

It was in September of that year when Leslie Henson was informed that the commanding officer wished him to produce a Christmas pantomime. Leslie got straight down to business and the cast was selected from his own party and from 'The Encores'. Mr. Monkman was landed with the part of a Yorkshire comedian.

Rehearsals for the great show were actually being held, I understand, when a number of 'The Encores' went on leave. They returned to find that the events of the War had taken a dramatic turn and that everybody was going off to Germany.

Source: *The Telegraph and Argus* (1932)

Percy Monkman

The branch manager at The Westminster Bank, Bradford (August 1952).

The Westminster staff magazine reprinted this short speech given by the manager at the main city centre branch in Kirkgate, Bradford, on the occasion of Percy's retirement.

On 11 August Percy Monkman retired from active service of the bank. He had always been at Bradford and was the last of a few who had given continuous service to the bank at this particular branch. So far as his actual banking is concerned, as First Cashier not only had he for many years been popular with every class of customer, but he had acquired a fund of knowledge which it will be quite impossible to replace.

At the customary gathering when he was congratulated upon reaching his retirement full of the joy of life in good health and heart, the Manager referred to him thus:

*M is for Monkman, an artist of rank
Far too artistic to be in a bank*

Speech by Ferdy Roberts, life-long friend and President of Bradford Arts Club at the 'Percyversary' (May 1974)

Apart from JB Priestley, Percy did not have many friendships dating from his schooldays, the sad impact of heavy losses in his generation fighting the First World War. One who did know him well from an early age was Ferdy Roberts who, some ten years younger, remembered him as a young Sunday School teacher. Ferdy was also a very well-known figure in Bradford, being one of the best rugby union players from the city. He was also a member of the Arts Club.

I would first like to welcome you all on this memorable and eventful occasion. It's good to see so many who have come to congratulate and pay tribute to one of our most illustrious members, who celebrates the 50th anniversary of this club.

Percy Monkman, I know, will be the first to admit, as many of us humbly do, that through his association and membership he has found great happiness, joy and pleasure, that he has reaped many rewards (richly deserved) for his many endeavours, and that in the process he has made countless lifelong friends who respect and admire him, but, what he has put back into the club is immeasurably greater. We cannot fail to recognise and admire his outstanding dedication and loyalty to the Club throughout all these years. We have to thank him for his unselfish service in all matters of administration – he has occupied the chairmanship for over a decade.

In the field of entertainment he has been invaluable and irreplaceable – not only has he compèred all the shows so admirably (in fact, as you see, he is even doing it for his own party!) but he has also been responsible for arranging, organising and enlisting the

An Extraordinary Bradfordian

services of the artistes (several of whom I am glad to see are here tonight) and I would like to take this opportunity of welcoming them and thanking them sincerely for all the wonderful entertainment they have given us on so many occasions.

But, above all, Percy – by his personality, skill and talent as an artist – has greatly enhanced the reputation of the Club, directly and indirectly, has raised its artistic standards and preserved its dignity and integrity. For all these things, we owe him a debt of gratitude we cannot hope to repay.

To mark this wonderful record, on your behalf, I have the happy privilege of making a humble but sincere presentation. This privilege, incidentally, falls upon me partly because of the honoured office I hold, and partly because (and, I think I'm right in saying this) I have known Percy longer than anyone else in the club. When I was about eight, I was sent to the local Sunday School to start my English religious education and it is there that I met Percy who was assigned as my pupil teacher. That he didn't make a very good job of it is abundantly clear, but it wasn't his fault; he was working on raw and difficult material! I, therefore, bear him no grudge. On the contrary, we have been staunch friends ever since.

You can imagine the difficulty we had in deciding what form this presentation should take. Many and varied were the suggestions. We all agreed it should be something which we hoped would give him great pleasure, peace and contentment.

We further agreed that he always looked the happiest, most relaxed and at peace with the world behind a good cigar – not necessarily a good one, he's not all that 'choosy'! So, mainly because I happened to know a sympathetic and friendly wholesaler, I was given the task of obtaining the cigars.

So, now, Percy, I would ask you to accept this small token of our gratitude, esteem and affection.

Percy Monkman

'This is your life' by friend Joan Crib recited at the 'Percyversary' (May 1974)

Joan Crib, a member of the Arts Club, composed and recited this piece at the party celebrating Percy's 50-year membership. Hardly mentioned elsewhere in Percy's documents, she was not a close friend, but clearly had fond memories of him.

My duty and my pleasure is a statement categorical
We meet tonight to celebrate a jubilee historical
When Percy joined the Arts Club, it was 1924
Making 50 years of membership – we hope for many more
An actor, and an artist, and a man of versatility,
A raconteur, a banker and a man of great ability.
A 'little low down' – we'll make it pretty cursory
In order not to spoil this very happy Perciversary.
You have acted with the Civic, in roles of great variety.
Your after-dinner speeches were a model of propriety.
But at Christmas in the Clubroom, we know it never fails –
That very ribald laughter – for Percy and his tales.
You have painted many a landscape, transposing with tranquillity
To comments from the locals, throwing doubts on your ability.
They had their pints of bitter and were certainly 'well-heeled'
'Them ruddy cows a'int right' they'd say, 'they're in't wrong bloody field'
You're very well acquainted with matters mathematical,
Like Gilbert's Major General? Whose equations were quadratical.
You've juggled long with figures – at a local bank in town
Where for hours you've subtracted or added with a frown
The accounts for Jones & Taylor or somebody called Parkers,
But your figures at the life class are absolutely starkers!
Well, Percy, we're most happy with the Club's administration,
And we hope you'll still be active through another generation.
From all our members here tonight, accept our thanks and love
We'll never have a better man – as Chairman of the Club.

As a corollary to this piece of light-hearted verse comes another in the form of an invitation declined to his second celebration in 1974 – the special lunch for his honorary life membership of the Bradford Civic Playhouse.

Please accept my apology and what a pity
Last time I missed Percy, a character in Bradford City
So many talents, and very witty and wise
An expert in the art of improvise
When I see some Modern Art I feel
His outlook is much more understood and real
Some I see as a Sinful Waste of paint
Makes me Spit and I feel Sickly faint
I like Percy's way and admire his Style
His clean comedy has made thousands Smile
I must do my duty as a County elected member
Best wishes Percy Monkman beginning 3rd November

M Duggan, County Councillor

An Extraordinary Bradfordian

Extract from article in *Telegraph & Argus* by John Hewitt (July 1982)

John Hewitt was for many years the *Telegraph & Argus* arts reviewer. Here he wrote the following feature in 1982 as Percy approached his 90th birthday.

Out in the country, camping at Hebden near Grassington, the young and nervous Percy Monkman set up his easel for his first attempt at an outdoor watercolour.

He had been careful to choose a quiet day when the lanes were empty, but so intent on his work was he that he failed to notice a small knot of locals gathering behind him. Carefully he dotted in the yellow of a far-off rick.

'Ay, oop,' came a voice behind him. 'He's putten Joe Thomson's rick in t'wrong bloody field.'

Through his 60-year painting career Percy Monkman has had to put up with incisive artistic criticism of that kind. He's taken it all in good part and it's given him some good stories for his lectures.

Now coming to his 90th birthday on August 11 – an anniversary which he doesn't relish – this dapper Baildon artist who sports a bow-tie and keeps a natty collection of 25 hats, is recognised as the grand old man of Bradford's art world. He is president of the Bradford Arts Club where he has been a member for nearly 60 years, and on July 10 is putting on an exhibition of his work at the club rooms in Mansfield Road, Manningham.

He still paints and it's not studio painting either. Though he sits in a car with his box of watercolours, he is happy to attempt a painting in any weather.

'The other day I went up to Oxenhope and it was so misty you could hardly see across the road, but I came back with a painting,' he says.

On his wall is a splendid, dramatic watercolour. He painted it at Thornton in a vicious thunderstorm with the windscreen wipers working twenty to a dozen.

Even his work as chief cashier at the Westminster Bank in the centre of Bradford didn't stop him drawing. His colleagues were often amused by the sketches and cartoons he left on the telephone pads. It also led him to produce his most popular series of paintings.

'On Bowling Tide the bank was closed but someone had to stay behind to man the phones. I got the job, but I was at my wit's end for something to do. So I climbed on the counter and looked out on the quiet city'.

That resulted in the first of his two large watercolours of Bradford as it was in 1952 before the huge changes which transformed Forster Square and a great deal more of the city centre. So popular did they become that he had a series of prints made which have gone to expatriate Bradfordians all over the world.

Percy Monkman is something of a character. He is devoted to his art. I don't think he **could** give up!

Percy Monkman

Letter of condolence from Sam Carter, friend from entertainment years (May 1986)

Throughout his adult life as an entertainer Percy worked with a large number of groups of performers, often organising with them whole programmes of entertainments. Here, we have a tribute from a member of a singing quartet with strong affectionate memories of working with him for a number of years. In truth, Percy had many much closer friends who appeared regularly in the family home. This was not one of those friendships, but the relationship was nevertheless maintained until Percy's death.

From the early 1950s when I first made Percy's acquaintance as Secretary of the Fletcher Singers Male Voice Quartet, I developed a great admiration for his exceptional ability as an entertainer, notably his subtle humour and his unfailing presentation of clean spontaneous fun. He endeared himself to a host of listeners at our many concerts, was a great favourite with my fellow members of the Quartet. I spent many happy and companionable hours with him, and ever since we have kept in touch once a year at Christmas, a few appreciative words from me, one of his own sketches and happily chosen words from Percy

I admired him greatly and came to love him for his wit and versatility, so that, while accepting that 93 is a pardonable age to die, I shall always keep a very warm corner in my heart for a man whose integrity, wonderful sense of humour and exceptional attributes in other spheres leaves me feeling very proud to be honoured by his friendship.

Letter of condolence from Rev RH McMurray Adam, minister at Shipley United Reform Church (May 1986)

Percy was brought up in a strong non-conformist background. Much of his early social life was centred around Girlington Congregational Church, just off Toller Lane and from that his reputation as an entertainer spread to the much wider non-conformist community of the city. When in 1952 he moved out to Baildon, about six miles away, not having a car, he also moved away somewhat from this community.

In my lifetime, Percy lost the habit of church-going (or 'going to chapel', as he would have said) except for a period in the 1970s when from time to time he attended Shipley United Reform Church (incorporating the Congregational Church), a short bus ride from Baildon. Here he became friendly with the minister who, writing to Percy's daughter Dorothy, clearly had a very fond memory of his artist friend before he transferred to another ministry in Northumberland.

I extend to you my sympathy, while at the same time giving thanks for all he put into life, for his friendship and the gaiety of his spirit.

I shall always be grateful for the privilege of knowing him in the Shipley years, and every day I am reminded of him as I look at the pictures in my rooms, pictures, his own pictures which he gave me in his generosity.

He lived to a ripe age and he 'lived' all the years, when one thinks back it is his 'putting into years' which stands out.

Your father was one of 'the greats' I encountered in my years of ministry. I shall always be grateful for having known him and being one of his friends.

An Extraordinary Bradfordian

Article in *The Dalesman* **by friend Ken Feakes (April 1992)**

Percy at easel aged 85 (August 1977)

Striking a friendship with Ken Feakes was one of several that Percy made in his retirement, which developed out of a shared passion for painting and a mutual need. Ken was keen to learn how to paint and Percy was keen to have a chauffeur. So, on a regular basis, Percy would be driven to a part of the Dales or Bronte country that he knew so well and he would then help Ken choose a suitable subject and give him tuition in painting it.

Six years after Percy's death Ken volunteered this article for *The Dalesman* magazine as a record of such days.

Like many southerners I had always nursed a mental picture of Yorkshire as predominantly an area of pitheads, slag heaps, dark satanic mills and 'where there's moock, there's brass, philosophy of life. Then in the early seventies we moved to Baildon, and this ill-informed assessment underwent swift and radical revision.

I was assisted in this smart about-turn by my luck in making the acquaintance of Percy Monkman, a watercolourist of high repute who was for many years Chairman and later President of the Bradford Arts Club. Percy

Percy Monkman

was then in his late seventies, and still a very active painter with a studio in Kirklands Villas, Baildon. But Percy had never learned to drive car and was dependent upon others for trips into his beloved Dales.

Having some time on my hands I was more than happy to oblige him, my reward being to become as familiar with dales and moors as Percy himself. And they were by no means fair weather journeyings. I remember particularly one raw, cold day in March when we set off for Malham, Percy being intent on 'getting' the Tarn before the leaves were on the trees.

We took the narrow road past Gordale Scar, went through two gates under the cold scrutiny of ewes with their frisky lambs, and reached the moor road to Arncliffe. Here we spent some time driving back and forth searching for a suitable standpoint.

By the time Percy had settled for the best available position, the grey clouds were sending down a dismal drizzle that I thought would put a dampener on even his dauntless enthusiasm. But not so, donning an old raincoat he had prudently brought along, he clambered out, and with me in the driving seat holding inside the car a board with his paper attached, and him standing out in what had become a steady downpour, he set about his work with all his usual gusto. In 15 minutes he had got down all he needed to do on the spot and, rain dripping from his raincoat and the old felt hat he invariably wore on these expeditions, he got back in the car without any indication that the circumstances were anything other than normal.

As always I was impressed by his total absorption in the work in hand. He had paid no more heed to the cold and the rain than had the sheep grazing the verges nearby, and, I must add, given no thought to me struggling to hold the board steady despite my cramped position behind the wheel, beyond an occasional grunt of encouragement.

Percy died in 1986. He was in the 94th year of his life, and he was painting almost to the end. Whenever I now go in the dales and on the moors I have a picture in my mind of Percy at his easel, striving always to express in paint his abiding love of the county of his birth.

Source: *The Dalesman*, 1992

An Extraordinary Bradfordian

Memories of family life by daughter Dorothy Greenwood (sometime in the 1990s)

After his death, Percy's daughter wrote some scenes of family life, based on holidays in Wharfedale and her father's habits as a painter. Here is an extract about his painting habits, and family holidays remembered from childhood.

For many years a holiday in the Dales in the spring or autumn or at cottages in Grassington, Kettlewell or Malham for long school breaks at as little as a pound a week self-catering with our family, a wonderful opportunity for painting and enjoying the countryside. We remember the thrill when the millstone changed to limestone on the way.

It was so incredibly reasonable to have these holidays over 50 years ago, cheaper than staying at home! We didn't have a car – the train to Skipton, followed by a bumpy bus ride, when we giggled and joked all the way to our chosen village to be met by a friendly Daleswoman who declared she did not know which was worst – fishermen or artists – with their tackle.

My father always stood up to paint in all weathers. A calendar day with a blue sky was not what he was wanting. He often wore a French beret that was too small and always a bow tie, the sort you have to fix yourself, nothing else would do. A well-worn paint-box and an odd collapsible water container that dripped, it was patched. A tube of brushes, the 'right' watercolour paper if it ever could be found, a board and an old easel with a temperament! His pockets were always full and numerous – charcoal for drawing mixed up with everything else, including his pipe and some dusty mints. His raincoat often got splashed with paint, not worrying him in the least.

He carried a small sketch book everywhere and filled all the empty spaces of the 'stop press' columns in newspapers with doodles. He resented wearing gloves and only painted from inside a car when it was impossible otherwise.

The sketch book was always at hand so that he could do a quick impression, often in unsettled weather, with colour notes, to be made into a picture in the studio. When possible he would do the whole composition on a board in the open air, whilst coping with onlookers, farm animals, passing tractors and rough ground. He used to say it was a 'germ', his fingers were itchy.

Friends used to take him in their cars out into the country. If they were aspiring artists, tuition would be offered on the way and on arrival.

Percy Monkman

A graphologist (date unknown but no later than the 1940s)

Finally, a very interesting portrait of Percy that backs up the testimony of the contributions made by people who knew him well comes from an unexpected source, someone who did not know him except from his handwriting.

Sometime before the Second World War, Percy commissioned an analysis of his handwriting from the Institute of Handwriting Analysis Ltd in London. We know little about the methodology used at the time, except that it was based on 50 words written by the subject, in ink on unruled paper. Unfortunately we have no record of the date. However we do have the character description produced and it is remarkably accurate.

The only point of detail that does not hit the right note is the reference to love of music. Although Percy would have sung thousands of times on stage as part of groups and choruses, the music would be humorous rather than purely musical. He was not really a great connoisseur or lover of music.

He has two outstanding characteristics – first and foremost is a 'joie de vivre' and secondly a fine sense of reality and practical matters in spite of the fundamental artistic-creative trend. There are the necessary ingredients for a most charming interesting and successful person. One feels one would like to have a dose of his keen sense of humour, his wit and not least have the experience of seeing life through his eyes.

He is not always easy to get on with, he is critical and wilful and though he is kind-hearted and good-natured one finds signs of temperamental outbursts, and it will so happen that he feels the need for solitude and meditation at times, and gets most annoyed if one disturbs him then.

He has a solid common sense, and he is certainly intelligent, quick-witted and not easily at a loss. He is not an intellectual, not one who splits non-existent hairs, but a person who admires beauty, and who will try to make the ordinary life more beautiful without disturbing or interfering with his strong ideals. He is fond of everything good, solid, natural and sincere, and extends this to the kind of people he chooses as his friends. Nothing will annoy him more than a person who shows bad taste, ill manners and no appreciation for those things in life he admires and needs.

He is, as said before, not at all a mere idealist, he sees the material side of life clearly, and enjoys, for instance, a good meal and some of the comforts that money can buy. His family feelings are strong and he will be a loyal, attached and helpful friend. He is sensual, and will find great pleasure in the company of the gentle sex. He also will love animals, nature, strong colours, music and to some extent literature. In his work he is reliable, enduring and persevering. Though he is sensitive to higher thoughts, and rather intuitive, his religious feelings are suppressed, probably owing to a disappointment he had in this direction. His life was altogether not free from setbacks and emotional upheavals.

Altogether one has the feeling of having met an inspiring, pleasant, creative person, a born teacher. Not of dry routine stuff, but of a good attitude towards life.

CHAPTER 10

ARTISTIC ACHIEVEMENTS

Not only did Percy show tremendous energy and activity in pursuit of his main artistic interests, but he reached a high professional standard in each that can be measured in a number of ways (eg awards, press reviews and the respect of his peers). Moreover, he was largely self-taught and his unique combination of gifts earned him such a strong reputation in Bradford and the West Riding as an entertainer, actor and painter.

Volume of activity

The figures are startling. Percy wrote, on a number of occasions, of having performed in about 300 shows entertaining the troops behind the front line in Northern France over at least two years. We know that during the winters between 1920 and 1931 he participated in more than 100 shows as a 'humorous entertainer', but there may have been many more in the 1930s. Percy himself estimated that he organised and participated in over 600 concert party evenings for forces and charities in the Second World War. And we know of many more such entertainments post-war. That covers just his career as an entertainer.

As an actor he appeared in 27 plays and nearly 160 performances between 1935 and 1955, over 90% at the Bradford Civic Playhouse.

That leaves the painting. His catalogue lists just over 2,400 paintings over his lifetime, 60% of them sold and another 14% were used as gifts. He was a regular exhibitor at a host of art shows, many becoming a regular feature (eg the summer shows at Harrogate). He also gave around 130 talks about painting during his retirement between 1952 and 1980.

Finally, we should not forget some 50 cartoons that were published between 1925 and 1960. In addition he drew many unpublished caricatures and cartoons.

In terms of volume, this is an amazing output for somebody with a full-time job for his adult working life.

Self-taught

But counting the numbers barely scratches the surface of Percy's achievement. What matters is the quality of the work. We will come to that shortly, but we should remember the critical point that he received no formal training in any of the skills involved.

We can guess that being an entertainer between the ages of 19 to 21 in six events, before he joined the army, stood him in good stead when he turned up to join an entertainment troupe. However, we have no record of how he made those initial steps as a 19 year old; certainly no mention of any training or even preparation. We do know that he was an avid collector of jokes and stories from an early age until well into middle age, at least. This clearly is the mark of someone who wanted to increase his ability to amuse and entertain.

The experience of entertaining troops day in day out in the First World War was an excellent apprenticeship. In later years Percy recognised that this was the best possible way of becoming a 'professional entertainer' and was excellent training for his future on stage.

When he joined the Bradford Civic Playhouse as an actor in 1935, he had had substantial experience as a comic actor doing short reviews and sketches from his time in the army and during the 1920s. However, he received no formal education in drama, unlike those youngsters 10 years later who were trained at the Northern School of Drama, linked by Esme Church to the Civic Playhouse. Although appearing in an entertainment troupe or concert party was valuable experience, it is not quite the same as appearing on stage in more serious drama.

As for painting, we know that school was no help and that after a few early attempts (eg drawings at Cambrai in 1919) he went to evening school at the Bradford College of Art. He also sought every opportunity to develop his techniques through the Bradford Arts Club network, including the 'Carnegie' weekends linked to Leeds University, and many talks by visiting experts. Years later, speaking at a school speech day, he described his time at the Arts Club as 'still going to school', which indicates that he saw this as a learning environment, even aged 70.

Collecting 'gags', observing skilled actors or learning from more experienced painters all indicate strong motivation to improve oneself. Percy was driven all his life by becoming better at his artistic interests.

Not only was he largely self-taught in terms of what you might call his artistic skills, but he had no support in terms of marketing and promotion. Yet he became very adept at doing this. He had no agent, or publicity assistant, nor of course anything that approaches the reach of today's social media. He relied totally on personal contact, word of mouth and mentions in the press generated by shows, talks and exhibitions.

Appearing before a large number of audiences as an entertainer or actor and being seen at exhibitions and talks made him visible to thousands of people over the years. Even in his day job, every day he came across scores of local people using the bank, one of the major banks in the centre of Bradford. In short, he had plenty of opportunity to promote what he was doing face-to-face and via the press, and he became very successful in making the most of that opportunity.

Professional standards

In looking at Percy's achievements, we should consider first the professional standards of his work.

As an entertainer, he clearly would not have survived without immediate positive feedback. However, many press reviews indicated that he was indeed very funny and we know from his diary of engagements that he had many repeat invitations. We can also recall that in the First World War it was said that one army general told him that his talent was in danger of being wasted.

We also know from many letters from event organisers that he commanded fees of up to three guineas in the 1920s. In 1919 he received an annual salary of £120 plus bonus on restarting work for the bank. Such fees for, say, half an hour or an hour's appearance were substantial. Yet Percy was not mercenary, sometimes appearing for no fee, and he was never tempted to secure an agent.

When he moved into acting, the standards were also high for what was a dramatic society. The Civic Playhouse, though, was semi-professional (directors and producers were paid, though actors were not). Plays attracted full houses. Its president (JB Priestley) was a national literary figure. From 1944 the theatre

An Extraordinary Bradfordian

was led by a director with a national reputation (Esme Church) who influenced the careers of many young actors and who became famous through the connection with the Northern School of Drama, co-located with the theatre. The choice of plays performed also showed that it was a serious theatre, a cut or two above the usual amateur dramatic society.

As for painting, the activity is much more an individual activity rather than a team enterprise. Entertainersand actors can only be successful as a group and they need a paying audienceto flourish. Painters can opt for a quiet life and still continue to paint, but those such as Percy constantly strive to improve, exhibit and, if they can, sell their works.For many exhibitions Percy's works had to be selected in competition with others as meeting a required standard. For others he was invited to exhibit because of his track record. Most important of all, there is a clear end product that can be judged against firm criteria such as being selected for art exhibitions by panels with independent experts, winning national competitions and being published in credible journals and magazines.

Awards for painting

During his career as a painter, Percy received a number of awards and accolades. His first major break was winning first prize in an annual competition, in 1935, for employees of the Westminster Bank. This was followed by similar first prizes in 1936, 1937 and 1938. Unfortunately on each occasion he was unable to attend the awards ceremony (probably on grounds of cost of a trip to London).

With 1,100 branches, by 1939 the Westminster Bank was a very large enterprise and so the annual exhibition was a major event. For example, the invitation Percy received for the award ceremony in 1938 indicated that the exhibition was held for one week at the Guildhall in London and opened by the Lord Mayor of London. The independent adviser to the bank for selecting awards was a Mr RO Dunlop, who was a member of the Royal Academy.

Another accolade in the mid-1930s was in having two of his paintings selected for an exhibition at the City of Birmingham Art Gallery (Brontëland villages and Ilkley from Addingham Moors, both painted in 1935). These were selected by a panel that included eminent artists Dame Laura Knight (among the most successful and popular painters in Britain) and Edward Wadsworth (Yorkshire-born and Bradford-trained, as it happens).

Paintings shown at Yorkshire Group of Artists in the 1930s included works by Sir William Rothenstein (also Bradford-born).

Percy submitted works to the Royal Academy's (RA) open summer exhibition during the 1930s and 1940s, but they were never selected. After many years of not submitting works, he tried again and in 1961 had one painting, of

Lothersdale near Skipton, selected. This was the only time that he made the RA summer exhibition.

He had more success with the Royal Society of British Artists where he exhibited twice in 1954 and 1955 with two scenes of Bradford Forster Square plus a rainy day at Lothersdale (again!).

He did even better with the Royal Institute of Painters in Water Colours (the RI). He exhibited ten times between 1957 and 1971 (and two pictures in five of those years) at the RI annual exhibition, which was open to non-members. Buoyed by this success, he applied to become a member, but this application in 1964 was rejected. He will have been disappointed with this rejection. He probably shared the same hostile views as Ashley Jackson about the bias by the London art establishment when he (Ashley) received a rejection from the RI in the form of an admission that he was nearly invited to join.

Finally, Percy was accepted into the newly-formed Yorkshire Watercolour Society around 1982, which gave him the opportunity to exhibit a painting in the House of Commons in November 1983 at an exhibition opened by Lord (Roy) Mason of Barnsley.

Two celebrations in one year

1974 was a bitter-sweet year for Percy. It started with the very sad but not unexpected death of his wife, followed by two major celebrations, organised by peers from his painting and acting worlds. In between the two celebrations he suffered another family bereavement with the death of his youngest brother, Frank.

Doris had been declining gradually over five years and the end came, with relief to Percy and the family, on 9 April. It was doubly sad that the one person that made Percy's remarkable life possible was not present at two unexpected events that celebrated many of the achievements of that artistic life. One was the 50th anniversary of his membership of Bradford Arts Club on 4 May, celebrated with a special party, and the other was the award of honorary life membership of the Bradford Civic Playhouse on 9 November.

Thanks to Percy's habit of preparing important speeches, we are able to reproduce what he said on each occasion in thanks to his friends and colleagues.

An Extraordinary Bradfordian

The 'Percyversary' – 4 May 1974

Invitation – front

THE BRADFORD ARTS CLUB

You are cordially invited to a celebration marking the

50th Anniversary of Percy Monkman's Membership of the Club

on SATURDAY, 4th MAY, 1974, at 7–30 p.m. in the Club Rooms

Wine and Cheese gratis

R.S.V.P. Bradford Arts Club, 14a Mansfield Road, Bradford 8.

Invitation – reverse

The first celebration came from Bradford Arts Club when around 200 members were invited to a special party which was described as the 'Percyversary'.

The party included entertainment from some of Percy's concert party friends (organised as ever by Percy himself, the guest of honour). In the previous chapter we reproduced two quite different contributions from the event, but here is what Percy himself had to say at the start of proceedings:

A warm welcome to fellow artists and friends who conceived this unique 'Percyversary'. I'm sure our President had something to do with this wonderful title. It could, of course, have been worse. They could have called it the 50 Percentenary, couldn't they? I feel very honoured indeed to be first to gain this distinction. This must surely be the longest gestation period of anyone 'in the club'.

It was a total surprise to me. 50 years! The time has just flown. It's the fastest 50 years I've ever known. That's one of the wonderful things about painting. Time is forgotten when you get involved in a painting. (JB Priestley once said at Wakefield 'When I am writing, I'm looking at my watch. When I am painting, I have to be dragged away.')

When I joined the club in 1924, the membership was about 50. We had premises in a one-time hay loft at 81a Manningham Lane. In fact the original title was 'The Loft Arts Club' until they had a letter sent to 'The Lost Hearts Club' so the name was changed to its present title.

They once advertised for a model. The advert read: Wanted model (full figure). A lady of 14 stones applied and didn't get the job!

We came to our present premises in 1937, since when, of course, we had to buy the premises and make many improvements at considerable cost and effort. Now our premises and amenities are probably better than any of the Yorkshire Arts Clubs, for which we are justifiably proud.

Percy Monkman

To me the Club has almost been a way of life. I have always felt that there is so much to learn about painting. There is no finality about it. Our endeavour has always been to give the fullest possible assistance to members by life classes (the life class has always been a number one priority), lectures and demonstrations by distinguished artists, and the ready exchange of technical and aesthetic ideas by fellow members have been of great value towards more proficient standards of painting. But additionally and probably more important we have always fostered the spirit of comradeship. There is no class distinction amongst artists, which is a great thing.

An Extraordinary Bradfordian

Life member of Bradford Civic Playhouse – 9 November 1974

The second celebration came from the Bradford Civic Playhouse. Percy was made honorary life member of the Playhouse at the celebration of the 45th anniversary of its opening on 9 November, attended by the Lord Mayor and Lady Mayoress of Bradford. This was only the fourth such honour since the Civic Playhouse was founded.

Percy dressed for Bradford Civic Concert Party

Peter Holdsworth, the arts critic of the *Telegraph & Argus* wrote a piece in celebration (16 November 1974): *This delightful picture of Percy Monkman in one of his outfits for an old-time show captures the whimsicality and roguish good humour which have so endeared him to Bradford Playhouse members for as long as many of them can remember. Not only has he been a delicious Chapel Street character but his Playhouse performances in the past are memories cherished by those lucky enough to see them. No honour is more deserved.*

A special cake was made for him decorated with the caricatures in the 1939 booklet *Bradford Civic Playhouse Personalities*. As Percy wrote with some amusement in a letter to his Canadian nephew, '*It's the first time I have had my work reproduced on a cake!*'

Celebration cake for honorary life membership of Civic Playhouse (9 November 1974)

(Chapter 5 shows a close-up of the caricatures used to decorate the cake.)

Percy Monkman

Percy was guest of honour and made a short speech in thanks for the award:

What a great pleasure it is to be on this stage again and not worry about memorising lines and cues.

What's wanted now is a few serious words! (a catchphrase from JB Priestley's popular comedy When We Are Married, which would be certain to draw laughs from this particular audience).

Firstly, may I say how thrilled and surprised I was when I learned of the honour you are conferring on my today – life membership.

My first reaction was 'Why me?' when so many have given so much more to the Playhouse! Probably I'm the oldest member now, I don't know. What I do know is that joined the Old Civic in 1935 in the Jowett Hall.

Soon afterwards the old theatre was burned down. This was just a coincidence, by the way! So my membership covers about 39 years. Almost half my life, but what a good half it's been.

As my publicity agent would have said, if I had one, my vital statistics are many years of acting, some years on the Management Committee, organising of the Civic Concert Party, doing hundreds of shows for forces and charities, then later with the Old Time Music Hall show and, in between, kept the Art Exhibitions going in the café. Otherwise my main role was one of the supporting cast.

In some respects I suppose I was something of an oddity, as I was probably one of the few actors who didn't want a leading part. This was a bit crafty on my part because I loved doing portraits of fellow artists during the show.

During the period when Miss Esme Church, who we remember with great affection, was running the Northern School of Drama, many of her pupils were keen to play small parts. I did scores of drawings of them, and, as you all know, many of those pupils now are national figures in films, television and the theatre. Thus I fulfilled two of my best loved hobbies – art and acting.

Dear old Philip Robinson (stage manager) was a keen artist, and he soon found out I was, so we joined up in some exciting jobs for the stage. We even reproduced old masters and French impressionists at the rate of one per night.

As you may know during these times, I did a part-time job in a bank (from 9 to 5).

Fame at last? I owe a great deal to the Playhouse. I made many lifelong friends and, so far as I know, no enemies.

Showcase of Percy's talents

We can be impressed with Percy's energy in terms of the volume of his artistic activities, but we should not let that distract us from the quality of what he was capable of producing. This book contains a personal selection of his talent, including:

- Percy the entertainer with examples of his comic material and description of a very successful and oft-performed review sketch (Chapter 2)

- Percy the actor with one example of a major stage performance (Chapter 3)

- Percy the artist with four pre-war award-winning pictures and examples of nine post-war paintings (Chapter 4) and, finally,

- Percy the cartoonist with a pair of fine complementary cartoons about life in the bank (Chapter 5)

Together, they all illustrate his talent as a man of humour, performer and artistic creator.

Percy Monkman

CHAPTER 11

PERCY'S LOST CITY?

Percy's life reflects a time and a society long gone. The close-knit community of his Bradford gave him the opportunity, which he fully grasped, of making a name for himself in a number of related artistic fields. Looked at from a distance, that world would seem to have largely disappeared by the turn of the 21st century. In the last few years of his life, how much would Percy have realised that, like JB Priestley before him, the Bradford that he knew was fast becoming a lost city?

Percy's local community in the Toller Lane area in 1922. Source: Bradford Local Studies Library

Key:
1. 106 Toller Lane, the greengrocer's shop
2. 34 and 70 Jesmond Avenue, the Monkman homes
3. Girlington Congs, the local chapel
4. Saltburn Place, JB Priestley's teenage home
5. Masham Place, the Greenwood family home
6. Hartman Place, home of Doris' sister, Maud

Percy Monkman

A close-knit community

Toller Lane where Manningham, Heaton and Girlington meet is where Percy lived, both as a teenager and young man before the First World War and as a married man with children after the war. His father's shop was 106 Toller Lane, at the corner with Jesmond Avenue. He lived all his working life at two addresses in Jesmond Avenue – numbers 34 and 70. Years later when Percy lived at number 70, his newly-married son Harvey lived at number 34 for a short while.

Just across Toller Lane was Little Lane, the address of Girlington Congregational Church, where the Monkman family were regular attendees: it was the centre of his parents' social life.

A confectioner's shop on Toller Lane was owned by a Mrs Rawnsley. The shop was open until 11pm on Saturday evenings, selling home-baked pies that Percy and Harry bought before they went home. Today that would be a kebab shop or a curry house, serving the same purpose as the last stop on the way home. Mrs Rawnsley's daughter Maud was friendly with Doris Northrop, who became Percy's wife. Maud married Percy's brother Harry.

Running into Jesmond Avenue, at right angles, was Saltburn Place where the young JB Priestley moved in 1903 from his first home in nearby Mannheim Road. Two streets below Saltburn Place was Hartman Place, where Percy's wife's sister (another Maud) lived with her husband George Leach. Coincidentally, the street in between, Masham Place, was, from the 1930s, home to the Greenwood family, whose son Reg married Percy's daughter Dorothy in 1941.

At the top of Jesmond Avenue were the playing fields of Belle Vue School where teenagers Percy and JBP and their friends played soccer at every opportunity.

All this was about a mile away from Percy's school in Drummond Road, Manningham, down towards the city centre, which was a further mile away with a regular tram (later trolley-bus) service.

Until Percy moved to Baildon when he retired, his world was based in this tightly-drawn community where everyone knew everyone and where visitors dropped in unannounced.

An Extraordinary Bradfordian

Major social changes

Probably when I was a student, I recall a conversation with Percy about the massive changes that had taken in place in society since the pre-World War 1 days when he was a young man. In his day there were hardly any motor cars, little evidence of radio or telephone and no television, yet now (say, in the early 1960s) life had changed so dramatically. He talked about the only traffic, when he was a boy, being horses and carts and about memories of his father collecting manure off the streets for his allotment.

How did Percy feel about that? Regrettably, I cannot recall his response, but I realised very clearly at that time what major changes in society he might have witnessed in his lifetime.

What I did not realise in the early 1960s was that this was only a start. The truth is that since then life has changed even more dramatically, even if we take the mid-1980s as the starting point. The internet, the mobile phone, social media, mass tourism and increased choice in food and eating outare just a few examples of the continued pace of change.

When you are living through these broad social changes, it is easy not to realise their impact. However, closer to home, towards the end of Percy's life changes were taking place that he could not have failed to notice. Percy was experiencing how his Bradford was changing and gradually disappearing.

Percy's perception of troubled times

Three institutions that he had closely identified with were going through difficult times.

First, Bradford Arts Club, with which his life was closely bound, was no longer popular. He had been a major contributor to its success from when he first joined in the 1920s and had helped to build its reputation. Being able to buy the property in Manningham, near Lister Park, gave the Arts Club a real home and base for its many activities. Compared with other arts clubs in the West Riding, which did not have such a home, this was a major strength.

Yet gradually declining membership in the 1970s led to serious questions being asked by members who did stay loyal. This, in turn, led to a major split between those who wanted to hold on to their property asset and those who wanted to sell up because it was becoming far too expensive to maintain. In addition, it was becoming an unsuitable inner city location and, in the late 1970s, women members in particular had been deterred by the Yorkshire Ripper murders (in fact, he did come from nearby Heaton). In his President's address of 1980 Percy indicated that this had affected attendances adversely. He was horrified by the idea of selling such an asset that he had worked so hard to build up during his 50 plus years of membership and resisted such a change.

Three months after Percy's death, the President of the Arts Club wrote to the Treasurer to describe how the club's reputation had plummeted around 1980:

The club was dead. It contained few working members. It was really only a matter of winding it up. No Honorary Secretary, no Honorary Treasurer, a large committee in which argument took pride of place and helping hands were practically non-existent.

The letter then goes on to show how this dire situation had been retrieved over the next five years, finishing with this more positive message:

May I give you and the team my heartfelt thanks for the steadfast contribution towards the rebirth of The Bradford Arts Club in 1986.

Even though by this time Percy no longer had any formal role in the running of the club, he will have been aware of this recent upturn in fortune, but he will also have been upset and shaken about how the club had declined in the previous years.

In reality, the club premises were sold soon after Percy died, when the costs of essential maintenance from dry rot and wet rot became unsustainable. The club rented new premises in the centre of Bradford, near the old Bradford Civic Playhouse, for four years, before rising rents led them to renting out a village hall in Heaton. Today it continues to meet every Saturday but with a much reduced membership of around 30.

Second, the Bradford Civic Playhouse had lost its sparkle of the 1940s and 1950s. In the 1990s it was to suffer a major fire and then a succession of financial crises which threatened its existence. Latterly, under new management, it has recovered. No longer active in the theatre, by the mid-1980s Percy would have been well aware that the theatre's reputation was in decline.

Third, his beloved Bradford City suffered from a major fire disaster at its Valley Parade stadium. The club had started when Percy was eleven years old, enjoyed early success and then over many years a gradual decline. As we have seen, less than a year before he died, Percy was to observe at first hand the wreckage of the main stand. It took 18 months before the club gradually recovered and started to enjoy happier days, but Percy at the end of his life would only have seen the darkest of days, which at times threatened the club's existence.

Finally, in the unlikely event that he had observed and taken an interest in changes in banking practice, Percy would have realised that technology had already revolutionised tasks that he carried out every day of his working life. All the receipting processes that he applied so diligently for over 40 years had been automated and 'hole in the wall' cash machines were being introduced. Banks were becoming quite different places. His job, as he understood it, had ceased to exist.

In short, not only was the Bradford that had been familiar to him all his life changing fast, but new social forces had also become quite visible in the life and community of the city.

An Extraordinary Bradfordian

A different Bradford today

In 1958, as we have seen, JB Priestley was commissioned by the BBC to make a film about his *'Lost City'*. This documented his feeling of loss of the Bradford pre-First World War that he had grown up in. JB Priestley never again lived in Bradford after the war, although he was a frequent visitor.

Percy grew up in the same Bradford and experienced a similar feeling of loss for the same reasons, no doubt agreeing with JB Priestley's perception. For example, both had worked in offices in the old Swan Arcade, already in disuse but finally pulled down in 1962 in the cause of modernisation of the city centre. However, unlike his friend, Percy never left Bradford, but, by the time of his own death in 1986, another wave of social changes were taking place to reinforce further the perception of Bradford becoming a lost city for someone of his generation.

The community that Percy had grown up in and in which as an adult he had flourished had started to change in a new and radical way. We have already seen how three institutions that were a major part of his life were in decline by the time of his death and how his day job had been replaced by automation. However, much deeper changes were having an impact on the Bradford that he knew.

The main reason was immigration from Pakistan and other parts of Asia. From the late 1950s Pakistani families had started to settle in Bradford, initially finding work in the mills. Shortly before this development Percy had made his retirement move to Baildon some five miles away, on the edge of the moors, and so had little direct experience of this change in Bradford's society. However, had he not made this move to Baildon and remained in the Toller Lane area, the changes would have been highly visible to him much earlier.

By the time of the 2011 census, 67% (352,317) of the city's population was classified as white and 27% (140,149) as being from Asian ethnic groups with the remaining 6% from other ethnic groups. Bradford, in fact, had by that time more Pakistani residents than any other city in England and Wales. By 2017 the city council had 28 councillors from an Asian background out of a total of 90.

The largest religious group in Bradford is Christian (47% of the population). Nearly one quarter of the population (25%) are Muslim. Just over one fifth of the district's population (21%) stated that they had no religion.

If we look at the electoral districts where Percy had lived, Manningham and Toller had the highest concentration of Asian groups (90% being Pakistani), whereas Baildon came 29th out of 30 areas as being ethnically the least diverse area (with around 1% from Asian groups). In 1952, a few years before this wave of immigration had started, Percy had moved from an area where it would soon have a major social impact to an area where it would have minimal impact.

If we look specifically at where Percy used to live, the impact is quite stark. From 1919 to 1952 he lived at two addresses in Jesmond Avenue just off Toller Lane. Today's electoral roll shows that all but two of 96 households in this road are from Asian (presumably mainly Pakistani) backgrounds, the two being Eastern European. Percy's father's greengrocery at the corner of Jesmond Avenue and Toller Lane is now an Asian travel agent, specialising in the journey of Hajj to Mecca.

The Victorian terrace houses in close

interlocking streets have stood the test of time well. They look as robust and well cared-for as they have ever done. No doubt they continue to house close-knit communities, even though they are now South Asian communities rather than the largely white English ones they were in Percy's day.

These radical changes have from time to time caused tensions and conflict, although little surfaced in Percy's life time. Ironically, an early such episode concerned the headmaster of Percy's old school in Drummond Road, Ray Hunniford, who made a public statement in the 1980s that multi-culturalism was not working in education. Strangely, this became the focus of a national controversy and led to him being sacked before being reinstated.

The most significant conflict occurred much later, in three days of rioting in July 2001 as a result of heightened tension between the large and growing British Asian communities and the city's white majority, escalated by confrontation between the Anti-Nazi League and far right groups such as the British National Party and the National Front. These riots also flared up in other Northern towns such as Oldham and Burnley.

Percy grew up in a strong non-conformist family whose social life revolved around the local church, just two minutes' walk away, which had up to 200 members. By the time he moved to Baildon this influence was rapidly waning, not just for his family but through society around him becoming much more secular. By the time he died, the Congregational Church had merged with other non-conformist churches such as the Methodist Church, the Presbyterian Church and the Moravian Church to become the United Reform Church. In fact today what was in Percy's day Girlington Congregational Church in Little Lane has been subsumed under the name of *Little Lane Church – a partnership of Baptist, Methodist and United Reform Christians* and even in this form its regular congregation is down to just 30. Moreover, in the Toller Lane area where he grew up, the best attended place of worship has become the mosque, as Islam has replaced Christianity locally as the dominant religion. Such a trend over Percy's lifetime would have been inconceivable even when he retired in 1952.

Had Percy experienced at first hand the impact of Pakistani immigration in his locality, he would have certainly felt the loss of the old Bradford that he knew. Liberal and fair-minded, he would not have been critical or bitter about these changes. It is far more likely that he would have criticised those who spoke out against immigration than being amongst their number. It is also likely that he would have sought out the humour in any cultural differences. Had he realised, however, that representational art is banned by Islam, he would have been disappointed, especially as there would have been little chance of the new immigrants buying his paintings or even taking an interest in them.

Nevertheless, one would not be human to have some regrets about the loss of the life that he knew so well and that had sustained him for so long. In his last few years he had become well aware of the decline of key institutions that mattered to him but, by virtue of his move away from the locality he had grown up in, he mighthave been insulated from the deep social changes taking place in those inner city suburbs.

So, like JB Priestley before him, Bradford was perhaps becoming a lost city to Percy, too, by the time of his death in 1986.

An Extraordinary Bradfordian

No longer a Bradford family

Not only has the place of Bradford changed, so has the family.

When Robert Monkman eventually settled in Bradford around 1870, some of his family also followed him. Then, his son Edwin's generation was completely rooted in Bradford, being born, living and dying there.

For most of Percy's life his generation also remained in Bradford, with the exception of brother Gordon who emigrated. However things started to change in his lifetime. On retirement Percy moved out to Baildon and, well before they retired, brothers Harry and Frank moved a few miles further out to Hawksworth and Ilkley.

Nobody in the next generation lived in Bradford. Percy's children settled in Baildon and his nephews and nieces settled further afield in Yorkshire with the exception of Harry's daughter who moved to Lancashire.

Finally, Percy's grandchildren, great-nephews and great-nieces, and all their children are now dispersed across the whole country (eg Warwick, Germany, Halifax; Dorset, Thirsk; Enfield, Bristol, Oxfordshire, Sevenoaks, Lewisham, Edinburgh and Halifax). Moreover, only some of the Canadian Monkmans retain the Monkman name.

Percy Monkman

CHAPTER 12

EXTRAORDINARY BRADFORDIAN

Entertainer, actor, painter, cartoonist, football fan, life-long friend and family man, Percy was a person of many parts for many people. However they knew him, everyone saw Percy as a character. Looking back at his life, we can identify several extraordinary facets to what gave him such a reputation.

A big step in the world

When, around his 17th birthday on 11 August 1909, Percy first stepped into the imposing building of Becketts Bank on the corner of Kirkgate and Cheapside opposite the equally imposing Midland Hotel in the centre of Bradford, he must have scarcely believed his good fortune.

A couple of miles away, his parents struggling as ever to make a living out of selling fruit and vegetables in the streets of Manningham, must have been very proud of their eldest son. Percy was already going to do well. He was the first Monkman to take and pass an examination, the first to gain a white collar job and the first to have the opportunity of job security and, beyond that the carrot, if he did well, a pension – an unheard-of benefit in his family. Percy's four brothers would also have to do well to keep up with their eldest brother, who already seemed to have one step on the ladder to a much more prosperous life.

Three of his grandparents had died in straitened circumstances in their early 40s. His father's father, the only grandparent he ever knew, had died earlier in 1909 in a workhouse, having had 12 children, three wives and a variety of jobs in country and town. His father had grown up in a large struggling family, had lost his mother when very young and his stepmother had been jailed for stealing. He started working as a street-hawker. Percy's mother had worked in the mill since the age of seven at the same time as going to school, had lost her own mother when a baby and her father when 13 years old.

This was not a family background to guarantee success and prosperity. It is a credit to his parents that they provided some stability for their five boys through hard work and doggedness. They would have added the value of being abstemious and God-fearing and following a Christian way of life.

We know that Percy was disappointed that his formal education stopped at 14, because his father did not value it. Yet in spite of that he was starting to do well. We can contrast this experience with his contemporary JB Priestley. JB's father, being a head teacher at Green Lane Board School in Manningham next door to Percy's own school in Drummond Road, did value education. As a result, JB went to Belle Vue Grammar School and thence to Cambridge University. For Percy it was only the next generation – his future son-in-law who was able to tread the same path.

In the course of time the bank proved not to be such an exciting career. Percy's life became so full outside his job that he could joke that he worked part-time at the bank. However, we should not underestimate Percy's success, and that of his brothers, in escaping from the type of life their parents had experienced. For Percy this experience proved to be the foundation for a remarkable set of achievements in artistic fields.

Unexpected impact of First World War

Percy was firmly a man of his time and place. Like so many men in 1914 his life was changed for ever by the war, but unlike many of his contemporaries, in his case the war led to better things.

The start of the First World War was a pivotal moment in Percy's life. Unlike his two younger brothers, who joined a year earlier, Percy seems to have been reluctant to enlist. With the benefit of hindsight, the unfolding nightmare of the war makes this reluctance fully understandable.

For those of us who have never had to face such a decision, we can easily underestimate the significance of this moment. And after the decision was made, it is almost impossible to imagine what it felt like to have joined the army in Northern France – the horror, the squalor and the boredom. Percy's response was pragmatic. He spotted an opportunity for some relief from the war, that played to his emerging interest in, and talent for, entertaining. He made the most of this opportunity in a way that was to shape his future life back in Bradford.

It gave him the immediate impetus to continue with his entertaining, which then led into the acting in the mid-1930s. While waiting to be demobilised in 1919, he also completed his first pair of drawings and that encouraged him, in the 1920s, to paint and draw cartoons and caricatures.

In hindsight, this experience shaped the direction of the rest of his life.

An Extraordinary Bradfordian

Entertaining the troops in two World Wars

When we then look at Percy's activity in the Second World War, we see another unusual feature about his achievements.

In the First World War he spent two to three years as a full-time entertainer of troops on the front-line. As there were only about 90 concert party troupes similar to the one in which he was involved, this itself was a relatively unusual activity for someone on military service.

Yet some twenty-two years later, in the Second World War, Percy was again fully involved in another concert party, organising and leading entertainments for returning and injured servicemen several nights a week. This commitment lasted for four to five years.

We do not know exactly how many times he trod the boards across both world wars, but in each case it was certainly hundreds. His total live audience might well have run well into six figures.

There can be very few who can boast such an unusual war record across both world wars.

A job in banking, a life in the arts

We have already stated that the other major influence on Percy's life was his decision before the war to train and then work for the bank. At the time it certainly represented a big step up, but after the war this might have lost a little of that aura.

In reality he had quite an ordinary job but outside work he lived an extraordinary life. The contrast between the two parts of his life, how he earned his living and how he chose to spend it, is quite startling. It may well be that without the security of the job he would never have had the energy, courage and motivation to develop his various artistic activities to such a high standard.

On return from the war he might have been tempted to become a professional entertainer, having had an intensive introduction to the role during the war. Had he gone down that route, he would have had to be very focused and hard-nosed about it to be successful in the long-term. He might well have found it difficult to develop his interest as a painter. As it was, the stability of the day job allowed him to develop his different interests.

The possibility of him becoming a professional artist rather than a professional entertainer was less realistic as his painting experience developed more gradually. By the time he had acquired the skills and a reputation, it was almost certainly too late to change direction. As it was, especially after the Second World War, he was able to earn a very useful second income without sacrificing his pension.

Percy Monkman

High artistic standards in each activity

After the First World War, Percy's Bradford roots sustained him in his artistic activities, building on both a strong community network into which he was born and a strong cultural tradition that gave him role models.

These factors allowed him the freedom to achieve the most with his talents. Not only did he end up entertaining night after night in both world wars tens of thousands of servicemen, but he was also an integral part of the most successful theatrical production on a Bradford stage in the 20th century. Finally, he became one of the best and most well-known and prolific of watercolour painters in Yorkshire.

Largely self-taught, he engaged with the public with all his artistic activities, making him open to their criticism. On the stage he performed both music hall entertainments and serious theatrical productions; in galleries he exhibited paintings and newspapers published his cartoons.

Another common theme of his work is that he was highly respected by his peers. In each activity he achieved a professional standard rather than just being a seriously committed amateur. He also collaborated with national figures (eg Leslie Henson as entertainer, Esme Church as actor and Ashley Jackson as painter). And in 1974, within a space of six months, he was celebrated by his peers in the two institutions that were such a strong part of his life – the theatre and the arts club.

Contrast with his three brothers

The four Monkman brothers who lived to retirement all had successful lives, considering their humble start and basic education. They were self-made achievers who became prominent members of their local communities. However, Percy's achievements were quite different from his three brothers'. He was unconventional where they were much more conventional.

One might even suggest that from birth their routes through life might differ. For a start Percy even had a much more unusual name than his brothers. Then, when they became young adults, they dressed a little differently. Percy almost always wore a bow-tie and they wore conventional ties.

Even in the First World War, their experiences differed. The two (Gordon and Harry) who were old enough to fight joined the Bradford Pals, fought on the front line and survived. Percy joined in a non-combatant role and also survived, but by following an unusual and highly individual path via an entertainment troupe.

After the war their lives certainly followed different paths.

Gordon, Harry and Frank all had to work hard to secure their living in a way that Percy did not. They all entered the wool trade, Bradford's staple industry until well into the 20th century. They all ended up managing their own businesses and eventually living prosperous lives, even if they struggled to find their feet in early adult life. They were all active members of their local communities and keen on active sport, especially golf. There would

An Extraordinary Bradfordian

be many Bradfordians of their generation who experienced such a life.

Percy's path was unique. His achievements were artistic, highly individual and unusual, being entirely focused on his leisure time, rather than his day job. He was extremely energetic; perhaps, running their own businesses, his three brothers did not have quite the same energy to put into their leisure activities as Percy.

Finally, in death, Percy did things differently in outliving each brother by at least 10 years and, despite being the eldest, was the last to die.

Unusual friendships

Throughout his life, Percy's artistic activities created long friendships with a fascinating mixture of people from entertaining, acting and painting, who shared similar passions and eccentricities.

The most prominent, and important friendship was, of course, with his close contemporary JB Priestley, Bradford's most celebrated person of their generation. The international fame for the nation's most famous man of letters who was a boyhood friend from the next streetand who played in the same football team provided great encouragement for Percy developing a reputation locally in their two areas of common interest – acting and painting.

However, Percy enjoyed many other friendships that grew from his interests. Entertaining and acting brought with it a strong camaraderie of shared experiences on the stage. Painting then brought him into contact with many eccentrics, driven, like Percy, to capture on canvas the essence of some moment or scene and to improve this skill at every opportunity.

Percy Monkman

Sense of humour

Perhaps the one quality that his wide range of friends recognised and pervaded everything that he did, whether family or friend, was his sense of humour. His reaction to almost all situations was to look for the funny side.

Percy was always seen as a character and his natural humour was a strong part of his persona. Being the comic turn both at formal events and in informal settings came naturally to him. It was no surprise that during the Second World War he was billed as 'Yorkshire's King of Mirth'.

The few people who knew him who are still alive remember his sense of humour above all. Iris Galey (nee Boetschi) recalls him as being an amusing man with many jokes who represented normal family life in contrast with her own childhood nightmare of a life. David Waddington, Arts Club friend, remembers him as an engaging and humorous companion, as he ferried him, over many years, between Baildon and Bradford. Ashley Jackson, fellow passionate watercolourist, remembers him as a 'lovely Capo di Monte type fella from Bradford'. Great nieces Nicki Godfrey and Mandy Tapper remember him as the 'grown-up' who made them laugh and let them use his paints. Finally, as his grandson living in difficult family circumstances, I remember him as the one person who represented normality and a sense of fun when it mattered that someone played this role as I was growing up.

A life no longer possible

It is difficult to imagine someone living the life today that Percy did.

In a pre-television age, when people largely had to find their own entertainment, he built a life initially around the music hall tradition, now completely disappeared, then around serious amateur theatre, which, too, today is hard to find. Alongside these activities he then built a life around watercolour painting which is no longer fashionable (eg steep decline in membership of Bradford Arts Club, from over 200 members to around 30 at the current time). His success in all these activities owes much to the close community where he worked, living close to all his family and friends and not far from the city centre where he worked – a community that no longer exists. Or perhaps it has just been replaced by a new community with a very different culture.

Even his pattern of a working life has gone out of fashion. No longer do people work for one organisation, least of all a bank, for forty years.

Almost all the aspects of Percy's life, his upbringing and his environment are firmly rooted in the early 20th century. This is now a lost world. Society has changed greatly since Percy's death. Bradford, too, was already changing before his death and has continued to change.

An Extraordinary Bradfordian

Living to a good old age

However, there is one aspect of his life that is extremely relevant to the current day. Percy died when 93 years old, a long life for someone born in 1892. Today that is the equivalent of living to be 100. Data from the Office of National Statistics shows that 1.1% of men born in England in 1892 lived to be at least 93 years old. The same percentage of men born in 1924 and living to be 93 years old today (2017) would now enjoy an extra seven years of life. Remarkable in so many other ways, Percy was also a man in a hundred when it came to longevity.

Everyone's life expectations in the developed world have increased considerably. For example, in 1917 King George V only had to send telegrams to 24 centenarians. In 2016 his granddaughter Queen Elizabeth II sent 6,405 such cards of congratulations. When William Beveridge, the thinker behind the welfare state, recommended retirement at 65 for men at the end of the Second World War, half the male population with manual jobs would die before they were 70. In the 1950s and 1960s, retirement was considered a period of rest after a long working life.

Perhaps the biggest challenge for those living in the 21st century and beyond is how to adjust life styles for much longer lives. This affects education, work and retirement. Percy, unusually for his time, spent one third of his life 'in retirement', which coincided with the time that I knew him. The thing that kept him going in this last phase of his life was his obsession with his interests, especially painting. He was lucky enough not to suffer from any illness associated with old age. Conversely, one might say that he lived the kind of full life that reduced the risks of such an illness.

There probably is no universal secret to living to a good old age. If you had asked Percy for his secret, he would undoubtedly have said quite simply, as he told pupils at a school speech day in Saltaire in 1962: *'One of the biggest problems of the future will be the use of increasing leisure. To live a full and happy life, we must take advantage of leisure, and use it, not waste it. And I don't know anything more satisfying than creating something, that is a result of your skill and imagination, something that's got you in it.'*

However, Percy's life does not quite do justice to his own advice. One might suggest that financial security, a good social network, a clear purpose, a constant search for personal development and a strong sense of fun are all likely ingredients. Percy's story shows that he had these in abundance and that in this respect at least he was a man ahead of his time.

In a rare moment of contemplation he wrote in 1978 to his Swiss friend Iris Galey: *'The great thing is making the most of your potential, but above all finding contentment in your family life and counting your blessings (voice of his mother again!). As Shakespeare said "The fault, dear Brutus, is not in our stars but in ourselves, that we are underlings". To use the gifts we have as fully as we can brings the greatest satisfaction to all. Aren't we getting philosophical?'*

Percy Monkman

FURTHER INFORMATION

Books and articles (in date of publication sequence)

Follies of the Forces
By Howard N Cole, 1938
Unpublished: full draft available at Imperial War Museum, London

Men of the RAF
By Sir William Rothenstein and Lord David Cecil
Published by Oxford University Press, 1942; no ISBN available

Socialism over sixty years: the life of Jowett of Bradford
By Fenner Brockway with preface by JB Priestley
Published by Allen and Unwin, 1946

Victorian Cities
By Asa Briggs, 1963
Published by Odhams Press
Out of print

Education in Bradford
By Bradford Corporation, 1970
ISBN: Not available
Out of print: Copy at Bradford Local Studies Library

Banking in Yorkshire
By WCE Hartley
Published by Dalesman Publishing Company Ltd, 1975
ISBN 0-85206-264-8

Wissenschaft in Worstedopolis: Public Science in Bradford, 1800-1850
By JB Morrell
Presidential address at meeting of School of Social Sciences, 12 May 1984
https://www.cambridge.org/core/journals/british-journal-for-the-history-of-science/article/wissenschaft-in-worstedopolis-public-science

Ruskin and Bradford: An Experiment in Victorian Cultural History
By Malcolm Hardman
Published by Manchester University Press, 1986
ISBN 0-7190-1765-3

I Couldn't Cry When Daddy Died
By Iris Galey
ISBN: 978-0941300100
Published by Mother Courage Press, 1986

Class Formation and Urban-industrial Society, Bradford 1750 to 1850
By Theodore Koditschek
ISBN 0-521-32771-7
Published by Cambridge University Press, 1990

The Rebel Tyke: Bradford and JB Priestley
By Peter Holdsworth
ISBN 0-907734-36-7
Published by Bradford Libraries, 1994

Theatre at War, 1914-18
By Larry Collins
ISBN: 978-1-90073-428-8
Published by Jade Publishing Ltd, 1998

Building Jerusalem: the rise and fall of the Victorian City
By Tristram Hunt
ISBN: 978-0-75381-983-8
Published by Weidenfeld & Nicholson, 2004

JB Priestley's Bradford
By Dr Gary Firth
ISBN: 978-0-7524-3865-8
Published by Tempus Publishing Ltd, 2006

Ashley Jackson: An Artist's Life
By Chris Bond
ISBN: 978-1-84563-104-8
Published by Pen and Sword Ltd, 2010

Bradford Through Time
By Mark Davis
ISBN: 978-1-4456-0330-8
Published by Amberley Publishing, 2011

The Christmas Truce (Play)
By Phil Porter
ISBN: 978-1-78319-214-4
Published by Oberon Books Ltd, 2014

Room at the Top – The origins of Professional Football in Bradford
By John Dewhirst
ISBN: 978-0-9566984-5-2
Published by bantamspast, 2015

Useful websites

The Royal Bank of Scotland Group Archive on the history of British banking
www.rbs.com/heritage

JB Priestley Archive for all writings by and about JBP
www.bradford.ac.uk/library/special-collections/collections/j-b-priestley-archive/

Not Just Hockney on other famous Bradford artists
www.notjusthockney.info

Our World in Data on statistics about life expectancy
https://ourworldindata.org/life-expectancy/

APPENDIX 1
TIMELINE OF PERCY'S LIFE

Births, marriages and deaths in family

16 August 1862

> Birth of Martha Ann Collins (mother) at Heaton, Bradford

3 May 1864

> Birth of Edwin Monkman (father) at Hemsworth, West Riding of Yorkshire

17 November 1890

> Marriage of Edwin Monkman with Martha Ann Collins at Heaton Baptist Chapel, Bradford

11 August 1892

> **Birth of Percy Monkman at 6 Bavaria Place, Manningham, Bradford**

27 March 1894

> Birth of Gordon Monkman (brother) at 16 Heaton Road, Bradford

23 July 1896

> Birth of John Henry (Harry) Monkman (brother) at 16 Heaton Road, Bradford

13 December 1901

> Birth of Stanley Monkman (brother) at 16 Heaton Road, Bradford

13 July 1904

> Birth of Frank Monkman (brother) at 16 Heaton Road, Bradford

13 September 1918

> **Marriage of Percy Monkman with Doris Northrop at Girlington Congregational Church, Bradford**

27 May 1920

> Birth of Dorothy Eileen (daughter) at 344 Kensington Street, Bradford

28 April 1922

> Birth of Alfred Philip Harvey (son) at 34 Toller Lane, Bradford

19 June 1923

> Birth of Colin Gordon (son) at 34 Toller Lane, Bradford

12 January 1929

> Death of Stanley Monkman (aged 28)

17 April 1941

> Marriage of Dorothy Monkman with Reginald Greenwood at Girlington Congregational Church, Bradford

Percy Monkman

6 April 1944

Marriage of Harvey Monkman with Marjorie Galloway at Girlington Congregational Church, Bradford

6 January 1944

Death of Martha Monkman (aged 81)

29 July 1946

Birth of Alexander Martin Greenwood (grandson) at Mornington Villas, Manningham, Bradford

31 October 1947

Birth of Avril Rosemary Monkman (granddaughter) at Bingley Maternity Hospital

8 January 1948

Birth of Adrian Paul Tristram Greenwood (grandson) at Mornington Villas, Manningham, Bradford

15 February 1950

Death of Edwin Monkman (aged 85) at Thorn Drive, Bradford

2 July 1953

Birth of Andrew Harvey Monkman (grandson) at Shipley Hospital

14 March 1959

Marriage of Colin Monkman with Dorothy Chapman at Baildon Parish Church

17 May 1969

Marriage of Avril Monkman with Richard Newton at Baildon Parish Church

2 August 1969

Marriage of Martin Greenwood with Eileen Hall at Hornsea Parish Church, East Riding of Yorkshire

1 April 1972

Marriage of Adrian Greenwood with Marianne Elisabeth Teresa Wevers at Harar, Ethiopia

4 August 1972

Birth of Rachel Louise Newton (great-granddaughter) at Huddersfield

20 February 1973

Birth of Mark Toby Greenwood (great-grandson) at Clemens Hospital Munster, West Germany

6 September 1973

Birth of Daniel Martin Greenwood (great-grandson) at Wythernshawe Hospital, Manchester

9 April 1974

Death of Doris Monkman (aged 79) at home in Baildon

21 August 1974

Death of Frank Monkman (aged 70) at Scalebor Park Hospital, Burley-in-Wharfedale

25 April 1975

Birth of Rebecca Jane Newton (great-granddaughter) at Halifax General Hospital

An Extraordinary Bradfordian

22 August 1975

Birth of Sally Catherine Greenwood (great-granddaughter) at Royal Infirmary, Huddersfield, West Yorkshire

22 December 1975

Birth of Alexander Robin Greenwood (great-grandson) at Cuckfield Hospital, West Sussex

22 December 1975

Birth of Anne-Marie Ruth Greenwood (great-granddaughter) at Cuckfield Hospital, West Sussex

12 May 1976

Death of John Henry Monkman (aged 80) on holiday in Devon

25 May 1977

Death of Gordon Monkman (aged 83) in Peterborough, Ontario, Canada

2 December 1977

Death of Harvey Monkman (aged 55) in Baildon, West Yorkshire

1 January 1982

Death of Andrew Monkman (aged 28) in Grassington, North Yorkshire

29 April 1986

Death of Percy Monkman (aged 93) at Shipley Hospital, Shipley, West Yorkshire

Addresses

1896	6 Bavaria Place, Manningham
1893?	16 Heaton Road, Manningham
Pre-1911	106 Toller Lane, Heaton
1919	344 Kensington Street, Girlington
1921 or 1922	34 Jesmond Avenue, Heaton
1928	70 Jesmond Avenue, Heaton
1952	2 Kirklands Villas, Baildon
1976	25 Springfield Road, Baildon

Percy Monkman

Education and work

July 1906	Left Drummond Road School, Manningham
1906 to 1907	Worked as office boy for R Binns Stock and Share Broker, Swan Arcade, Bradford (six months)
1907	Worked as office boy for Manningham Mills (six months)
1909	Passed entrance examination for bank.
August 1909	Started work with Becketts Bank (Leeds) in Bradford branch
5 October 1915	Joined Royal Army Medical Corps (RAMC) as Private
30 June 1919	Demobilised from Royal Army Medical Corps (RAMC) as Lance-Corporal
July 1919	Rejoined Becketts Bank (Leeds) which, as result of merger in 1921, became the Westminster Bank
August 1952	Retired from the Westminster Bank after 40 years' service

An Extraordinary Bradfordian

Artistic achievements

January 1912	Made first recorded appearance as entertainer
1924	Joined Bradford Arts Club
1935	Joined Bradford Civic Playhouse
1935	Winner of 1st Prize for Water Colours (The Westminster)
1936	Winner of 1st Prize for Water Colours (The Westminster)
1937	Winner of 1st Prize for Water Colours (The Westminster)
1938	Winner of 1st Prize for Water Colours (The Westminster)
1950	Became Vice-Chairman of Bradford Arts Club
December 1960	Solo actor in *The End*. awarded one of the Ten Best Cine-Films of 1960
1963	Became Chairman of Bradford Arts Club
4 May 1974	Celebrated 50th anniversary of membership of Bradford Arts Club ('Percyversary')
9 November 1974	Awarded honorary life membership of Bradford Civic Playhouse
March 1977	Became President of Bradford Arts Club

Percy Monkman

Appearances on stage at Bradford Civic Playhouse

	Season	Times performed	Play	Author
1	1935/36	6	*Moon in the Yellow River*	Denis Johnston
2	1938	6	*The Inspector General*	Nikolai Gogol
3	1938	18	*When We Are Married*	JB Priestley
4	1940	12	*When We Are Married* (revival)	JB Priestley
5	1941	6	*What say they?*	James Bridie
6	1941	6	*Distant Point*	A Afinogenev
7	1942	12	*When We Are Married* (revival)	JB Priestley
8	1943	6	*Libel*	Edward Wooll
9	1943	2	*The Beaux Strategem*	George Farquhar
10	1943	6	*The Corn is Green*	Emlyn Williams
11	1944	6	*The Corn is Green* (revival)	Emlyn Williams
12	1944	6	*Ghosts*	Henrik Ibsen
13	1944	8 *	*When We Are Married* (revival)	JB Priestley
14	1944	12	*They Came to a City*	JB Priestley
15	1945	6	*Much Ado About Nothing*	William Shakespeare
16	1946	6	*The Tempest*	William Shakespeare
17	1947	10	*Johnson over Jordan*	JB Priestley
18	1947	6	*Johnson over Jordan* (revival)	JB Priestley
19	1948	10	*It Depends What You Mean*	James Bridie
20	1948	10	*Quay South*	Howard Clewes
21	1948	10	*Hog's Blood and Hellebore*	Jonquil Anthony
22	1950	10	*The Lady's Not for Burning*	Christopher Fry
23	1952	10	*When We Are Married* (revival)	JB Priestley
24	1953	6	*Penny for a Song*	John Whiting
25	1954	6	*The Man Who Came to a Dinner*	Hart and Kaufman
26	1956	6	*Hobson's Choice*	Harold Brighouse
27	1958	6	*When We Are Married* (revival)	JB Priestley

Note: * indicates that this was an outdoor production played in August in Bradford's five largest parks.

INDEX

Notes

1. All Percy's family are listed in terms of relationship to Percy (eg mother, daughter).
2. All other individuals are listed in terms of roles (eg friend, artist).
3. Main references to people are by surname, but a cross reference is also given to Christian name if the person appears more than once.
4. Except for people with national reputations, individuals are only included if it is thought that Percy met them.
5. All references to Percy are omitted, including photographs etc, unless they show other people.
6. All specific local place names (eg streets, parks, districts) are assumed to be in Bradford, unless otherwise stated.
7. All general references to Bradford are omitted, unless it is part of a name (eg Bradford City AFC).
8. Items are not given for references in the main preface, in the prologue or in the short preface to each chapter.
9. Items also exclude references in Further Information and in Appendix 1.
10. All items shown in bold are items of visual interest (eg photos).
11. All items shown in italics refer to titles (eg plays, books).

Entry		Page
16th Battalion	also Bradford Pals	17
90th birthday		143
Aberdeen		120
Addingham		151
Adrian Greenwood	see Greenwood, Adrian	
alcohol		129
Alhambra		32, 53
Allerton		132
Amateur Cine World		53, 55
Ambleside		63, 116
ambulance		**18**
An Inspector Calls (Priestley)		98
Anderson, John (actor)		43
Andrew, Monkman	see Monkman, Andrew	
Angel Pavement (Priestley)		98
Angus Rands	see Rands, Angus	

annual dinner		71
Appletreewick		63
Appleyard, Joe (friend)		74, 118
Archies		21, **22,** 26, 129
Armistice		27
Army		17
Arnott, Robert (journalist)		24, 139
art education		11, 59
Arthur Tetley	see Tetley, Arthur	
Arundel, Jimmy (friend)		107, 108
Ashley Jackson	see Jackson, Ashley	
Ashley Jackson: An Artist's Life		117
Asian ethnic groups		163
Atherton, John S (friend)		106, 108
Audrey Woodrow	see Woodrow, Audrey	
Austwick		62, 73
awards		153
Baildon		65, 67, 67, 71, 72, 84, 87, 114, 132, 147
		162, 165, 166
Baildon Moors		80
Baildon Players		51, 51
Bank Street		67
banking		12,169
banking cartoons		**94**
banking technology		162
Baptists		6
Barden Tower		63
Barker, Edward		110
Barker, Jean (friend)		63
Barnsley		117
Barnum and Bailey		11
Barstow, Stan (novelist)		103, 103
Basel		112, 113
Battle of the Somme	also Somme	133
Bavaria Place		8
BBC		100, 163
BBC Radio Leeds		103, 113
Becketts Bank		12, **12,** 167

Belle Vue Grammar School		121, 160, 167
Bentley, Phyllis (novelist)		101
Berlin		131
Bernard Hepton	see Hepton Bernard	
Bill Briggs	see Briggs, Bill	
Bingley		61
Bingley Fair (painting)		77, **77**
Binns R (Swan Arcade)		11
Birch Lane		88
Birmingham City Art Gallery		61
Black Swan		100
Blore, Eric (actor)		26
'*Blow in the bag*' (cartoon)		**93**
Boetschi, Trudi (friend)		112, 112, 113
Bolling Hall		116
Bolton Abbey		63, 63, 64
Bond, Chris (writer)		117
Bonney, Peter (friend)		62
Book-keeping certificate		12
Bosher, Donald (artist)		71
Bowen, Owen (artist)		74
Bowes, Laura (sister-in-law)		135, 135
Bowling		1
bow-tie		131, 143, 170
box of paints		58
Bradford Alhambra	see Alhambra	
Bradford Arts Club		48, 71, 71, 73, 97, 100, 107, 109, 111, 112 116, 132, 140, 143, 145, 152, 161, 162, 172
Bradford Beck		2
Bradford Cartwright Hall	see Cartwright Hall	
Bradford City AFC		99, 121, 123, 125, 134, 162
Bradford City AFC cartoon vs Nelson (1927)		87, **87**
Bradford City AFC FA Cup		13
Bradford City AFC fire disaster		115, 124, **124, 124**
Bradford City Charter 1897		7
Bradford City Council		78, 163
Bradford Civic Playhouse	see Civic Playhouse	
Bradford Civic Playhouse Personalities		90, **90**, 110, 155
Bradford Civic Playhouse Personalities: celebration cake		**90**

185

Bradford College of Art	70
Bradford Diocesan Adult Religious Education Committee	49
Bradford family	165
Bradford Forster Square	6
Bradford Grammar School	7, 71, 68, 115
Bradford Interchange	6
Bradford Northern (rugby league club)	88, 123
Bradford Pals	17, 97, 133, 170
Bradford Park Avenue	88, 88, 99, 122, 126, 134
Bradford Pictorial	82
Bradford Players	49
Bradford School of Art	93, 119
Bradford Spring Exhibition see Spring Exhibition	
Bradford Voluntary Wartime Entertainers Association	31
Bradford YMCA	121, **121**
Bragg, Melvyn (writer)	103
Braine, John (novelist)	101, 103
breathalyser	93
Brian Walker see Walker, Brian	
Bridlington harbour (painting)	77, **77**
Briggs, Bill (friend)	**Cover,** 111
Brighouse	72
Bright Day (Priestley)	98
Brighton	119
Bronte country	57, 62, 64, 119, 153
Bronteland hamlet (painting)	76, **76**
brothers (Monkman)	133
Brown Muff & Co	67, **67**, 68
Brown, Ian (friend)	63
Brundrit, Reg (artist)	58
Bryson, Geoffrey (performer)	35, 110
Buckden	63
building regulations	4
Bullock, Sir Alan (historian)	92, **92**
Burnsall	63, 63, 64
Butterfield, Harry (friend)	62
Cambrai	60, **60, 60,** 150
Cambridge University	98, 136, 167

Canada	105, 128, 133, 135
Canadian Monkmans	134, 165
Canal at Dockfields, Shipley	81, **81**
Carnegie weekends	71, 150
Carter, Sam (friend)	144
cartoons	87, 89, 94, 149
Cartwright Hall	11, 31, 48, 73, 78, 92, 107
cashier	140, 143
Castle Bolton	109
catalogue of paintings	69
Catford	18
Cawston, Richard (TV producer)	100
celebration cake	90, **90**, 155, **155**
Census (2011)	163
centenarians	173
Central Library	98, 103
Certificate, book-keeping	12
Chapel Street	46, 155
Chapman, Stanley (artist)	72, 117
Cheapside	167
Cheetham, Barbara (performer)	110
Chelsea	119
cholera	2, 3
Christmas 1923	132
Christmas card	66, 93
Christmas party	71
Church, Esme (director)	42, 43, 45, 150, 151, 155, 170
Church Treasurer	130, 131
Churchill, Sir Winston (politician)	25, 59
Cine-films, ten best in 1960	54
City of Birmingham	151
City Hall	7
City Hall Square	75, 101, **101**
City of Birmingham Art Gallery	61
City Rains (painting)	78, **78**
Civic Concert Party	31, 33, 34, 52, 108, 155, **155**
Civic Playhouse	31, 39, 39, 40, 42, 44, 44, 50, 50, 51
	62, 97, 100, 104, 110, 113, **115**, 120, 142
	150, 150, 152, 155, 156, 162

Clem Pulman	see Pulman, Clem	
Clock House		68
close-knit community		160
clown		**23**
Cole, Howard N (author)		24, 25
Colin Monkman	see Monkman, Colin	
Collins, Martha (mother) also Monkman, M (after marriage)		3, 5, 8
Collins, Thomas (grandfather)		3
commissions		65
competition winner		76
concert parties		24, 151
concert party		21
Congregational Church		164
Congregationalists		6
Conistone		63, 67
conscription		17
Constance Pearson	see Pearson, Constance	
contemporaries (artists)		106
Cooper, Harriet (grandmother)		3
Corporation		4
correspondence with JB Priestley		102
Cousin Jinny	see Jinny	
Cow & Calf Rocks		63
Coxwold		62
Crib, Joan (friend)		142
cricket		6, 126
Crosby, Tommy (friend)		22, 25, 26, 105, 105, 129
Customers and their Customs (cartoon)		98, **98**
Daisy Hill		19
Dales	see Yorkshire Dales	
Dales holidays		146
Dalesman magazine		73, 106, 107, 108, 145
David Giles	see Giles, David	
David Waddington	see Waddington, David	
David Hockney	see Hockney, David	
de Greasley, Mike (friend)		103
death, Monkman, Stanley (brother)		135
death, Priestley JB (friend)		103

death, Monkman, Doris (wife)		137
death, Monkman, Harvey (son)		137
death, Monkman, Andrew (grandson)		137
death, Monkman, Frank (brother)		152
death, Monkman, Doris (wife)		152
Delius, Frederick (composer)		7
Deloittes		68
dementia		136
demobilisation		28, 60
Derwentwater		69
Dews, Peter (director)		44
Dick Hudson's		65, 118
Disorderly Room (review sketch)		25, 26, 42, 105, 139
Distant Point (A Afinogenev)		45
Dobrudden Farm		65
Doris Northrop	see Northrop, Doris	
Dorothy Monkman	see Monkman, Dorothy	
Dorothy Greenwood	see Greenwood, Dorothy	
Dorset		61, 61
Doullens (Northern France)		18
Dresden		131
Drummond Road		160
Drummond Road Board School		10, **10**, 169, 166
dyer		3
East Riding		2, 3, 3
Education Act (1870)		5, 10
Edwardian Bradford		13
Edwin Monkman	see Monkman, Edwin	
Edwin Smith	see Smith, Edwin	
Elite picture house		19
Elland		3
Elland Road, Leeds		88
Emmerdale Farm		65
Encores' concert party		139
Engels, Friedrich (political philosopher)		1
English Journey (JB Priestley)		39
Engstrand (*Ghosts*)		46
ENSA		24

entertainer		169, 169
entertaining troops		21
Entertainments National Service Association (ENSA)		24
Eric Pollard	see Pollard, Eric	
Esholt		65
Esme Church	see Church, Esme	
Eurich, Richard (artist)		71
Evans, Norman (comedian)		32
Examinations, shorthand		12
Examinations, Institute of Bankers		12
examples of humour		36
exhibitions		73
FA Cup		122,124
Factory Act		5
family life		146
Fattorinis (jeweller)		122
Feakes, Ken (friend)		63,73,145
Feather, Lord Vic (trade unionist)		75
Ferdy Roberts	see Roberts, Ferdy	
Filey		61, 65,126
fire service		4
first concert		20, **20**
First World War		16, 21, 42, 60, 79,105,123,140,149 150, 168, 170
Fleming, Eric (buyer)		65
Fletcher Singers Male Voice Quartet		144
*Follies of the Forces (*Howard N Cole*)*		24, 25
football		6, 121, 122, 123
Football gossip (cartoon*)*		88, **88**
Forster Square		5, 12, 14, 68, 75, 79, **79**, 81, **81** 101, 143, 152
Forster, WE (politician)		5
Fox, Nora (actress)		39
Frank Monkman	see Monkman, Frank	
Freeman of Bradford (JB Priestley)		98, 101
friendship		97
Frizinghall		100
fruiterer		8

gags	see jokes	
Galey, Iris (friend)		112, 113, 172, 173
Game Cock Inn, Austwick		73
Gaskill, William (director)		42
Geoffrey Bryson	see Bryson, Geoffrey	
George Jeakins	see Jeakins, George	
German		7, 8, 25, 131, 133
Germany		65, 131
Ghosts (Henrik Ibsen)		46
gifts of paintings		75, 105
Giles, David (director)		44, 44
Gill, Charlie (friend)		111
Girlington		8, 129, **159**, 160
Girlington Congregational Church		19, 28, 119, 129, 130, 134, 160, 164
Godfrey, Nicki (great-niece)		172
golden wedding		27, 130, **133**
golf		126
Gordale Scar		109, 145
Gordon Monkman	see Monkman, Gordon	
Goronwy Jones (*The Corn Is Green*)		49
Grange-over-Sands		61, 62
graphologist		148
Grassington		61, 62, 63, 63, 64, 64, 69, **82**, 137 143, 146
Green Lane Board School		171
Greenfield Congregational Church		9, 129, 130
greengrocer's shop		129
Greenhalgh, Tony (friend)		63
Greenwood, Rhoda (grandmother)		3
Greenwood Menswear		67
Greenwood, Adrian (grandson)		128, 136
Greenwood, Dorothy (daughter)		3, 11, 73, 74, **74**, 101, 105, 110, 112 114, 116, 129, 129, 130, 132, 137, 137 146, 160
Greenwood, John F (friend)		71, 119
Greenwood, Martin (grandson)		128
Greenwood, Muriel (performer)		110
Greenwood, Reg (son-in-law)		136, 160
Guildhall		151
Guiseley		86

Halle Orchestra		6
Hamburg		131
Harewood House		31, 48
Harrogate		72, 73, 74
Harry Monkman	see Monkman, Harry	
Harry Tout	see Tout, Harry	
Hart, Rex (performer)		29
Hawes		61
Hawkes, Jacquetta (JBP's wife)		103
Hawksworth		165
Haworth		64, 119
Hayrick, The (painting)		76, **76**
Headingley		126
healthy life-style		131
Heap, FW (customer)		75
Heaton		3, 8, 8, 61, 69, **159,** 160, 161, 16**2**
Hebden		143
Hemsworth		8
Henson, Leslie (performer)		24, 24, 25, 25, 139, 170
Hepton, Bernard (actor)		44, 44
Herbert Soppitt (*When We Are Married*)		**40**, 43, 100
Hewitt, John (journalist)		143
Hickson, Nancy (friend)		103
Higgins, Jack (novelist)		103
High Bradley		63
Hill, James (actor)		44
Hobson's Choice (Harold Brighouse)		49, **49**
Hockney David (artist)		98, 103
Holdsworth, Peter (critic)		42, 44, 116, 155
Holland		65, 131
Holmes, Katharine (artist)		109
Holmfirth		118
Horrocks, Alfred. (friend)		111
Horton		1
House of Commons		72, 152
Hubberholme		63
Huby		65
Huddersfield Examiner		29

humorous entertainer		28
I Couldn't Cry When Daddy Died (Iris Galey)		112
Ilkley		63, 64, 116, 119, 134, 165
Ilkley Moor		3
immigration		163, 164
Impressionists		107
Institute of Handwriting Analysis		148
insurance agent		3
Iris Galey	see Galey, Iris	
Islam		164, 164
It Depends What You Mean (James Bridie)		45
Jackson, Ashley (friend)		72, 117, 118, 170,1 72
Jane Smith	see Smith, Jane	
JB Priestley	see Priestley, JB	
Jeakins, George (artist)		103
Jesmond Avenue		160, 163
Jim Heeler (*Hobson's Choice*)		47
Jimmy Arundel	see Arundel, Jimmy	
Jinny (father's cousin)		9
Joan Tout	see Tout, Joan	
Joe Appleyard	see Appleyard, Joe	
Joe Pighills	see Pighills, Joe	
John Braine	see Braine, John	
John F Greenwood	see Greenwood, John F	
John S Atherton	see Atherton, John S	
Johnson, Linda (customer)		75
joining army		15
joke books		151
jokes		19
Jones, Fred (artist)		71
Jowett Fred (politician)		14
Keighley		73
Ken Feakes	see Feakes, Ken	
Kettlewell		61, 63, 63, 64, 146
Kilnsey Crag		63, 69
Kirkgate		12, 140, 167

Kirkgate Market		100
Kirklands Farm, Baildon		84, **84**
Kirklands Lane, Baildon		85, **85**
Kirklands Villas, Baildon		112, 145
Kirkstall Abbey		1
Kitchen, Olive (performer)		35, 110
Knight, Dame Laura		151
Kramer, Jacob (friend)		108
Labour Party		5
Lady in the Bath (mime)		113
Lake District		62, 63, 65, 69, 116
Lakeritis (cartoon)		**88**
Lamprett Bellboys (*Penny for a Song*)		**48**
Lancashire		58, 61
landscapes		63
Langton (near Malton)		3
Laura Bowes	see Bowes, Laura	
Laurence Scarfe	see Scarfe, Laurence	
Lawson, Fred (friend)		109
Leeds		6, 13, 64, 72, 73, 78, 108, 109, 119, 119
Leeds & Liverpool Canal,		65
Leeds City of Varieties		30, 33
leisure time		6, 173
Leslie Henson	see Henson, Leslie	
leukaemia		131
Lewis, Ivy (friend)		115
life membership, Civic Playhouse		90, 138, 142, 152, 155, 156
Light opera! (cartoon)		92, **92**
Lille		25
Lilycroft		13
limestone country		59
Lincoln City		124
Linton		63
Lister Park		6, 13, 29
Lister, Samuel (factory owner)		5
Lister's Mill		3, 5, 5, 8
Little Germany		7, 37
Little Lane		164

Littondale		63
Liverpool		21, 105
longevity		175
Lord Mayor of Bradford		31, 101, 103, 157
Lost City (TV programme)		100, 163
Lost Hearts Club		153
Lothersdale		152
Low Springs		65
Lowry		72
Lugano		62
Lytham St Annes		61, 61
Main street, Grassington		82, **82**
Maine Road, Manchester		122
Malham		64, 64, 109, 145, 146
Malton		3
man with lute		**29**
Manningham		1, 3, 5, 8, 8, 8, 8, 88, 116, 130, 143, **159**, 160, 161, 163, 163, 167
Manningham Lane		6, 71, 83
Manningham Mills		11
Manningham RFC		122
Market Street		13
marketing		150
marriage		27
Martha Monkman	see Monkman, Martha	
Martha Collins	see Collins, Martha	
Mary Whitehouse (actress)		41, 110
Masham Place		160
Mason, Lord (Roy) (politician)		72, 154
McIntyre, Donald (artist)		71
McMurray Adam, Rev RH (friend)		144
Men of the RAF (Rothenstein)		43
Methodists		6
Midland Hotel		6, 12, 167
midwives		9
Military Cross		133
military service		17
miscarriage		8, 9
Mitchell, Bill (editor)		73

Monkman family	127, 130
Monkman, Andrew (grandson)	128, 137
Monkman, Avril (granddaughter)	128
Monkman, Colin (son)	128, **128**
Monkman, Doris (wife), also Northrop, D (before marriage)	**27**, 102, 111, 112, **128**, 128, 132, 132, **133**, 136, 136
Monkman, Dorothy (daughter) also Greenwood, D (after marriage)	**128**, 128
Monkman, Dorothy (sister-in-law)	134
Monkman, Edwin (father)	3, 3, 5, 8, 8, **10**, 19, **127**, 129, 129, 165
Monkman, Frank (brother)	127, **127**, 133, **133**, 134, 134, 135, 165, 170
Monkman, Gordon (brother)	**10**, 66, 102, 127, **127**, 128, 133, **133**, 133, 133, 133, 135, 165, 170, 170
Monkman, Harriet Leaf (step-grandmother)	3
Monkman, Harry (brother)	*iii*, 17, 20, 127, **127**, 133, **133**, 134, 134, 135, 165, 170, 170
Monkman, Harvey (son)	89, **128**, 128, 137, 160, 165, 170, 170
Monkman, Herbert (cousin)	133
Monkman, Martha (mother), also Collins, M (before marriage)	**9, 10**, **127**, 129, 129, 130
Monkman, Robert (grandfather)	3, **3**, 5, 12, 165
Monkman, Roseanne (step-grandmother)	3
Monkman, Stanley (brother)	127, **127**, 135
Monty Python	134
Moon in the River (Denis Johnston)	45
Moorside, Baildon	80, **80**
Morecambe	61
Morrell JB (historian)	2
Mrs Mops	88
Much Ado About Nothing (William Shakespeare)	44, **44**
'Mucky Duck'	100
mud in First World War	**18**
Muff, Bernard (baritone)	110
Mullings, Frank (tenor)	92
multi-culturalism	164
music	148
Nathanson, Teddy (performer)	33, 110

Nazi Germany	133
Nelson (City's 9-1 victory)	123
nervous breakdown	131
New Zealand	112, 134, 135
Newcastle United	122
Nixon, Bronwen (friend)	116
Non-conformist	6, 130, 130
Northern Command	30, 32, 33, **33**, 50
Northern France	28, 31, 69, 133, 168
Northern School of Drama	44, **44**, 150, 156
Office of National Statistics	173
Old Time Music Hall	34, 35, 35, 51, 115, **115**
Oldfield, Jean (performer)	110
Olive Kitchen	see Kitchen, Olive
one eye trick	**114**
Open air show at Harrogate	74, **74**
Order of Merit	98
Otley	60, 64
Otley Chevin	63, 86, **86**
Oxenhope	64, 119, 143, 146
paint box	146
painting outdoors	**70**, 145
painting philosophy	57
painting prize	59
paintings	149
Pakistanis	163, 164
Palmerston (Lord)	7
Paris	65
Park Avenue	see Bradford Park Avenue
passion for painting	69, 106
Pearson, Constance (friend)	64, 109
Peel Park	6
Pennine moors	118
Penny for a Song (John Whiting)	**46**
Percyversary	140, 142, 151, **153**
Peter Holdsworth	see Holdsworth, Peter
Peterborough (Canada)	66, 134

Peterborough Cathedral		66, **66**
Petheridge, Edward (actor)		44
Philip Robinson	see Robinson, Philip	
pierrot		21, **23**
Pighills, Joe (friend)		64, 117, 119
pipe-smoking		133
Playhouse	see Civic Playhouse	
police		4
Pollard, Eric (producer)		55, 56
population		1, 7
portfolio of paintings		63
portraits		63
Postscripts (Priestley)		98
Pratt, Bessie (actress)		141
Priestley, JB (friend)		11, 13, 14, 31, 39, 40, 42
		50, 57, 62, 75, 89, **89**, 90
		91, 97, 98, 98, **99**,100, **103**
		104, 118, 121, 153, 157, 160, 163
		164, 167, 171
Prince Arthur of Connaught		139
productions		149
professional standards		150
programmes (1920s)		30
promotion		150
publicity		73
Pudsey		132
Pulman, Clem (friend)		119, **119**, 128
Quay South (Howard Clewes)		47, **47**
Queen Victoria		11
Rackhams		68
RAF Linton-on-Ouse		43, **43**
rainstorm		58
RAMC		17, **18**, 28, 139
Rands, Angus (friend)		71, 74
Rawnsley, Mrs		160
Rawnsley, Maud		160
Read, Roger (pianist)		110

Reg Greenwood	see Greenwood, Reg	
retirement		12, 58, 131,1 40, 173
Richardson, Tony (director)		44, 44
rioting (July 2001)		164
Rita Scully	see Scully, Rita	
River Aire		64, 65
River Wharfe	also Wharfedale	63, 69
Robert Arnott	see Arnott, Robert	
Robert Monkman	see Monkman, Robert	
Roberts, Ferdy (friend)		97, 140
Robin Hood's Bay		65
Robinson, Philip (friend)		41, 50, 156
Roger Suddards	see Suddards, Roger	
Roni Vine (actress)	see Vine, Roni	
Rothay Manor		116
Rothenstein, Sir William (artist)		7, 43, 61, 72, 151
Rotterdam		131
Royal Academy (RA)		106, 119, 151, 151
Royal Army Medical Corps	see RAMC	
Royal College of Art (RCA)		61, 103, 119, 119
Royal Command performance		25
Royal Institute of Water Colour Painters (RI)		106, 117, 152
Royal Society for the Encouragement of Arts, Manufactures and Commerce		12
Royal Society of Art (RCA)		106
Royal Society of British Artists (RBA)		119, 152
rugby union		6, 126
Ruskin, John (artist)		7
sales of paintings		61, 75, 116
Salt, Sir Titus (mill-owner)		4, 65
Saltaire		5, 64, 173
Saltburn Place		99, 160
Saltburn United		99
Salter, Mona (accompanist)		110
Scarborough		65
Scarfe, Laurence (friend)		71, 97, 119
Schofield, Mary (actress)		42
School certificate	**11**	

school (Drummond Road)	see Drummond Road Board School	
school attendance		11
school log book		11, 11
school-leaving		11
Scotchman Road		121
Scott, Harry (editor)		73
Scouts		134
Scrub (*The Beaux Strategem*)		45
Scully, Rita (performer)		35, 35, 110
Second World War		31, 50, 62, 132, 169, 169
self-taught		149, 170
sense of humour		172
Shakespeare, William (playwright)		173
Shipley		81
Shipley United Reform Church		144
Shipley Congregational Church	see Shipley United Reform Church	
Shipley Glen		65, 75
Shipley Hospital		115
Shipley Times & Express		53
Shorthand examinations		12
sickness		11
Silverdale (Morecambe)		61
Singing Waiters (sketch)		**34**
Sir Winston Churchill	see Churchill, Sir Winston	
sketch book		147
Skipton		63, 147, 152
Slade School		108
Smith, Edwin (performer)		35, 35, 110
Smith, Jane (actress)		41, 41
Snowden Street		83
snowscenes		58, 83
social changes		161
Somme	also Battle of the Somme	1, 18
Sooty		34
Speech Day talk		59, 173
sport		6, 87
sporting cartoons		87
Spring Exhibition		60, 73, 92
St Cecilia		49

St Georges Hall		6
St Luke's Hospital		32
St. Johns Ambulance		17
Stanley Monkman	see Monkman, Stanley	
Starbotton		58, 63
Stephens Robert (actor)		44, 44
Stratford-upon-Avon		101
subscription concerts		13
Suddards, Roger (friend)		34, 35, 61, 68, 75, 115
Sunday School		130, 140
Sunday School teacher		130, 140
Sunday Times		124
supportive wife		132
Sussex		65
Swaledale		64
Swan Arcade		11, 13, 14, 100, 163
Swansea		119
Switzerland		62, 65, 112
Sykes, Tom (artist)		117
talks on painting		57, 149
Tapper, Mandy (great niece)		172
Teddy Nathanson	see Nathanson, Teddy	
teetotal		131
Telegraph & Argus		13, 14, 26, 35, 41, 41, 42, 44, 45 51, 51, 65, 70, 75, 76, 87, 88, 89, 90, 92, 98, 101, 109, 139, 143, 155
temperance		2
Tetley, Arthur (comedian)		41, 41, 110
The Beaux Strategem (George Farquhar)		45
The Christmas Truce (Phil Porter)		
The Corn is Green (Emlyn Williams)		45, **46**
The Dalesman	see *Dalesman* magazine	
The Disorderly Room	see *Disorderly Room*	
The Encores		26
The End (cine-film)		53
The Friendly Bank (cartoon)		95, **95**
The Gaieties		25
The Good Companions (Priestley)		98
The Guardian		109

201

The Happiest Days of Your Life (play)	51
The Inspector General (Nikolai Gogol)	5
The Lady's Not for Burning (Christopher Fry)	48, **48**
The Rebel Tyke (Peter Holdsworth)	42, 116
The Tempest (William Shakespeare)	47, **47**
The Westminster	76, 94
Theatre Royal	6, 83
They Came to a City (JB Priestley)	**91**
Thornton	143
Thorpe	63
Throup, Sam (farmer)	63
Timble	69
Titus (Sir) Salt — see Salt, Titus	
Toller Lane	8, 9, 9, 13, 27, 99, 129, 130 130, **159**, 160, 163
Toller Lane Cricket Club	126
Tommy Crosby — see Crosby, Tommy	
Tout, Harry (friend)	35, 35, 50, 97, 110, **110**
Tout, Joan (friend)	35, 35, 97, 110, **110**
Town Hall	7, 14
'Track-less'	77
training	149
Treasure Hunt (play)	51
Tributes to a Yorkshire legend (JB Priestley)	103
Trinculo (*The Tempest*)	49
trolleybus	79
Trudi Boetschi — see Boetschi, Trudi	
Tyrell Street	67
Uniques	19
United Reform Church	164
University of Bradford	98, 115
Valley Parade	122, 124
Valley Road	58
Verges (*Much Ado about Nothing*)	46
Victoria Hotel	6, 71, 101
Victorian, turn of 19th century	1
Victorian	4, 67, 79

Vine, Bill (performer)		110
Vine, Roni (actress)		41, 41, 110
Voluntary Wartime Entertainers Association		31
Waddington, David (friend)		63, 172
Wadsworth, Edward		151
Wakefield		3
Walker, Brian (friend)		63, 124
Walter Williams	see Williams, Walter	
Ward, Ossie (comedian)		110
Warwickshire		65
water		4
watercolour		63, 118
Webster, Muriel (actress)		41, 41
wedding		27, **27**
Wensleydale		61, 64, 109
Wesson, Edward (artist)		71
West Riding		73, 120
West Yorkshire Regiment	also Bradford Pals	133
Westminster Bank		12
Westminster Bank annual art exhibition (1935 to 1938)		61, 76, 140, 143, 151
Wetwang		3
Wharfedale	also River Wharfe	63, 63, 64, 82
Wharfedale Films		55
Wharfedale Group of Artists		106
When We are Married (JB Priestley)		40, 41, 42, 42, 44, 44, 49, 62, 98, 100, 156
Whitby		61, 65
White Abbey		13
Whitelaw, Billie (actress)		44
Wild Violets (play)		51
William (Sir) Rothenstein	see Rothenstein, Sir William	
Williams, Walter (friend)		35, 41, 41
Wilson, Bernard (compere)		110
Wilson, Judy (actress)		44
Wood, Newton (performer)		110
Woodrow, Audrey (performer)		35, 110
Wool Exchange		6, 67
wool trade		170
World War One	see First World War	

World War Two	see Second World War
York	65
Yorkshire artists	106, 117
Yorkshire Dales	61, 62, 63, 69
Yorkshire Evening Post	48, 87, 88
Yorkshire Group of Artists	61, 72, 73, 153
Yorkshire Observer	45, 48, 49
Yorkshire Post	41, 45, 45, 46, 47, 75, 101, 103
Yorkshire Ripper	161
Yorkshire Sports	126
Yorkshire Watercolour Society	72, 73, 117, 152
Yorkshire's King of Mirth	**30,** 172
Young performer	**20**